The GI Generation

The GI Generation

A Memoir

Frank F. Mathias

THE UNIVERSITY PRESS OF KENTUCKY

Publication of this volume was made possible in part
by a grant from the National Endowment for the Humanities.

Editorial and Sales Offices: The University Press of Kentucky
663 South Limestone Street, Lexington, Kentucky 40508–4008

04 03 02 01 00   5 4 3 2 1

Library of Congress Cataloging-in-Publication Data

Mathias, Frank Furlong.
    The GI generation : a memoir / Frank F. Mathias
        p.   cm.
    ISBN 0-8131-2157-4 (cloth : alk. paper)
    1. Mathias, Frank Furlong. 2. United States—Social life and
customs—20th century. 3. Depressions—1929—Kentucky—
Carlisle. 4. World War, 1939-1945—Personal narratives, American.
5. Carlisle (Ky.)—Biography. I. Title: G.I. generation. II. Title.

CT275.M46444 A3 2000
973.91—dc21   99-089854

For Florence

Contents

Preface *ix*

1. Lucky and Nannie   *1*

2. Carlisle and Maysville   *10*

3. Our Main Street Neighborhood   *22*

4. Cigars and Cinnamon Balls   *37*

5. Hammering Catfish and Other Events   *49*

6. The Uncommon Cold and the Specialty Man   *61*

7. Major and Minor   *72*

8. The Forces of Nature   *83*

9. They Called Him Lucky   *99*

10. A Shoeshine and a Smile   *109*

11. Burma Shave and Buzzard Roost   *119*

12. Foo-fighters and Kinniconick   *130*

13. Making Do with the Great Depression   *140*

14. Cops, Robbers, and Characters   *153*

15. Summertime   *168*

16. Hanging around Town   *180*

17. Camp Black Hawk and Carlisle Christianity   *194*

18. Maysville on My Mind   *207*

19. The Queen City and the Kings   *220*

20. Life Went on as Usual   *237*

21. Poetry and War   *250*

22. The Music Goes Round and Round   *260*

Postscript   *268*

Illustrations follow page 146

Preface

On August 25, 1943, I entered the United States Army as an entirely willing eighteen-year-old draftee. I joined several million other lads born between 1910 and 1927, a spread of years catching most of America's World War II servicemen. As if to balance the biblical passage "A time to be born," these years embraced a time it might have been better to have postponed one's arrival, for we were the star-crossed "GI Generation" destined to help pull the world's blood-stained chestnuts out of the fires of fascism, then for the rest of the century devise a safe yet perilous path through the threat of nuclear war. We did these things, I think, because they had to be done, and it was up to us to do them. Exactly the same can be said for those lads who fought the Revolution, the Civil War, and World War I.

It can also be said that the decades preceding a war witness the sprouting, growing, shaping, and maturing of the men called to fight the war. And that is the major theme of this book. Although I reveal the thread of only one boy's life, along with that of his small community, it is woven thoroughly throughout the fabric of his entire generation, for the Great Depression notwithstanding, the two decades between the wars were years of national and social and cultural unity. We could not have won without it. Once in the army I found that my diverse comrades and I shared most of the same beliefs, tastes and distastes, education, music, humor, fears, and much else. Although much has been written about the GI Generation after they entered combat, practically nothing has appeared tracing the ins and outs of their lives as they grew to maturity between the two greatest wars of all time. This book proposes to show my life and through it the similar lives of that much greater entity now known as the GI Generation.

Readers younger than I may be surprised to find that life between World Wars I and II did not embrace expanded versions of the America one finds in the novels of F. Scott Fitzgerald, John Steinbeck, and Sinclair Lewis. Writers too often have overplayed the jazzy, jobless, or smugly conventional sides of life lived by some Americans during two of the most crucial yet interesting decades of the turbulent twentieth century. Most of us lived lives far removed from those of the Gatsbys, Joads, or Babbits. Like Einstein's realization that a falling man feels no force of gravity, we whose youth fell within these disordered decades lived reasonably happy lives, with little or no sense of the ever-mounting gravity of each prewar year. Who was I to know that ten of my playmates or pals would be killed in action just a few years down the road? We were chock-full of the optimism of youth and thoughtless of any future much beyond high school graduation. Moreover (although we were part of it), the phrase "GI Generation" would have been as meaningless to us as "ball point pen" or "tape recorder." In short, I intend to paint a much happier, more humorous, and truer face on these twenty-odd years between the wars. I shall also let the reader link the war to my pals and me by mentioning future battle deaths of playmates and pertinent or related experiences of my own during the war.

It may be hard for today's reader to grasp how quickly postarmistice World War I began converting itself into World War II. By the time of my birth, in 1925, World War II was, for all practical purposes, already in its planning stages. Germany and Russia were secretly violating postwar treaties to promote each other's military power. In return for Krupp know-how in building a Russian munitions industry Moscow set aside vast tracts of land for German training of young fighter pilots and for the testing of new tank formations as well as heavy artillery. William Manchester revealed this and similar shenanigans in his 1964 book *The Arms of Krupp.* Additionally, the ill-starred year of 1925 witnessed not only the withdrawal of French troops from the Ruhr but Adolph Hitler's publication of *Mein Kampf,* as he set about building a powerful Nazi Party. Mussolini, of course, had taken over and run fascist Italy for three years by this time. But as will be seen in the opening chapter, I was born into a Jazz Age Kentucky bungalow with nary a worry in the world. My parents, like nearly all Americans, believed World War I, "the war to end all wars," had "made the world safe for democracy." We lived, loved, and operated on that belief until the seventh day of December 1941. That's the day the entire GI Generation came of age!

There is no better example of what is meant by "coming of age" than that of my cousin Bob Mathias, the son of Uncle Harry and Aunt Catherine Marshall Mathias. Stephen E. Ambrose, in the prologue of his splendid book *D-Day, June 6, 1944: The Climactic Battle of World War II* ([New York: Simon & Schuster, 1994], 22–26) offers the wartime action of Bob and another young man as examples of what Hitler was up against in his overconfident belief that democracies produces weaklings:

> Lt. Robert Mason Mathias was the leader of the second platoon, E company, 508th Parachute Infantry Regiment, U.S. 82nd Airborne Division. At midnight, June 5/6, 1944, he was riding in a C-47 Dakota over the English Channel, headed toward the Cotentin Peninsula of Normandy. . . . The Germans below were firing furiously at the air armada of 822 C-47s. . . . Mathias had his hands on the outside of the doorway, ready [to lead his sixteen men out] when a shell burst beside him. . . . knocking him off his feet. With a mighty effort he pulled himself back up. The green light went on. . . . The crew of the C-47 could have applied first aid. . . . Instead, Mathias raised his right arm, called out "Follow me!" and leaped into the night . . . bleeding from his multiple wounds. . . . When he was located a half hour or so later, he was still in his chute, dead. He was the first American officer killed by German fire on D-day.

Ambrose concludes his prologue with a brief analysis of Mathias and most of the GI Generation. These, he maintains, were "the young men born into the false prosperity of the 1920s and brought up in the bitter realities of the Depression of the 1930s. . . . The literature they read as youngsters was antiwar, cynical, portraying patriots as suckers, slackers as heroes. None of them wanted to be part of another war. . . . But when the test came, when freedom had to be fought for or abandoned, they fought. They were soldiers of democracy. They were men of D-day, and to them we owe our freedom."

I have written this book as the historian I am, and not as an "old-timer" intent on gilding the lily. The events described here actually happened and have not been exaggerated. But errors do creep into a manuscript written years after the fact, and I accept sole responsibility for them. I have presented this story as it happened, letting the characters speak for themselves whenever possible. Gaps in my memory were often filled by conversations with, or letters from, men and women who shared many of the experiences described in this book. Names are sometimes changed to protect privacy. I do not claim exact memory of conversations set down in this book, but I do believe I have offered close approximations of them.

It is said that if one really needs something done go to the busiest man around, so I did. The renowned author-historian Stephen E. Ambrose won my lasting gratitude by his very generous evaluation of my memoir. The same can be said for Edward M. Coffman, a dear friend who also earned my special gratitude for his enthusiastic support and careful reading and marking of my manuscript. Speaking of enthusiasm, none had more for this project than my three children, Nancy, Frank, and Susan, and my shamrock-stained son-in-law Patrick Francis Sullivan.

What would I have done without the support of my hometown folks? The *Carlisle Mercury* staff, as well as Billy Dale Crawford, editor of the *Nicholas Countian,* were always there when I needed them, as were my colleagues of the "Old Farts Club," who were never at a loss for between-your-eyes advice. The late Ernest Sosby and Charles Gates, local historians, were unfailingly helpful, as were Jorita Anderson and the library staff. Total support came from Carlisle High School classmates and friends Joseph and Joan Conley, John and Emily Wolf, John and Linda Soper, Clay Hamm, James Cassidy, Bob Cunningham, Everett Earl Pfanstiel Jr., and Kay Fisher Hall. Gene Neal, bless him, was always there for me, as were Wendell, Virginia, and Barbara Kingsolver, Cleary Fightmaster, and Ben and Viola Pumphrey.

Maysvillians Glenn and Barbara Mattingly, Charles Brodt, and cousin James Clarkson kept my literary furrow straight as I plowed through a field of Ohio River memories and not a few dreams. Equal gratitude goes to Jane Wise, Anne Moore Pollit, Sharon Moore Legge, Ellen Walton, Woodson Wood, Wenonah Jones Merrill, Mary H. Campbell, Verna Ellis, Mary Lida and Nancy Comer. Library director Evelyn Gillespie Cropper and her staff merit my thanks, as do museum directors Louis and Dawn Browning and associates Sue Ellen Grannis, Rebecca Cartmell, Alice Kay Gallenstein, and Jane Hendrickson.

University of Dayton history department chairman Lawrence Flockerzie and secretaries Patti Martin and Jeaninne Chaffin stuck with me through thick and thin, as did my longtime buddy Jack Minardi, an old navy fighter pilot and, like me, a University of Dayton retiree.

Florence, my beloved wife for over forty years, lived through the literary clutter for three years. How lucky can one old-timer be to have a wife like this and supporters like that crowd above!

1

Lucky and Nannie

The British Colonial Office seldom hired missionaries or lawyers as diplomats, believing they followed either God or the law too closely for the comfort of other viewpoints. It might have rejected my mother, but I feel "Lucky," my father, would have been a star performer at some far-flung outpost of empire. I base this assumption on the evidence of his dealings with Brother Cedric Peel.

Almost annually Lucky and several of his fishing friends went for a try at the muskies said to swarm in Mazey Creek. This was a sixty-mile drive, the last half over dirt and gravel roads. The clear, cold stream flowed through sparsely populated Appalachian foothills, scenery excitingly different from the Bluegrass country of Dad's northern Kentucky homeland. The fishermen took pillows and blankets for their stay with Brother Cedric, but whether they slept in his little house or in his barn escapes my memory. As Cedric Peel, he ran a small grocery nearby, but as Brother Cedric he ministered to a congregation based in a typical "little white church in the wildwood." It was Protestant, but of what denomination, if any, I have no recall.

Charles "Lucky" Mathias was Catholic, and Catholics were instructed to avoid official Protestant services lest they seemed to sanction certain Reformation presumptions. Dad went along with this up to a point, but that point was reached on those fishing weekends at Brother Cedric's, for the proverbial "ox was in the ditch" for Lucky. The nearest Catholic church was over forty rough and rutted miles away. Lucky, never a quibbler, took the ox by the horns and joined his friends at Brother Cedric's Sunday service. Quite a few of the brethren stood outside near the open windows, smoking and chewing, refugees from Brother Cedric's lengthy hellfire sermons. Most, including Dad, seldom ventured inside to partake of the Lord's Supper.

One summer Sunday, after Brother Cedric had unleashed an exceptionally stirring sermon, he announced that he had run short of the fruit of the vine for the Lord's Supper: "I am substituting bourbon whiskey instead," he said. A quiet mumbling instantly ran through the outside crowd, followed by a hats-in-hands procession into the small church. Brother Cedric possibly marveled at the Lord's generosity in sending him a record number of communicants that day.

Once home, Lucky made a tactical error in telling Nannie what had happened. Mom's doctrinaire approach to Catholicism and Christianity in general would have terrified the British Colonial Office. "Why that's just terrible!" she said, with emphasis on *terrible*. "What a bunch of dumbbells, and you among them. Why, you couldn't even be a good Protestant!" My younger brother and I listened in and looked on as Dad took his lumps, but I sort of sensed that my traveling salesman and fishing-addicted father had done his best to be a friend and neighbor to everybody, including his own conscience.

Lucky seldom bragged about anything except Carlisle, his hometown. Often, when the noon whistle blew on the White Rose flour mill, he cocked an ear and smiled contentedly: "I've heard that whistle all my life and I hope to hear it to the end. They didn't nickname me 'Lucky' for nothing." Mom called him Charlie, but the rest of the world knew him only as Lucky. He was a reasonably happy salesman and family man. Except for a visit with his brother in Dallas when he was seventy-two, he had been no farther than two-hundred miles from home. He never saw an ocean. And Dad's wishes were granted, for he lived seventy-seven years in Carlisle, dying at high noon on a June day in 1958. The old mill was shut down for some reason that day, and almost as if in his honor, the whistle was silent.

My schoolteacher mother, Nancy Furlong, did not share Dad's

love for Carlisle; she was never quite certain about the place until late in life. "Charlie," she sometimes complained, "I never saw so many numbskulls gathered in one village of fifteen-hundred people in my life!" With this Nannie either started an argument or ended one. Dad was left mumbling about "river rats" in Maysville, her hometown thirty miles north on the Ohio River.

Nannie was correct insofar as Carlisle had endured more than its share of blunderers. Early on its leaders seldom set its sails in time to catch the winds of change. Something or someone was always around to spit in the soup. In 1816, when platting a county seat for Nicholas County, dumbbells anchored it on back roads three miles from the Maysville Road, the main area highway. Effectively dry-docked, it lost population and wealth and watched less isolated county seats leave it in their wakes. But worse was coming. State and local blockheads got politically busy in 1867 and carved most of tiny Robertson County out of Nicholas, sapping economic and political strength from both counties. But during the 1920s fair winds filled Carlisle's sails; it had become one of Kentucky's leading tobacco markets. Several million pounds of burley were auctioned annually from huge warehouses in and around the town. Then came ignoramuses who threatened corporate tobacco buyers with violence if they did not pay higher prices. The next season no buyers showed up. They had written the Carlisle market off their books forever.

Some said Nancy Browning Furlong was a natural-born teacher; dealing with the younger variety of "dunces" had long been her stock-in-trade. She was thirty-six and Lucky forty-three when they married, and although Nannie had earned a teaching certificate from what is now Eastern Kentucky University and done further work at Chicago's prestigious Gregg School of Business, she married a man with an eighth grade education. Lucky respected his dedicated wife's education and long years as a teacher, but he became touchy anytime his lack of advanced schooling came up. He eventually realized that her reference to some Carlislians as "dummies" was meant as more of an educational challenge demanding her attention than as an insult. After all, in her family of nine, just as in his of eight, most of the boys had gone little beyond the eighth grade. He loved her and she loved him, and this carried them through their thirty-four years together.

Nannie's thoughts about her origin differed mightily from Lucky's. Dad had a passive view of his past: "They were all a bunch of Black Forest clock carvers from a village named Endingen, not far from Freiburg in Baden. Old Joe [Joseph Anton Mathias], my grandpa, came to Chillicothe in 1834. My mother's gang of Harmeyers came over a little later from Freren village in Lower Saxony. I never met any of them that weren't damned glad to be here." Nannie, however, was aggressively Irish-American. She sang a lot, often accompanying herself on her mandolin. A song fastened as tightly as death itself to my memory is one she sang almost daily as she worked, a song aimed like a sword at the heart of England— "The Wearing of the Green":

I met with Napper Tandy, and he took me by the hand,
And he said, 'How's poor old Ireland, and how does she
    stand?'
She's the most distressful country that ever yet was seen,
They are hanging men and women there for wearing of the
    green.

My mother was the oldest of six sisters and three brothers. Her father was tall, handsome John Benedict Furlong, the son of Irish immigrant parents. He was born in Mason County in 1862 and later represented it in the Kentucky legislature during the 1920s. J.B. was a farmer most of his life and he married a farmer's daughter, Elizabeth Browning, in 1887. The couple owned and farmed forty fertile acres on Tuckahoe Ridge, a plateau above the Ohio River named for Virginians—"Tuckahoes"—who settled the area in the 1780s. Nancy Browning Furlong was born in their small frame farmhouse in 1888 and as "big sister" would pick up a sense of command and presence that never deserted her throughout a long life.

The Browning side of Nannie's family were Protestant Mason County farmers of English descent. Elizabeth Browning converted to Catholicism when she married J.B., but her family worshiped at Mount Carmel Christian Church. Unlike the Furlongs, the

Brownings had been in America a long time, branching off the Bramel family of Cheshire, England. My mother never fully accepted the fact that she was half-English, thus only half-Irish. The Furlong or Irish side of her nature invariably took precedent over the English or Browning side. She loved the Brownings—her mother was one— but somewhere along the line the English nation had fallen from favor from her having talked to many survivors of the English-induced Great Famine. She had very little good to say about the English nation for the rest of her life, yet when World War II's baleful shadow neared, she unhesitatingly backed the English people against the Nazis.

Just down the dusty road from the furlongs lived the Donovan family. Nancy and their son Herman became playmates and lifelong friends. Herman Lee Donovan later culminated a brilliant career in education by serving as president of the University of Kentucky from 1941 to 1956. Mom never tired of telling me that I could grow up to be as "fine a teacher as Herman Lee if you just show his gumption." Gumption meant initiative and common sense combined, as near as I ever understood it, but I knew she had me pegged wrong. Gumption or no gumption, my sights were set on becoming a dance-band musician, like those I heard playing aboard the excursion steamboats that docked at Maysville. I became tired of hearing about Herman Lee, never dreaming the day would come when I could check on Mom's pedestaled playmate.

I entered the University of Kentucky under the GI Bill in 1946 and a few weeks later saw President Donovan standing nonchalantly alongside the library steps. I approached him, my mind swimming with tales Mom had told of Tuckahoe and Herman Lee. I almost called him Herman Lee but caught myself in time. "Dr. Donovan, didn't you grow up on Tuckahoe Ridge in Mason County?" I asked, almost apologetically.

"Why, yes I did," he replied. "How in the world did you know that?"

"Well, sir," I said, "my mother is Nancy Furlong, and she . . ."

"Nancy Furlong! Your mother is Nancy Furlong! Is she all right? I haven't heard from her for some time. She's still in Carlisle?"

"Yes, sir, she's in Carlisle and she's just fine." I had not known what to expect, and his avid interest took me by surprise. He looked me over with a grin on his face. I told him my name.

"Frank," he said with elation-tinged nostalgia, "your mother and I were the best of playmates back there on Tuckahoe. We played up and down that dusty little road, chased butterflies across the fields, and got muddy wading in Lawrence Creek." We spent several minutes catching up on the Mason County Furlongs and Donovans and the Carlisle Mathiases. I left him with the feeling that a piece of life's jigsaw puzzle had finally been pressed firmly into place.

Nannie taught in the Mason County schools until she went west in 1916 to visit her sister Anna Martin, who, with her husband, Joseph Gilkey, had opened International Business College in El Paso, Texas, a successful venture. Nannie spent much of 1916 with them, absorbing the squally and exciting times along the U.S.-Mexican border. Her exceptional memory kept these times fresh for tales to her family. These tales appealed to my romantic nature, no matter how many times I heard them. She, my own mother, had seen and done these things in person, that is what impressed me. I had seen Mexicans, cowboys, and the Wild West in movies, but here she sat, a person who had really been there! Sometimes I brought in buddies—Joe Beatty, Spud Marshall, Louis Reibold, Joe Roundtree—to show Mom off. They came willingly, having passed favorable judgment on tales they had heard before. "Tell us about El Paso," I asked, showing off for my pals by saying that "El Paso means 'the pass.'"

"Are you sure you want to hear it again?" she asked as we nodded that we did. "Pancho Villa, as you know, was running wild along the border in those days. He and his horsemen wore big sombreros [we all knew that this meant hats and shook our heads knowingly at each other] and had already shot up several American towns. Mexico was having a revolution." We were all ears now, waiting to hear about her and the railroad cars. "Well, boys, my sister and I and some friends went down to the tracks along the Rio Grande and sat on top of a freight car. We could see people running in the Juarez streets across the river and hear shooting going on. But we got a lot more than we bargained for—let me tell you! Suddenly we heard thumping sounds in and around our freight car. Bullets were coming our way! Soldiers ran up and shooed us off the cars. Weren't we the dumbest bunch you ever heard of?" My pals and I did not think dumbness had anything to do with it. Here we sat in dumb old Carlisle while daring people like my mother must still be out west somewhere living exciting and worthwhile lives.

Gilkey connections got Nannie a teaching job in Greeley, Colorado. She spent the next several years teaching commercial subjects there and in Longmont and Boulder. There was also a three-month stint in a tiny, mountain mining camp where she lived in a tent between the school and a student's home. "The tent was nice," she recalled, "with built-in floor and siding, but sometimes I had to push snow off the sagging canvas above my cot to see if it was daylight and time to go to work." Another three-month job ended one week after it started when a student helper burned Hudson's one-room school down by using highly flammable tumbleweed for kindling in the stove.

Nannie eventually realized that her Gregg School of Business degree could get her better paying jobs than those in Colorado. She applied for and won a job teaching at Mason City, Iowa, High School. The pay was a whopping $114 per month. While there she taught Meredith Willson, a student destined for fame as a musician and playwright. Willson's senior photo in Nannie's 1919 *Masonian* yearbook reveals a beetle-browed lad with pompadoured hair typical of the era, one whom classmates assigned this prophecy: "Great men are not always wise." Whether wise or not, one would expect the composer of *The Music Man* to have been active in "River City" high school music, and he was. The legend under the photo lists him in "orchestra, band, glee club, chorus, minstrel show and opera."

Willson, of course, was a noted American composer long before he wrote *The Music Man*. Mom never let me forget it: "If you don't practice your saxophone you'll never be as good a musician as Meredith Willson." "Lord have mercy," I thought, "if it isn't Herman Lee, it's Meredith."

A teacher Nannie had worked with at Mason City wrote her from North Carolina in 1921 of an attractive opening in her field at a Rocky Mount high school. She got the job. Earlier encounters with Herman Lee and Meredith had their counterpart in North Carolina. Kay Kyser was in her typing class, a lad later to win fame as a swing-era bandleader and radio maestro of his "College of Musical Knowledge." Mom of course turned this to her advantage: "Listen now, one of these days you might play in a band as good as Kay Kyser's if you practice hard; he was one of my students." I practiced, hoping Mom was correct this time. As it turned out, she was.

After a year in North Carolina Nannie returned home to teach at Maysville High School. She thought of herself as an "old maid" of thirty-four but had hardly started teaching when she met an attractive traveling salesman; a new world immediately opened for both of them.

Charles Lindsey Mathias was forty-one when he and Nancy Furlong met. Lucky, however, had never been lucky in love. He had courted many women but for various vague reasons had never been able to lead one to the bridal parlor. One reason was religion, for his was an era of harsh anti-Catholic sentiment. Carlisle was a thoroughly Protestant community, and the idea of one's daughter marrying a "papist" chilled the hearts of more than a few parents. This prejudice worked both ways of course, but Lucky's problems went beyond that. He was the nature boy of his family, forever tramping the woods and streams, fishing and messing himself up with mud, bait, and fish smells. He probably talked far too much about such things to women who were generally uninterested. He had traveled no farther than Louisville and Cincinnati, and at thirty-seven he missed the draft and "gay Paree." Finally, his eight years of education neither excited nor opened his imagination to wider vistas, as it had for most of his brothers. Married or not, Lucky was stuck with Carlisle and Carlisle with him.

One might wonder what a well-traveled woman like Nancy Furlong would see in Lucky. At the time it was said that there was not much left for either one of them to choose from. A tad of truth there, no doubt, but there was more to it than that. Lucky was physically attractive, with wavy brown hair, good masculine features, tanned complexion, a muscular 155 pounds, and a healthy and vigorous spring to his walk—a true outdoorsman. He was a good talker and a good listener, always able to spice conversation from his readings in various novels, magazines, and newspapers. And he was humble, deferring easily to anyone who might object or offer a better opinion. His gentle humor was usually directed toward himself. In other words, he was an excellent salesman. But in addition, he had a superb mind. He saw through much of the social, cultural, and economic clutter of his era, but he was unable to pin it down in educated discourse. This caused him to overvalue education yet be suspicious of it at the same time. Mom forever walked a tightrope on this issue. But she never had any problems with him regarding loyalty, honesty, or integrity, for his entire family was solidly grounded in those virtues. In today's world, I think, he would have become a successful mechanical engineer, for he loved all things mechanical; he invented several items that sold well but never won a patent.

Lucky and Nannie met at a farmhouse party during the summer of 1923. Within minutes they were earnestly talking to each other, ignoring the rest. There could be no thought of playing the waiting game. Courting proceeded full-time and culminated in their June 1924 marriage at Carlisle's Catholic church. They pooled their $5,000 in savings and built a two-bedroom bungalow on an East Main Street lot next to Grandma and Uncle Joe Mathias, the home I loved and lived in until I was drafted in 1943. Crooner Gene Austin's hit ballad "My Blue Heaven" might have been written with such a little Jazz Age bungalow in mind. It was painted pale yellow with dark brown trim, had a "veranda" with typically fat wooden pillars, a cozy fireplace framed by polished wooden bookcases, a small breakfast nook, stylish French doors connecting the front and living rooms, and a small unfinished basement with a coal furnace. A bright, airy interior was assured by banks of windows in each room. Finally, there was a floored but unfinished attic that would make a nice playroom for any children that might arrive, and one was soon on the way.

Two of Nannie's sisters, Alma, a registered nurse at Maysville's Hayswood Hospital, and Lillian, soon to be one, insisted that she do the "safe and modern thing: Have your baby at the Hayswood where we can be your nurses." It was an offer a happy Nannie could not refuse. I was born there on May 23, 1925, and named Francis Furlong, to me a sissy sounding name I later dropped for Frank.

2

Carlisle and Maysville

I was born into America's first modern decade, a tangled time struggling to live with Prohibition, the recent advent of radio and jazz, Sigmund Freud, "scandalous" feminine fashions, and the lurid revival of the Ku Klux Klan. For all I know, the fright the Klan gave my mother during her honeymoon may account for my somewhat nervous disposition. The honeymooners were Louisville-bound but stopped for the night in Frankfort. They chose the wrong night. That evening a mile-long parade of hooded, torch-wielding Klansmen marched past their hotel. The lovely honeymoon room quivered in the flickering torchlight. The procession was venomously anti-Catholic, anti-black, and anti-Jewish. Dad was enraged and Mom limp with fright. Their honeymoon got off to a good start next day at Louisville's fine Seelbach Hotel.

The Klan carried evil seeds of destruction within itself. A few years later, the Indiana grand dragon raped, bit, and chewed on his secretary to the extent that she died of her wounds. Subsequent trials exposed the true nature of the Klan to the unsophisticated and rather foolish membership. They quit in droves, and by 1930 the KKK was mostly a memory.

Lucky could never hold a grudge and said his hometown Klansmen "just wanted something to join for a little excitement, but when they found out what they really *had* joined, they quit." Nannie and others were not so sure. The KKK revival elicited unpleasant thoughts among Carlisle's tiny Catholic minority. Although there were no overt acts against Catholics and blacks, postwar Protestantism had become something to reckon with and, for a time, to fear.

The human story, most will say, is woven as deeply into the fabric of small towns as it is into that of cities. In both there is a bewildering and jarring mixture of good, bad, mediocre, old, and new to contend with on a regular basis, but in a small town it is usually done person to person. The anonymity of a city is an emotional luxury denied the small-towner. Lucky, for example, knew who the local Klansmen were, and he knew that they knew he knew. Dad had to forgive and forget if he intended to make his living in Carlisle.

As Uncle Joe said, "If this town has any secrets, I never heard of 'em." In other words, few people, things, or events escaped some form of happy or cruel publicity in Carlisle, whether through gossip, sermons, or editorials. Just observing the town through four seasons was enough to sense the varied but sometimes painful publicity surrounding almost all people, things, and events: hoboes knocking on doors for handouts; dwarves, freaks, strippers, Gypsies, and magicians in traveling carnivals; hellfire sermons shouted in public tent meetings; orange quarantine disease signs tacked on front doors; earthy odors of animal manure on streets and human manure in privies, both generating clouds of flies; perfume from flowers and tree blossoms floating in clean, smogless air; spittoons and related spatterings on store floors; jerkily walking, whiskey poisoned "jake-leggers"; calcium-deficient bowlegged adults and children; smiles often gleaming with gold teeth or painfully darkened with rotten ones; string bands playing wonderfully original "hillbilly" music for square dances; kids swirling by on steel-wheeled roller skates or on sleds; the nonchalant use of racial slurs; "addled" folks freely cavorting or leering on the streets; death looking from the waxen, pale face of tubercular men and women; dusty Ku Klux Klan robes and swords abandoned in closets and played with by boys and girls; rabid dogs occasionally cornered and shot by police pistols; and the town's sleepy silence punctuated always by bells: church bells, fire bells, school bells, train engine bells, dinner bells, and the friendly baritone voice of the big courthouse clock bell, tolling the time for the town. It took a year for this partial parade of life in Carlisle to pass, for most of these things were sprinkled through the seasons like salt and pepper on bland food.

Physically speaking, Carlisle was not much. Few small towns are. But size is not everything. During the late 1800s a dozen or so Victorian brick and stone business buildings and churches were built around Courthouse Square, as was a fine new courthouse. Taken together, the scene would make a completely authentic setting for a period movie. Lucky loved them all, often boasting that he had "watched them build the whole shebang."

Small towns often ignore or disparage their past, and Carlisle was no exception. At school we learned the names and dates of the presidents, the state capitals, the English kings, and the biggest battles, but we learned little of the history of our own community. Yet history surrounded us. Slavery, with its human conflicts and drama, had lived and breathed in our streets. The Reverend John Rankin, later to found the most important station on the Underground Railroad, had been a minister at a Carlisle church, yet nary a word of this. Daniel Boone and son had farmed nearby, yet their cabin was falling into rack and ruin. President Andrew Jackson's famous veto of the Maysville Road Bill set federal highway construction back a century, yet no mention of this even though this road was the county's one major highway.

Charles Dazey, a noted playwright, was born near Carlisle in 1855. His play *In Old Kentucky* became a Broadway favorite starring Lillian Russell. In 1936 it appeared as a movie starring Will Rogers, but, as I say, nary a word of this. And although there was mention of the savage Battle of Blue Licks, and of Governor Thomas Metcalfe, few students could have identified or discussed either the event or the person with any depth. For that matter, fewer still could have identified or discussed Marxism, fascism, totalitarianism, and other between-the-war "isms" that were rapidly leading all of us into another global war. Most Carlislians believed that World War I had "made the world safe for democracy." But in spite of the above, Carlisle's virtues far outweighed its faults.

The town itself sits on the rim of the state's fertile Bluegrass region, some thirty-five miles northeast of Lexington and seventy miles southeast of Cincinnati. It was not only the county seat but had long been the kind of place and society Thomas Jefferson had in mind when he advocated a nation based on small farmers and mechanics. There was no person or family of real wealth in the vicinity, nor was there any factory or mill to seek economic and political privileges at the expense of the people. Small farmers, businessmen, craftsmen, and the like made up the entire population. A few lawyers and physicians attended to their relatively simple needs. Nearly everyone was white, Anglo-Saxon, and Protestant, with only a sprinkling of African Americans in the county, no Jews, and only eighty Catholics.

The climate is that of the Ohio Valley, with four distinct seasons and below-zero temperatures several times each winter. Agriculture provided the entire economic base, and tobacco farming brought in most of the cash income. The Great Depression caused no real problems of want or hunger in this rural setting; moreover, the people stuck together, helping those who needed it, and were firmly optimistic in the belief that better days were coming. Victorian values were still practiced in Carlisle, and I can testify that they were easy values to live with. My parents lost the keys to our house in 1930 and never locked the doors again until the place was sold in 1970. Every street was safe to walk for anybody at any time of the day or night. I never really valued or cherished the simple peace found in my old hometown until I returned after nearly two years in an army infantry division.

The first memorable event of my life probably started in Carlisle but came to fruition in Maysville. In early June 1928, I was at Granny Furlong's house. She led me to the front porch and confusion gripped me! My mother was carrying a baby up the front steps. She smiled at me, but all I could see was that baby in her arms. Perhaps I thought I was to be replaced, but my memory is neutral, with overtones of neither fear nor joy. Charles Lindsay Mathias Jr. completed our family. He arrived a year before the Great Depression and in the midst of one of America's most cantankerous presidential races. Later known as a lad with little patience for windbags, bigots, triflers, and simpletons, he could hardly have arrived at a worse time!

The Hoover-Smith race ignited bad feelings throughout America in 1928. Religion was the main issue, for cataclysmic faults in the economy remained hidden. Some said if Al Smith won, the pope would dig a tunnel under the Atlantic and invade the United States. (I heard this absurdity parroted as late as the 1960 Kennedy campaign!) Lucky and Nannie were Smith supporters, not only because they were lifelong "straight ticket" Democrats but because they believed it was about time for a Catholic to sit in the White House. I picked up their fervor and showed I was ready to fight for the "Happy Warrior."

Dad spit on a comb, slicked my hair, and took me uptown to show me off to friends and acquaintances seemingly forever loafing at the corner of Main and Broadway. Some seemed to do no more than watch the town's new stoplight switch from red to green and back again. Dad introduced me to the crowd. I liked it when they stooped to shake my tiny hand, but I did not like what one of them said next. "Lucky, you know that boy of yours looks just like Hoover; let's call him 'Little Hoover' from now on." I remember his jovial fat face as he bent over, asking: "Do you mind if we call you 'Little Hoover' from now on?"

I sensed that whatever Hoover was, was bad, so I swung my fists as hard as I could, hitting him around the legs. The crowd got a kick out of this and so did Dad. The teaser won me over by giving me a toy elephant, probably with a GOP symbol on it. For the next decade I was hailed as "Little Hoover" by the crowd of part-time farmhands and jobless clerks and laborers hanging around that corner. Achieving "recognition" is easy to come by in a small town!

I may have been Little Hoover to the uptown loafers, but in the rambling old frame house next door I was a beloved *Enkel* (grandson). Dad had built on a vacant lot next to his widowed mother, my Grandma Mary Harmeyer Mathias. My Uncle Joe, a lifelong bachelor, lived with her. As a toddler I spent a world of time sitting in the ample lap of *Meiner Grossmutter*. Although her family gave up speaking German owing to vicious poison pen letters during the Great

War—a typical message received was this one: "All you damned kratheads and huns ought to be whipped back to Germany where you belong"—Grandma pooh-poohed them all and spoke the old language as often as she used English.

Grandma loved to talk to me in German, and I loved to visit *das Haus meiner Grossmutter und meines onkel Joseph*. I learned that to say, "*Guten Morgan, Ich habe Hunger*"—brought a hug and a sweet reward if I also said *Bitte*—please. She held me in her lap when she taught me to say the *Vater Unser*—Our Father—in German. I sensed there was one way to speak *mit meiner Grossmutter* and another way to speak to everyone else. I think Mom was sometimes irked when I came home blabbing baby talk *auf Deutsch*. She also had to reconcile the fact that Dad, with only an eighth grade education, understood Grandma and me but she did not. I was four years old when Granny died.

The events surrounding Grandma's death remain branded in my mind. The complications of old age brought her to her deathbed, where she lingered for several weeks. As life ebbed, a score of Covington and Cincinnati relatives came to Carlisle, staying with us or with neighbors. Their names were pure German: Bedinghaus, Rolfe, Ebbing, Merkel, Keller, Speiker, Hermes, and, of course, Harmeyer. They were physically impressive people, but I was puzzled to note that some of the men wore knickers. I had only seen knickers on schoolboys.

The day before Grandma died Mom dressed me up and led me to her bedside. A circle of friends and relatives stood in the room; several patted my head as Mom led me through them. *Meiner Grossmutter* took my hand briefly, smiled wanly at me, and whispered something I could not understand. Perfume and tobacco smells hovered in the big room, and I liked them as I stood in the corner after seeing Grandma. Then I overheard them. Several men were talking about a "death clock." One said he had heard it ticking inside the walls of the old house. Another agreed, saying that he too had heard it: "When the death clock starts," he said solemnly, "life must end."

This scared me; I ran home to mother. I told her breathlessly what I had heard. She belittled the whole episode as something dreamed up by a bunch of superstitious Germans: "Germans are that way," she said condescendingly, "hearing clocks in the wall instead of in the steeples. Your Granny Mathias is sick from old age but she's not going to die because of clocks in the walls or anywhere else. Go on out and play." I felt relieved until the following morning when Dad came home crying; his mother had died a few minutes earlier. I was saddened to see him crying, so I cried too.

I later learned that the Irish easily outdistanced the Germans when it came to superstitions. Mom and the Furlong kinfolk were quick to tell us kids about leprechauns: "They are wrinkled little creatures who live under trees and rock fences. They wear pointed hats and shoes, with green jackets and tight pants. If you're able to catch one, he'll tell you where to find a pot of gold."

I thought these "wee people" were okay, saw them portrayed cutely in magazines, and believed they might exist. But things worsened quickly concerning Irish superstitions when we visited an old Irish immigrant widow on a weedy, overgrown Montgomery County farm twenty miles from Carlisle. We had spent a summer afternoon at Uncle John King's farm. He was husband to Dad's sister Katie, was Irish, and had many Irish friends and relations in the county. We left early, for Dad wanted to visit the old widow, long a friend of his and Uncle John's, but one I had never heard him speak of before.

Aunt Hattie lived far off the road in a run-down, two-story brick farmhouse overburdened with brooding spruce and fir trees. It was dusk and it was windy, with occasional sheet lightning. We entered, and I saw she had no electricity but used two coal oil lamps. There was a dank, cavelike closeness in the unkempt old house. It was a perfect setting for what was to come. We exchanged greetings. Aunt Hattie was wearing an ankle-length black dress with white lace near her neck; she spoke with a clipped Irish accent and somehow seemed relieved to see us. She laughed at Dad's usual salesman's jokes, then the two of them chatted about her late husband, her farm, and the New Deal. But Aunt Hattie suddenly shifted the conversation drastically: "Lucky," she said pointedly, her eyes flashing, "I've heard the wail of the banshee outside these very windows on many a night this summer. The claws of the creature scrape against the gutters and windows as it tries—saints preserve us!—to get at me here inside!"

My eyes popped wide open as windblown spruce branches began thrashing against the eaves and cracked windows of the drafty old structure. I scurried out of the flickering shadows to Dad's side. The old woman was truly frightened, and so was I. Dad tried to talk her out of her fear, but she would have none of it: "Lucky," she said grimly, "the banshee always knows when death is near."

Death was not near for Aunt Hattie that night; she lived two more years. A neighbor found her dead on the floor of her living room when he called on her one morning. The night before there had been a howling windstorm.

Tragedy struck the Furlong family on July 24, 1930. Nannie's brother Bill, an electrician, was electrocuted by a frayed wire while working inside the boiler at Cincinnati's First Presbyterian Church. A younger brother, Andrew, had been killed in a 1916 accident while working as a fireman on the Southern Pacific Railroad. Bill's death left only John of three Furlong boys, and it also left his widow and two children to face the Great Depression, just getting well under way in 1930.

Dad drove us to Cincinnati for the funeral. I was five years old when I saw the big city for the first time; I was impressed. Lucky stopped for brief visits with several of his German-speaking cousins. We then went on to the funeral, where I met cousins I had never seen before, and this was fun, but the trip home turned into an ordeal. My two-year-old brother became sick and began running at both ends. On top of this, our Model T had several flat tires. Dad busily patched one while I wandered up a weedy creekbed. Suddenly I thought I was lost and began shouting and crying. Mom startled me when she rose like a genie up from weeds not ten feet in front of me. "Will you shut up!" she commanded. "I'm trying to wash the poop off of Charles and get him back to sleep. Go back down the creek to Daddy before you become a bigger nuisance." It was long after dark before the old Model T limped into Carlisle with boots bumping the tires and a headlight out. The seventy-mile trip had taken over five hours.

Bill's death and the onset of the Depression finished off Grandpa

Furlong's political career. He represented Mason County in Frankfort during much of the Roaring Twenties. I knew little of this, but I knew he cut an impressive figure: a slender six feet tall, always dressed in a neat black suit with a glistening gold key chain, silver hair and mustache, and a ready laugh and twinkling eyes when he stooped ceremoniously to shake my hand and call me "governor" when I visited.

All of us liked to hear Grandpa recall incidents during his campaigns, and he loved to tell us, relating each one with gusto. "One day," he said, "while campaigning out in Orangeburg, a fellow in the audience shouted up at me and asked, 'How much are you giving for a vote?' I roared back that I wasn't giving anything, neither money, liquor, nor anything else. The fellow squinted up his eyes at me and popped his next question: 'What did you say your name was?' 'Furlong,' I replied with understandable pride. 'Well, sir,' he snorted, 'you're jist about as fur long as you're gonna git!'" J.B. also had early insight into his times, being one of the few who expressed a critical assessment of "Adolph Hitler and his 'Nasties'" as possible fomenters of another great war.

Although Grandpa won in 1929 without this vote-seller, he retired from politics when his term ended in 1932. A *Maysville Independent* editorial noted that "Furlong served his people faithfully and well . . . and there was not the semblance of a suggestion that he did not in every way carry out his pledges to the voters and capably represent the county. . . . He made a difference in the General Assembly." J.B. was fifty-nine when he entered politics in 1921 and seventy when he retired.

During Grandpa's last term of office I gained an understanding that the world might have more to offer than even my family. Dad often drove us to Maysville to watch construction of the great Ohio River suspension bridge, this combining nicely with visits to Mom's many relatives. The Furlongs' hillside home is five blocks south of the river but is perfectly aligned with the bridge deck, its three second-story windows staring down the center stripe. Usually we watched from the house, but Dad sometimes took me with him downtown for a closer view. On one of these jaunts I watched workers swing in giant two-hundred-foot arcs back and forth, high above the river, as they shepherded dangling cables for connection to a continually growing deck and roadway. It was a stunning scene. I was enthralled. Poet Robert Frost later made much ado about being a "swinger of birches," but for a five-year-old boy that day, he would rather have been a "swinger of bridges" any old time!

Maysville's role in my life was next only to that of Carlisle. The Maysville I knew between the wars might, at first glance, have passed as a sister to Meredith Willson's "River City." It was a historic and very attractive nineteenth-century river town of seven thousand, with brick streets, antebellum homes galore, and quaint little open-sided trolleys chattering in a neighborly way alongside a world-class river. Few could live in this community without absorbing some of its charm and history.

Maysville became a leading Ohio River port before Cincinnati and Louisville were much more than campsites for surveyors and a few settlers. Virginia governor Patrick Henry awarded a military warrant to John May and frontiersman Simon Kenton in 1785 for the settlement soon called Limestone and then Maysville. It became a logical clearinghouse and target for travelers, whether going into or out of Kentucky, or east or west on the big river. People passing through Maysville include Henry Clay, James Monroe, John Quincy Adams, Daniel Webster, and America's favorite Frenchman, Lafayette. One who became the most famous frontiersman who ever lived took business advantage of the flood of travelers. Daniel Boone wrapped items and poured drinks for them in his store and tavern. He left Maysville in 1790, later describing his seven years there as the happiest of his life.

Perhaps none won the fame of Boone, but others of note have a touch of Maysville in their backgrounds. Harriet Beecher (Stowe), then a young teacher, came upriver from Cincinnati in 1833 as a guest of one of her students, Elizabeth Key. During this visit Stowe witnessed slavery and a slave auction firsthand and incorporated much of this into her balefully destined *Uncle Tom's Cabin*. Ulysses S. Grant attended the Richeson and Rand school, picking up "Toad" as a schoolboy nickname. "Toad" Grant probably passed young Albert

Sidney Johnston while walking around town. Grant later had his hands full of Confederate general Johnston in 1862 at the terrible Battle of Shiloh. Even the United States Supreme Court has strong Maysville connections. Local historians Jean Calvert and John Klee, in their fine book *The Towns of Mason County,* reveal that Thomas and Mary Keith Marshall are buried here and, more to the point, that one of their fifteen children was Chief Justice John Marshall, the uniquely great legal mind whose Court established the ground rules of American government. Although Marshall was a native of Virginia, Justice Stanley Reed of the New Deal called Maysville home. According to Gary Moulton's *Journals of the Lewis and Clark Expedition,* two of those known as the "Nine Young Men from Kentucky" enlisted at Maysville when William Clark barged down the river in October 1803. John Colter later became a famous "mountain man" and "discoverer" of the present region of Yellowstone Park, while George Shannon assisted Nicholas Biddle in the preparation of his valuable history of the expedition and afterward was a governor of Missouri.

My favorite Maysvillian is Judge Roy Bean, self-described "Law West of the Pecos" after migrating from Maysville to the West Texas frontier. The colorful judge held his court at one end of his saloon bar and once fined a corpse $40 for carrying a concealed weapon at a funeral! A modern Maysville favorite is Rosemary Clooney, who left town to become a nationally known singer of jazz and popular music. She is my third cousin, and had she been older, winning fame back in the 1930s, Nannie would certainly have included Rosemary along with Herman Lee, Meredith, and Kay as a goad to my musical and educational well-being.

Nannie was never one to ignore any goad, negative as well as positive ones, she might use to improve her sons. Among the negative ones were the shantyboat people. They were said to drift lazily in and out with the seasons, fishing and lightly "taxing" farmers' riverside crops and gardens and shunning work beyond that required to buy a few necessities. Several shantyboats were usually tied up at the river end of Commerce Street, the men working hard at unloading sheet metal to make cans at the Carnation Milk Company factory. Others worked elsewhere, but most were good citizens doing their best to make it through hard times.

Many Maysvillians saw them as a shifty lot, perhaps jealous of the tax-free and easygoing lives they were believed to enjoy. After all, they could drift down south for the winter—"just like millionaires!" Grandpa chortled. He was a friendly politician to many of them, and he liked them. His daughter Nannie, however was not to be fooled: "If you don't show some gumption and study harder you'll wind up just like those kids on the shantyboats!" She was never to catch on, but this was one goad that always backfired.

"Like those kids on the shantyboats!" I though elatedly. "Boy, oh boy, would I like to live like them!" I entered my usual dream world at such times: "They don't go to school and just fish and swim off their boat any good old time it suits them. . . . Go up and down the Ohio and Mississippi and see all sorts of things. . . . Even Huck Finn didn't have it any better than them. . . . Here I sit piddlin' around doin' nothin' worthwhile. I wish Mom would shut up about the shantyboat kids; what does she know anyway?"

It was no shantyboat that caught my attention during a pre-Christmas shopping trip to Maysville in 1937 but an American gunboat, the USS *Panay*. Japanese bombers had sunk her in a Chinese river, inflicting numerous casualties. Newsreels, newscasts, and newspapers were full of this unprovoked, viciously arrogant attack. Dad and my uncles Walter "Doc" Hines and Simon Clarkson were enraged, generally deciding that it might be better for the United States to jump Japan now and "get it over with." I was twelve years old and confronted for the first time with the insecure feeling that even my powerful homeland was not immune to attack. But the war scare, like most others, quickly subsided, for neither Japan nor the United States was prepared to carry the issue further.

3

Our Main Street Neighborhood

Sinclair Lewis knew what he was doing when he chose *Main Street* as the title for his sensational novel of 1920. The title linked his overly satirical story with most small towns in America, for nearly every one of them had a Main Street. My hometown's Main Street was about like the rest, I suppose. It lived up to its name in telling where the action was. Sunday mornings it gave way to churchgoers, but Saturday afternoons found farmers and tradesmen, matinee movie fans, shoppers, courthouse denizens, and coveys of kids scurrying back and forth with all the hurly-burly of a football scrimmage. A dozen or so tobacco-chewing citizens always loafed at Cole's corner, where Main and Broadway met, idly watching traffic and ogling women. The smooth sandstone sidewalk was dangerously slick with their tobacco droolings. Mom despised them as a unit, invariably saying when Dad drove by, "I just wish you'd look at that germ-spitting bunch on the corner; there's not a thought among the whole lot of 'em!" Dad chewed tobacco, and I knew he numbered friends among that "germ-spitting bunch," but he always kept quiet and drove on.

Our house was two blocks east of Courthouse Square, on Main Street. The big brick Growers' Tobacco Warehouse was across the street near a busy intersection with Dorsey Avenue. Autos, strollers, and schoolkids passed almost continuously in front of our house, but everything considered, I was sort of proud to live on Main Street.

It was not "Silk Stocking avenue"—Sycamore Street was that—but I believed that a street named Main Street had to be important. After all, there was not another street in town where a kid could sit in his window and watch Louisville and Nashville (L&N) trains puffing smoke and whistling as they crossed nearby Dorsey Avenue!

Our neighbors toward town were Grandma Mathias and Uncle Joe. Everyone in Carlisle called him Uncle Joe. This gentle and friendly little "Dutchman" was a living image of everybody's favorite uncle. He was five feet six, weighed 170 portly pounds, smoked a big curved pipe, and tilted from side to side as he walked and talked his way around town taking care of a modest hail and fire insurance business. When younger he had been Carlisle's fire chief, standing as high as a Napoleon on the smoky steam fire engine as the teamster sent the fire horses galloping and clattering toward flaming homes and business. Later he delivered a rural mail route as his full-time job. When my Grandpa Mathias died in 1915, Joe set himself up as a tailor in the vacant cobbler's shop. "Store-bought" clothes finally ended this effort and led him into insurance. But he was always a character. During the Spanish Civil War Joe's angry mispronunciation of Communists as "com*mun*ists" led listeners to think he was hard set against Spaniards taking communion or the Lord's Supper!

When Uncle Joe ate Sunday dinner with us he usually took the opportunity to tell about several recent articles he had read in his beloved *National Geographic*. His collection of these magazines dated back to 1909. But he was also likely to note that some dish Mom had served up was "Good, but not quite like Mother used to make it." Nannie bit her lip but kept quiet. After he left Lucky usually said that "Joe sure was spouting and blowing today." Mom answered that "if he hadn't been such a momma's boy he would have been eating in his own home all these years."

Uncle Joe was my favorite uncle; he had a lot more going for him than showed at our dinner table. It was no secret that he had long entertained a burning desire to be a "hogger," the engineer on a fast train. He absolutely met every passenger train that came through Carlisle. His presence was an accepted part of the attractive, tile-roofed Louisville and Nashville station, like the tracks or baggage carts. Engineers, firemen, and brakemen knew and liked him, for he never hid his admiration for them or their jobs. They gave him a "ride in the cab" any time he wanted to go to Maysville or Paris. This was undeniable proof to Spud Marshall, Davey Harper, all my other pals, and me that Uncle Joe was truly a man to reckon with.

We could tell that he liked us. When we were at the station, he often treated us to a peek behind the scenes. The telegraph operator smiled at Uncle Joe and his flock of wide-eyed kids as he clicked out and received his dots and dashes. At other times Uncle Joe turned teacher, telling about dreaded "hot boxes" on axle ends or explaining why engines gave out vaporous sighs only in the station yet huffed and puffed mightily out on the open track. Pennies to use in the gumball machine were handed out at the end of each lecture.

A ramshackle one-and-a-half story building ran from Uncle Joe's back porch almost to ours. It was half the size of our bungalow and called the "hoot owl house" after the owls that nested in its attic. Dating back to 1830, it was packed full of stored items which today would be valuable antiques and conversation pieces. When Joe retired as a tailor, he stored his stock and equipment here, thus there were thousands of beautiful and interesting buttons of silver, leather, glass, coral, wood, horn, ivory, and various metals. His shop's set of pressing irons was there, each iron in its slot around the charcoal-fed heating cylinder. Charles and I and our friends banged on several attractively designed but woefully out-of-tune pianos. We dressed up in derby hats and spats and other out-of-date clothing lying around. Grandpa's cobbler bench, tools, and pegs gathered dust in a corner. Although we kids were told to stay out, we sneaked in at every opportunity. But be it said emphatically that we never ever sneaked into the ramshackle old hoot owl house after dark.

The crumbling old structure, with its patchy whitewashed wooden sides, had an eerie voice of its own. Creaks and groans from its settling walls, or the rustle and cries of birds and rodents, issued from it at odd times. We suspected, however, that its truest voice came from ghostly beings much more formidable than mice, weasels, or owls. Our suspicions were based on knowledge that the hoot owl house served as slave quarters for those who owned it before the Civil War.

There was a meticulously built, stone-walled, walk-in basement under half of the building. Twelve heavy iron rings were irremovably set into the stones, most with crudely forged chains and shackles hanging down from them. Any slave under risk as a runaway was presumably chained to one of these rings. Since one in every six people in pre–Civil War Nicholas County was a slave, slave auctions were frequent events. These were held regularly at Courthouse Square, little more than a block away. It may well be that the sturdily built and chain-equipped basement was used as a holding pen for defiant black men headed for the auction block.

Household slaves—men, women, and children—were born, lived, loved, and died upstairs in what we called the single "big room" of the hoot owl house. Thoughts of these things meant that after dark the hulking old structure was totally free of kids playing hide 'n seek or anything else. We resembled exactly the timid soul who said, "I don't believe in ghosts . . . but they're there."

As has happened all too often in Carlisle, Uncle Joe's old home and the hoot owl house slave quarters were torn down in the 1970s. A grocery store parking lot was deeply dug and walled into the site. The ghosts may still be hanging around, however, for something— or someone—keeps causing the wall to crack and collapse back into the lot.

Slavery left many stains on the social, cultural, religious, and economic life of Nicholas County. As for me, growing up in former slave territory attuned me more to the past than if I had lived elsewhere. It added spice to life, as evidence the hoot owl house, but it also instilled a sense of the human tragedy. I felt as if history had happened to me. I had no trouble identifying myself, my homeland, and my sentiments with those of the Reverend James Dickey as I later read of a scene he witnessed in 1822 along the Maysville Road a few miles from Carlisle, quoted by Joan Conley in her masterful *History of Nicholas County:* "Forty black men were all chained together . . . in rank and file. A chain perhaps forty feet long was stretched between the two ranks, to which short chains were joined which connected with handcuffs. Behind them were, I suppose, about thirty women, in double rank, the couples tied hand to hand."

My schoolteacher mother became aware of the tie between Nicholas County and the Reverend John Rankin's risky Underground Railroad station secluded on the steep Ohio River bluff above Ripley, Ohio. Her Tuckahoe Ridge birthplace was only a few miles southeast of Ripley. Rankin, Carlisle's Presbyterian minister, spent years denouncing slavery from his and other of the county's pulpits. He made little progress, but when convinced of his abolitionist calling, he moved to Ripley to meet slavery head-on. Escaped slaves were shunted from his place north to Canada.

Nannie was never one to let an interesting subject die a natural death. She took notes on the Carlisle-Rankin-Ripley connection, finding proof in J. Winston Coleman's popular *Slavery Times in Kentucky* that Nicholas County slaves had probably passed through Rankin's station. I have one of her notes to that effect, written in her attractively legible penmanship, honed by years of teaching the subject. She copied an article Coleman had taken from the Paris *Kentucky State Flag* of December 17, 1855: "Runaways drowned! . . . A party of six slaves ran away from . . . Millersburg. One belonged to Mrs. Emily Taylor of Bourbon, one to Mr. Miller, of Irish Station, in *Nicholas County,* and the others to persons in the *latter county.* . . . The negroes attempted to cross the river [near Maysville] in a skiff about daylight. . . . The skiff overturned and the three women and child drowned" (italics Nannie's).

Mom's motives in running such information to the ground were several and not all of them purely intellectual. She of course fed the information to Charles and me as a mother robin might feed her young. And she was always ready to boost Lucky's allegedly low-octane educational estate. But she was a competitive soul and sought ways to keep up with friends in the PTA and high school teaching staff.

Nannie was never to understand that her sometimes stated belief that "Mason County is ahead of Nicholas in so many ways" was not shared by most Nicholas Countians, including Dad. He was "tolerably embarrassed," he said, when she told a mixed group of his friends that the Reverend John Rankin could do nothing with Nicholas Countians and had to move to Ripley to carry out his calling. This is probably true, but it was not the kind of thing homefolks wanted to hear. Dad always peeked at Charles and me, winking whenever Mom was "feeling her Mason County oats," as he called it.

The county's African American population skidded from 1,800 at the Civil War's end to perhaps 250 by 1930. They lived in a shacky village adjoining Carlisle called Henryville. They had no running water, no sidewalks, and owing to their tiny tax base, little chance of getting either. Children of high school age were bussed over forty miles to and from a segregated school in Montgomery County. Their parents worked in service jobs or as laborers; several, however, were successful barbers, mechanics, ministers, and craftsmen. I neither heard of, nor saw, any physical mistreatment of these citizens, but they were fully expected to "know their place." Sometimes they broke this unwritten rule. A widely whispered "scandal" of the 1930s concerned the son of a leading citizen who had "run off and married that Henryville woman" and settled in Ohio.

My pals and I accepted the racial situation as normal, and seldom actively questioned it. Indeed, trips to Ohio convinced me that the Buckeye State, when compared to Kentucky, was hypocrisy-ridden. At Cincinnati and Columbus swimming pools I often had to "join the club" or pass some sort of "inspection"—"keeps blacks out," it was whispered. Even worse was a sizable highway sign at the entrance to an Ohio county seat advising pointedly that "Negroes do not spend the night here—do your business and move on." The swimming restrictions and the sign perplexed me but made me smugly glad to live in Kentucky, where, I naively believed, "colored folks are treated right." It would take the Nazis and the Japanese to teach the GI Generation the horrible dangers of race hatred.

Few boys are as lucky in neighbors as I was. On one side was an uncle who seemed likely any day to blossom into a railroad "hogger," while on the other lived an honest-to-goodness genuine cowboy! Edwin G. Metcalfe was a Christian preacher's son who punched cattle in Montana for fifteen years, then spent a frigid three more working in Yukon gold mines. Patriotism, fifty-below-zero thermometer readings, and the unpleasant presence of swarms of huge and hungry Yukon mosquitos all caught up with him by 1917, so he sailed to France with the American Expeditionary Force. Most AEF vets, like Metcalfe, saw no combat, thus their tales left my generation with the erroneous idea that war must be loads of fun! Ed was forty-two in 1919 when he returned to Carlisle. He relished telling what happened next: "I never intended to be a nester after twenty years of roaming, but I got captured by a redhead and never got away."

The "redhead" was Elsie McIntyre, daughter of a local dentist who died in 1920, shortly after Ed and Elsie were married. Ed became man of the house in the old McIntyre home next door, where Andrew, an only child, was born. We could not have had better neighbors, for "Uncle" Ed, "Aunt" Elsie, Ed's mother-in-law Sarah Parsons "Bummie" McIntyre, and son Andrew fit into the Mathias family life better than most of our blood relations. Andy was like an older brother to me. The two families shared all, from the latest jokes to fears the Depression was going to do us in.

Ed was a natural storyteller, whether in his small uptown grocery or in his front porch swing; he was ever ready to spin a yarn. Listeners felt the freedom yet empty loneliness of the Great Plains, or shivered with him under the Yukon's coldly beautiful northern lights or peeked shyly at a doughboy using a "pissery" (pissoir) on a Paris street. Some of his tales were published in a postwar *Louisville Courier-Journal* article, but his friends and neighbors had enjoyed these stories long before this. Perhaps I can recreate some of them.

"I can't forget the spring of '99," he said slowly as heads turned his way. "I was twenty-two and handed the big job of driving two hundred horses from northern Montana's Sweet Grass Hills, with orders to sell them in North Dakota. As we moved by a forest late one afternoon I saw shadows flickering through the trees—wolves!" He paused to let that sink in. "The herd was healthy with no stragglers, so I wasn't too worried. I settled for the night at a water hole, ate, then rode guard 'til dawn. During that long trail I saw nary a fence nor cross trail. It was open country, but all I needed to get my bearings was to look west at the snowy peaks of the Rockies."

Uncle Ed was never one to gild the lily when he told his tales. One day my pal Bobby Cunningham and I were in his store ogling the candy. Bobby was a Christian preacher's son, as was Ed. I had told Bobby about my fabulous neighbor, painting a word picture in keeping with movie cowboys. My pal had an important question ready: "Mr. Metcalfe, how many rustlers did you shoot with your six-gun when you were a cowboy?" Aunt Elsie was standing nearby, and she chuckled along with her husband.

"You're a preacher's son, Bobby, and I'm going to tell you the truth—none! Why, boy, I never even owned a pistol. You and Frank have seen too many movies. Nobody I ever rode with ever warbled songs around campfires. We dressed about like the hands at Tickie Fisher's lumberyard here—big work shoes, cotton shirts, and jeans." Bobby and I could not doubt Uncle Ed, but we still closely followed the likes of Tom Mix, Bob Steele, Buck Jones, and other movie cowboys. We overlooked their fancy boots and clothes so long as they did not kiss anything but horses.

Ed's tales of the Yukon were relished by listeners as much as his cowboy stories. Sometime before World War I he left Montana to try his luck in the Yukon, Canada's bitterly cold province along Alaska's eastern border. A personable, muscular six-footer, Metcalfe soon had work as a sharpener of drill steel in a gold mine. The placer mines of gold rush days had given way to shaft or quartz mines.

Ed's friends soon included Robert Service and Sam McGee, both destined for literary fame. The three roomed together for a time. Service wrote poetry while working as a bank clerk in White Horse, and McGee, a Canadian rancher, came north for lengthy visits. Service got a laugh throughout White Horse when he published *The Cremation of Sam McGee*:

The Northern Lights have seen
Queer sights,
But the queerest they ever did see
Was that night on the marge of
Lake Lebarge
I cremated Sam McGee . . .

"Bob tricked Sam with that one for sure," Ed recalled, "but it didn't take Sam long to get back at his friend." Metcalfe now tensed his audience, telling how McGee and Service were skiffing along a flood-swollen river when McGee's oars snagged, upset the boat, and hurled the two into the river. Some men nearby pulled them from the swirling, icy water, but McGee, after getting his confidence back, pretended to the crowd of laughing onlookers and rescuers that the snagged oars were no accident. "He raised his fist," Ed said, "and shouted that 'Bob damn near froze me to death in that oven so I just decided I'd drown him!'"

Edwin Grubbs Metcalfe's Nicholas County roots go back to 1800, the year Thomas "Stonehammer" Metcalfe, his great-grand-father, arrived from Virginia. He was a stone mason turned politician who was elected Kentucky's governor in 1829. The governor and his family are buried in a graveyard behind Forest Retreat, a lovely home he built early in the nineteenth century. The Metcalfes often took me with them when they put flowers on the graves on Decoration Day. In short, history happened to Ed Metcalfe, and through him to his friends and associates.

History had also happened to Sarah Parsons McIntyre, his mother-in-law. She survived America's worst war as a child. Sarah was seven in 1862 when her dad, Thomas Parsons, rode away with the Fourteenth Kentucky (Union) Cavalry. He left three children and his wife behind. The next year he was captured during a fight with John Hunt Morgan's raiders. While he was awaiting exchange at Camp Chase, near Columbus, Ohio, word arrived that his wife was deathly ill from the effects of measles, probably pneumonia. For two days and nights he struggled desperately to get home, traveling two hundred miles by foot, train, wagon, and ferry. He did not make it in time. His wife's sister lay sobbing on a floor pallet when he arrived. Sarah sat with her brother and sister on rumpled bed-clothes, their faces scaling from measles and all of them crying. His wife had only died minutes before his arrival.

Uncle Joe sometimes said that "Elsie Metcalfe is sound as a dollar." This might not mean much in today's economy, but in the 1930s it meant that there was an unimpaired wholeness about her, that she had integrity. Elsie was an attractive and energetic woman who mirrored her husband's sense of humor. Both were about the same age as Lucky and Nannie.

Andrew Metcalfe, an only child, was born in 1920 and was a truly reliable friend to me until he was killed in action in World War II. As a toddler he was unable to say "mummie," thus fixing "Bummie" as a family and neighborhood nickname on his grandmother McIntyre.

Bummie wore ankle-length dresses and a bonnet. She held that children should be seen and not heard but was never cranky about it. Bummie and Elsie did their serious cooking on a large cast-iron range in their "dogtrot" kitchen. This was a one-room shed with a covered walkway built behind their house in 1829 for fire protection. Lighter cooking was done on a coal oil stove inside the home. They often let me watch them if I fetched fuel for them and agreed not to become "pestiferous." They started the fire in the "fire box" by layering corn cobs, kindling, and coal, adjusting these for heat as long experience dictated. Their cooking top offered six eight-inch lids. There was one three-ring sectional lid to fit different-sized cooking utensils and an antiscorch lid to prevent burning of cereals and the like after long cooking. The big stove did two things for them in addition to oven baking: an eight-gallon "reservoir" heated water and a "warming closet" kept food warm until served. Bummie and Elsie did all of their canning and baking here and were usually willing to hand out a hot slice of bread and jam to kids they knew. I saw rousing games of cowboys and Indians disintegrate when the smells of hot salt-rising bread or blackberry cobblers got in the way of the action.

Verna and Maud Stone and their daughter Pauline lived in our neighborhood on the other side of Uncle Joe's house. Like the Metcalfes, they ran a store on Main Street and were good friends. Their ample yard was the western edge of a block-long play area for neighborhood children. Maud and Vernie were about the same age as Lucky and Nannie; in fact, nearly every couple on the block was of their generation. But there came a time when Maud Stone was held in very low repute by my ten-year-old brother.

One spring Charles invested his savings by having Uncle Ed order him a dozen Plymouth Rock chicks. Groceries served hatcheries as middlemen, and before long twelve fuzzy little chicks arrived in special boxes. Charles was now in the chicken business and soon had healthy, white-feathered pullets in a chicken wire enclosure in the hoot owl house. He had not yet noticed that the Stones had built a nice chicken house in their backyard. It contained some white Plymouth Rocks about the same age as his, standing out against the darker barred Plymouth Rocks in the Stones' new coop.

One afternoon Charles was puzzled to find that three of his chickens were missing. It never occurred to him that a weasel, owl, or rat could easily have gotten into his lightly guarded chickens. It was then that he noticed the Stones' chicken coop and their white Plymouth Rocks for the first time. That did it! He immediately marched to their back door and knocked. Maud came to the door with her usual smile. "What is it, Charles?" she asked, perhaps expecting a plea to raid her large cherry tree.

"Mrs. Stone," the little boy intoned with chilling conviction, "you've been stealing my chickens!"

It took considerable time for all of us to convince my redheaded brother that there were no chicken thieves in the neighborhood. He lost a few pullets to varmints, then sold all but his pet to regain his investment. He named his pet "Don" after Andrew Metcalfe's male hound, and Don soon grew to be a broiler-size hen. She followed him around, sensing that she was special.

Mom told Dad one day to prepare a chicken she had tied by the back porch. She had water boiling and knew Lucky would have the bird ready in record time. And why not? He was an expert. After eighth grade Dad worked for two years as a fifty-cent-a-day chicken plucker for M.T. Ruddell's Bluegrass Produce House. I always watched in awe as he opened his keenly honed pocket knife—the one he also used to spear sardines from the can when eating on the road—grabbed the chicken, cut off its head, let it run headless around the yard until it dropped, then dunked it in a bucket of boiling water. He pulled it out to cool a minute before scooping the loosened feathers off in several quick handfuls. After disemboweling and rinsing it, he cut it into pieces and took it to Mom ready for the stove. But on this day Nannie startled him, rolling her eyes at the ceiling: "Oh Lord, what have you done!"

"What do you mean, what have I done? I've got the chicken ready, haven't I?"

"It can't be," she cried. "I just saw my chicken through the window, still tied by the tiger lilies. You've grabbed Charles's pet by mistake!"

Evasive action was out of the question; we decided to eat the chicken before telling him. I soon backed out of the deal. Eating Don smacked of cannibalism so I told my brother what had happened. He cried and fumed for a week, getting sympathy and special treatment until Dad said, "Shut up boy or I'll have to take my belt to you." Charles, never a fool, shut up and got on with his chickenless life.

Each year when cold weather came—called "hog-killing time" in the country—the Earlywines and Mathiases got together for a hard times backyard cookout. Jake Earlywine and his attractive family lived behind us. "Little Jake" and Frances, his sister, were my playmates. Lucky and Jake bought a large hog each autumn. Verna Stone killed and bled it and delivered it to our backyard.

An afternoon of work began with scraping off bristles, then cutting out pieces and hams, and finally rendering the rest in a big cast-iron kettle over a smoky wood fire. Pure kitchen lard went into flat trays where it solidified. Remaining lard was mixed with lye, solidified in trays, and sliced into small blocks of powerful cleaning soap. Work over, we doused the fire, shooed stray cats from the scraps, cleaned the utensils and divided the harvest. We felt good as we looked at each other. We had shared a lot of work, but what we had came much cheaper than commercial lard, soap, or pork. Every Depression penny counted.

Anyone describing Miss Phoebe Henry would have to start by saying she was simply a sweet old lady. She was a bit older than Bummie but dressed the same way, with ankle-length skirts over high button shoes. Her small brick house was behind the Metcalfes', but she had long since surrendered her backyard to tall grasses, various weeds, wildflowers, and shrubby plants—altogether a much used junglelike hideaway for neighborhood kids.

Miss Phoebe emerged as a minor attraction for Andrew Metcalfe when he started dating. My pals and I, hidden in the undergrowth, watched him take girlfriends, nearly all whom were named Jane, to visit Miss Phoebe. She undoubtedly enjoyed the attention, but Andy had an ulterior motive. He discovered that his elderly neighbor saved cylindrical toilet paper "cores" and eggshells. The cores were tied in red and blue ribbons and placed in likely spots around her home. The eggshells were displayed like seashells in boxes and bottles. Miss Phoebe enjoyed her high school visitors, pointing proudly to the decorated cores and glistening eggshells. I envied Andy's expertise in things like this, for he not only won Miss Phoebe's affection but at the same time left his dates laughing.

On a nearby street, "Grandpa" and "Grandma" Smith lived in elderly peace until their stepson came back to town. He moved his wife and kids into the big but creaky Smith house. Although Shorty Smith looked "like a bantam rooster," as some said, he had the temperament of an opossum—playing dead if confronted with much opposition. Shorty soon had a low-paying job, and Charles and I became pals with Roy, his son.

Word soon got around that Shorty was a wife-beater. When his workweek ended on Saturday he got drunk and, depending on his mood, beat his wife and slapped the kids around. Roy verified that. Dad, Ed Metcalfe, and Jake Earlywine collared Shorty one afternoon and laid the law down to him—stop beating her or be dragged bodily to jail. That stopped him for at least that weekend.

Grandpa Smith came up with a more fitting "solution" several weekends later. Roy told me what his granddad had done, and we decided to hide in the bushes behind the house and see what happened. We were eleven years old. Grandpa Smith had discovered a pint of liquor Shorty had hidden on the screened back porch. He knew his stepson would grab it as soon as he came in from work. Roy had watched in fascination: "Grandpa poured half the whiskey out and then pissed the bottle full again!"

Roy and I watched Shorty come out on the porch. He snaked

the liquor out of its lair and bit into the cork, slowly pulling it from the bottle. It popped as it slid out. Shorty had been waiting all day for this. He smiled, lifted the bottle to his lips, threw his head back with the whiskey on high, and took a long draw: "P-p-p-f-f-f-t-t-t!" He spit and sprayed the telltale taste out of his mouth and through the rusty screen. "The old fart has done it! Damn 'im he's done!" he screamed. "I'll sure as hell get 'im for this!" he added, still spitting, fuming, and stomping back and forth on the sagging porch floor.

"Daddy looked all over the place for Grandpa," Roy said later, "but he had slipped off uptown 'til he figured it was safe to come home." Things seemed to run more smoothly at the Smith house after this. There was no more talk of wife-beating.

In the mid-1930s Carlisle's four big tobacco warehouses were torn down. They were skeletons of the once thriving tobacco market, now ready for economic burial. The brick one across from my home had long been a wet weather playground for east end kids. It accommodated Halloween get-togethers, church festivals, and most any childhood game. The silky smooth concrete basement floor was a favorite of roller skaters, while upstairs a fine wooden floor was brightly lit in daytime by scores of ceiling skylights. In today's world this big building would be seen as a public asset and purchased by the town. The depressed world of the 1930s dictated a different fate; it was torn down and the lot sold along with the bricks.

Great heaps of mortar-encrusted bricks were piled about the lot. Jobs cleaning them paid ten cents per hundred. Charles and I, Roberta and James Hughes, and boys and girls from all over the east end leaped at the offer. An old screwdriver or chisel and hammer were the only tools needed. It was the first paying job for most of us. Ten cents went a long way, yet after the first one hundred bricks we knew we were earning it. But the fine old warehouse was a neighbor we sorely missed from that time on.

Three favorite neighbors, the "Henry Girls," lived three houses east of me. "Miss Lucille," "Miss Jenny," and "Miss Jimmie," spinsters all, lived in a large frame home at the eastern edge of the unfenced neighborhood play area. Two gigantic sycamores rose between their sidewalk and Main Street, each with a horse hitching ring embedded in its trunk. Fatty King hitched his horse and ice wagon here while he made deliveries around the neighborhood, shooing boys away from scraps of ice when he returned. Kids passing those trees always grabbed the leather straps dangling from each ring and swung around the trees. A much greater attraction was the heavily laden gooseberry bushes behind the house. Flocks of kids and blackbirds descended annually on the berries, picking some for themselves and some for the "Girls."

A different kind of attraction gradually won my attention. Frances, the Girls' niece, often dropped by with Laddy, her beautiful collie. We three played together, as rough and tumble as I ever did with my buddies. "I like Frances a lot," I thought, "even if she is a girl." I had heard of sweethearts and wondered if she and I might qualify. "I'd better go ask Andrew," I reasoned, "'cause he's started high school and knows just about everything."

Andy loved this kind of question, being as thoroughgoing a romantic as I was. "Of course you're sweethearts!" he replied, shaking his head as if any fool would know that. "You're a Francis and she's a Frances—even your names go together. Say, what's the name of that pretty little Earlywine girl that lives up behind your house?"

"Frances," I replied.

"See there! See there!" Andy exclaimed, reveling in this unexpected addition to his clever answer. "You've got the whole neighborhood sewed up!" And we both laughed. I knew better than that but laughed with relief, perhaps because Andy's silly answers freed me from something I did not understand anyway. Even if Frances and I were sweethearts, I had not the slightest idea what came next. Instead, we played together as usual, but one day she showed up with a mouthful of metal.

"Gold teeth!" I exclaimed. "Boy, are they nice!"

She answered me with a resigned look on her face: "They are braces, silly, and I hate them."

So much for my first love affair.

4

Cigars and
Cinnamon Balls

The first grade beckoned. It was the day after Labor Day in Depression-ridden 1931. Dad kissed me and drove off to work; Mom walked me two blocks to Carlisle's one big public school building.

When Mom and I entered the first grade room, I looked it over and decided I was not going to like it. Miss McCloud, the attractive young teacher introduced herself as the bell rang. She began talking to the class, telling us how much she would enjoy teaching us. But as she talked the mothers left, slipping silently out through the cloakroom. I kept my eye on Mom. Miss McCloud distracted me with some chalk sketches on the blackboard. I turned around. Mom was missing—she had slipped out! I had been deserted. Fear crept into me. I was afraid to leave and afraid to stay. I wrangled with this problem for a few minutes, then panic struck. I ran out of the room and all the way home, not even stopping to say hello to Miss Phoebe as she puttered around on her back porch. Mom welcomed and comforted me, gradually making me think I wanted to try again. An hour passed, then she and I walked back. Mom waved to a smiling Miss McCloud as I walked in and took my seat. It was the rough beginning of a happy school year.

The first grade room was nestled into a first floor corner of the big brick school. It was a sunny room with rows of small desks huddled in awe of the teacher's big desk centered up front. Tall windows graced two sides of the room and slate blackboards the rest. Letters of the alphabet, numerals, and pictures of animals ran across the top of the blackboards. Impressive steam radiators stood below most windows. When winter came we were entertained and often startled by the hissing and popping sounds they made. Winter also set us staring intently from our desks up through the windows in the hope of seeing snowflakes silhouetted against the sky. When snow did come, the wooly smell of scarfs, gloves, and hats drying on the radiators filled the room.

I fit quickly into my new life, sensing I was now part of things beyond my home. I felt this keenly during my walk to school. After passing through Miss Phoebe's overgrown yard, I joined a stream of students of all ages. I admired boys clattering sticks across the up-right slats of an iron picket fence running alongside the Cox house sidewalk. I could do this as well as anybody, but I could not whistle like the older boys. And I was amazed the following spring when boys and girls made screeching sounds by blowing through maple seed wings held between tongues and teeth. Since I was dressed in short pants and long brown stockings instead of knickers, I sensed I still had a lot to learn.

During the first grade I gradually fell in love with my teacher. There was no chance she could beat Mom's time, but Miss McCloud had earned my affectionate attention. I made good grades because she was the teacher. When I discovered a pretty ring inside a Cracker Jack box, I knew what to do with it. Dad had just given Mom a ring for her birthday, making her happy. During the first grade's May picnic in parklike Mathers' Woods, I sat in the violet-dimpled grass next to Miss McCloud. "Here's a ring for you," I said, my eyes full of admiration.

"Why, thank you, Frank!" she exclaimed in pleasant surprise, slipping it on her finger. "You're a sweet little boy." She gave me a hug, and I knew I had done the right thing.

All but one of the twenty-one first graders fit easily into the class. The exception was an oversized, gawky boy with shaggy hair and shy demeanor. His mother came with him the first two months, sitting like a sentinel in a corner chair. Her black dresses touched the floor, covering men's work shoes. She kept her bonnet on during class. She was different, and her intelligent son knew it. If asked a question, she usually replied, "I can't rightly say." My classmates and I shamefully teased her son behind her back. Our parents scolded us for this but we did it anyway. Her son quit, I think, after finishing the eighth grade. I forgot about him until I opened a *Cincinnati Times-Star* decades later. There was a large photo of a noted Ohio banker standing proudly beside his award-winning bank manager. I read the manager's name, looked closely at the photo, and was pleasantly surprised to find that everything matched—he was the "Ugly Duckling" from grade school!

Whenever I walked home for dinner (no one said "lunch"), my competitive three-year-old brother made sure I did not hog Mom's attention. Anytime I seemed to do so, he dropped to the floor and banged his head up and down until noticed. Andrew Metcalfe thought this was the funniest thing he had ever seen—thus prompting Charles to perform regularly for him.

I liked the first grade and was vaguely unhappy when the school year ended. But before summer vacation, an unpleasant event came my way. No one could win a blue ribbon at the annual May Day festivities without proof of a general health examination, and this included teeth. With this in mind, Dad took me to see Stanley Hutchings, his dentist and longtime fishing friend. Although I knew and liked Dr. Hutchings, I did not know what to expect. When I saw the dental chair, I thought he ran a barber shop and sat down to get a haircut. He probed gently here and there in my mouth and found a cavity. Hutchings pulled his drill down and let me feel the stone-tipped burr spinning painlessly between my fingers. "This little drill won't hurt a big boy like you very much, will it?" he asked, grinning a typical dentist's grin and knowing all the while he was lying through his teeth.

I looked at Dad for reassurance, and he nodded and grinned in agreement with Hutchings, then took his false teeth out and snapped them at me. (It was my understanding that he and Mom had lost their teeth owing to "diarrhea," not learning until several years later, and with some relief, that the word was "pyorrhea," an infection of the gums and tooth sockets.)

I laughed at Dad's antics, but when the dentist stuck his drill into the cavity, the laugh was on me. The low-speed drill of that era heated the tooth as it slowly ground its painful way through the decay. When the pain hit me full force, I called a halt to the proceedings, saying: "I want to go home *right now!*"

"It will just take a little bit more, Frankie," Hutchings said sympathetically, "and then you will be set to get a blue ribbon and your name in the paper. What do you think of that?"

I liked what he said, so I stuck it out. But every year after that I endured a frightful May Day trip to the dentist's office, expecting the worst for my cavity-prone teeth. I laid a stick or object of some kind at the foot of the long stairs leading to Hutchings's forbidding office, saying to myself, "Boy, oh boy, will I be glad to pick this up again!" And I was, forgetting teeth forever and a year.

When I entered the first grade Dad was fifty and Mom forty-three. Some of my classmates' grandparents were younger. Charles and I experienced the ups and downs of children actually raised by grandparents. Moreover, the Great War dug an immense social, cultural, and moral trench between preceding generations and those that followed. At the time, however, few understood that the Roaring Twenties were ushering in the "modern world," least of all Lucky, Nannie, and their two boys.

Charles and I were of course unable to understand that our parents had grown up in a society far different from our own, nor could they be expected to tell us. They were Victorians, raised in the most optimistic of centuries, the nineteenth, when there was an almost sacred belief that all good things were possible. Townspeople of their generation, such as the Metcalfes, were just like them. World War I is said to have undermined these beliefs, and perhaps it did for battered Europeans, but most of the old ways lived on in battle-free America; at least they were in full flower in white, Anglo-Saxon, Protestant Carlisle. Although rejecting some Victorian values—Prohibition, for example—my generation held on to the old social and cultural unity necessary to overcome the near fatal challenge of fascism in World War II. But with Victorians for parents, my brother and I felt no little confusion as we explored a completely unmarked trail between the old and the new.

As far as Dad was concerned, the modern world could go its way and he would go his. Sports, for example, meant little to Dad for he had worked hard since leaving the eighth grade. His one great recreational obsession was fishing, which he shared fully with Charles and me. But he never pitched ball with us, nor did he know much or care about the Cincinnati Reds, the UK Wildcats, or even the Carlisle Musketeers. He never once criticized any sport or its fans; he simply walked his silent path and expected others to do the same.

The radio got Lucky somewhat involved in sports for the first time in his life, not as a participant, of course, but as a listener/fan. In 1927 he bought a Crosley radio. At first glance it seemed to be a spindly metal table with an absurdly thick top. On closer inspection, one found that the top had several tuning dials and that a saucer-size speaker hung on several wires under the top. Lucky strung some two hundred feet of fine wire over and around the hoot owl house for an aerial. He loved to tinker with the radio and aerial, and he kept both working so well we could pick up Havana.

Lucky became hooked on heavyweight title bouts and Notre Dame football. In tight bouts or games he became as loud and aggressive as a man half his age. One memorable 1933 heavyweight title bout pitted Jack Sharkey against Primo Carnera. Dad huddled by the radio, becoming fully and loudly involved as Sharkey and Carnera–the "Wild Bull of the Pampas"—battled it out. Suddenly, there was shouting and noise outside; people were running through our yard. Dad turned up the radio, but a torrent of noise now came in from across the street—the small combined grocery and dwelling next to the warehouse was on fire! By this time the uptown fire bell was ringing wildly, calling the volunteers to the engine. Help was obviously needed to carry out furniture and grocery stocks. "Charlie," Mom shouted, "you've got to do something!"

"Damn! Damn! Damn!" Lucky grumbled loudly as he stormed out the door. "That damned place would catch fire in the middle of the best fight of the year!"

Seventeen years later I was reminded of Dad and his addiction to championship prizefights. I was a ticket and customs agent for National Airlines at Miami International Airport. Someone cleared his throat while I was busily hunched over my desk. I looked up and was startled to be staring into the placid face of Joe Louis. I was thrilled.

"Hope I can get a ticket for Cuba here," Louis said in his low-key way.

"You're in the right place," I replied. "We've got six flights a day with plenty of seats on most of them. Say, I saw you fight an exhibition bout at Fort Benning back in 1945. Sugar Ray Robinson was on the same program."

"Yeah," he said, "I remember those days," nodding as I handed him his ticket. As he walked away, I pondered those bygone days when Dad and most white boxing fans followed Louis's fights with the express hope that a white man would finally beat him. Times had changed. I admitted to myself that Joe Louis had stood for a lot more than boxing titles.

Except for Notre Dame, Dad never had much to say for football. He had no deep knowledge of the game, and I am certain he could not have named the positions played by the eleven athletes. He may have had a vague religious identification with the school, but I never heard him say so. He loved to back a winner, however, and in the days of Knute Rockne and Elmer Layden the Fighting Irish walloped team after team almost as if from force of habit. He also put these games and boxing bouts to practical use, for they served as excellent conversation starters along his sales route.

Dad was little more involved in his sons' schoolwork than he was in sports, but Mom easily took up all the slack. My brother and I got advice and help only when we could prove it was "deserved." Nannie had a near uncanny knack of knowing whether Charles and I really deserved help with a lesson or whether we were trying to fool her into solving our problems, and help never came if we did not deserve it. She often filled in as a substitute teacher at the high school, so I thought of her in some ways as I did of my other teachers. It was good to hear classmates praise her as a typing and shorthand teacher, but as she often said, "It's so easy to teach when backed by a first-rate superintendent," and Carlisle had one.

Everett Earl Pfanstiel, called "Fanny" behind his back by the students, was appointed superintendent of Carlisle City Schools in

1926. An alumnus of Transylvania University, he held an M.A. degree and was a World War I veteran and a native of nearby Bracken County. Admirably equipped by nature and by training, Pfanstiel combined a sensitive sense of justice with a humorous, easygoing manner that in no way interfered with his consistent demand for quality or with his intolerance for cheating or serious student troublemaking. Any miscreant "sent up" to Fanny's office took a trip few wanted to repeat. In other words, his name meant discipline; education cannot take place without it.

Pfanstiel's public school domain boasted a commanding presence on a low hill overlooking the town. Grades occupied the first floor and high school the upper two stories. There was a large auditorium, with stage, usually called "chapel," with stained glass windows and church-type pews for seats. Chapel was held once a week. Protestant ministers and occasionally the Catholic priest often spoke to the four hundred or so students on such subjects as cheating, honesty, fighting and other nondoctrinal topics. The Lord's Prayer was recited here as well as in classrooms each morning. I heard no complaint regarding "violation of church and state separation," either from my parents or from anyone else.

I first met the superintendent when several of us first graders were inspecting a strange contraption in the "boys' basement." This was the boys' part of a basement underlying the entire school, with toilets and play areas. The girls had their part, as did the Penny Lunch and home economics department. Brick walls separated each part. The funny-looking contraption we first-graders puzzled over was a generator with protruding, long, paddlelike wooden blades set in a half-circle—at least, that is my best memory of the thing. Pfanstiel happened to walk by while we were inspecting it. "Don't you boys know what that is?" he asked.

"No, sir," we answered. We had heard a lot about him and were impressed that he had paused to talk to us.

"Why, boys," he replied, with a meaningful grin on his face, "that's my paddling machine."

We of course believed him, holding the thing in awe until it was removed, presumably for action in his formidable office.

Pfanstiel had a genius for showing up at the wrong time, a

characteristic my brother experienced when he lit a string of fire-crackers at recess in the basement. The elated smirk had hardly left his face when a big hand reached around a corner and grabbed a handful of his red hair, bending him over. A paddle blazed a trail across his rear end. Fanny released him but stood there with a quiz-zical look on his face, as if to ask how such a stupid thing could ever have happened. He was famous for this look. But Charles's respect for the superintendent soon increased greatly, for Fanny did not tell Lucky about the firecrackers. Had he done so, Charles would have gotten another paddling.

I, too, learned the hard way. One boring afternoon in study hall I embedded a pin in my shoe sole and hunched my foot across the aisle to jab Martha Barnett, two seats to the front. As I was midway into the act my rear end exploded, as if hit by a sky rocket. There stood Pfanstiel, quizzical look and all, holding his long, thin paddle. I was surprised it was not smoking. As he slowly made his way through the room, I was embarrassed; I hated to look at my classmates' smiling faces. They later pointed out my oversight. "Didn't you notice the silence when he came in through the cloak-room door?" Martha asked, more mindful of my plight than of my attempt to stick her with a pin.

"How come you didn't smell the cigar odor and the cinnamon balls?" John Hopkins wanted to know. He had me there, for every-one knew Fanny smoked cigars and chewed cinnamon balls, leaving a telltale smell wherever he went. I just rubbed my sore butt and shook my head, but I was thankful he would not tell on me. Parents backed the teachers and the students knew it. Discipline, in effect, came from within the student body itself.

"Professor" Pfanstiel, as the townspeople called him, had much more going for him than his paddle. One day Dicky Jones, as I shall call him, came to the superintendent's office with a puzzling request: "Sir, I want to be excused from attending graduation exercises."

"Why, Dicky," Pfanstiel said in a bewildered tone of voice, "you are a fine student and I want to know why you make such a request."

"Mr. Pfanstiel, I just don't have the money to buy a suit and all the other seniors are set to wear them."

Fanny immediately stood up, put his arm around Dicky's shoulder, and headed out the door. "We are going downtown right now and I'm going to buy you a suit." Although Jones was too proud to accept Pfanstiel's offer, the small town added this to a lengthy listing of Fanny's concern for his students.

Pfanstiel was ahead of his time in waging a continual antismoking campaign in behalf of student health and fire safety. Although he smoked an occasional cigar, he was determined to stamp out smoking on school grounds, especially in the boys' basement toilet and play area.

There were few if any campaigns against smoking in the 1930s, especially in a state and county where tobacco was the economic mainstay. Smoking and chewing seemed harmless to most Americans, but not to Fanny. We grade-schoolers were shown expensive full-color pictures of the dark, putrid lungs of heavy smokers, as compared to the rosy, healthy lungs of abstainers. Pfanstiel called cigarettes "coffin nails" and "nicotine sticks." The football and basketball coaches testified that cigarettes caused "short wind and low performance" in any athlete foolish enough to smoke them. As a result, I did not become foolish enough to smoke anything but a few Indian cigars until I was in the army.

Sometime during the mid-1930s the superintendent began mentioning the "Basement Puff Club" when he spoke at the Wednesday chapel assemblies. He created the title to designate a number of willful and habitual smokers in the boys' basement. One Wednesday he offered a challenge to members of the club. He said something like this: "I'll call members of the Basement Puff Club into my office from now on and tell each one which kind or brand of cigarette he was smoking and the exact time he did it. If I'm correct, the smoker will be honor bound to admit it, quit all smoking on campus, and accept a paddling."

One by one, and sometimes two by two, the "club" began losing members to Fanny's paddle. As he expected, the lads had tacitly accepted his terms and saw the thing as a game stacked in their favor: "Fanny'll play hell catchin' me" was the general feeling. But Pfanstiel did catch them, and all were perplexed as to how he pinned down the exact time, the brand of cigarette smoked, and often even the conversation and number of puffs taken by the smug youths of the "club." Although smugness was paddled out of them, they added to a student belief that Fanny had mysterious power to see through walls or read smokers' minds. Most have never learned his secret.

Students came closer to divining his secret than they knew; he was, in effect, "seeing through walls." I was a senior before I learned that the superbly built school had several walk-through ventilation shafts built into the three-story, thick-walled structure. It was possible, given a boost by a pal, to look down into some classrooms through small, ceiling-level, screened registers. (One could also peer into an uninspiring section of the girls' basement this way.) An innocuous looking door in the boys' basement led into the shafts. It had a misleading sign concerning electrical power plant dangers on its front and a hinge-hasp with an imposing but broken combination lock. One side shaft dead-ended in a home economics room closet where pies could be spirited away through a small opening. This seldom happened, for we "in-crowd" boys feared encountering Sandy Williams, the African American janitor and Fanny's spy, while in the shaft.

The crucial shaft for smokers ended in part of an abandoned basement furnace. The furnace door faced the boys' toilet area. Actually, the back of the furnace was missing, but the front half was fitted snugly over the shaft exit, not to trap smokers, of course, but to keep students out of the shaft. But now it played its fateful role, for anyone inside the shaft/furnace had a close-up view of the restroom through a partially open shaft regulator in the furnace door. Williams probably revealed the possibilities to his boss, thereby inspiring the creation of the Basement Puff Club. In any event, Williams did the spying and collecting of the damning information. Puff Clubbers knew Sandy was involved, for he sometimes sneaked in on them from the boys' basement itself, but they had no inkling that he usually did no more than peek through the furnace door, take names, note cigarette brands, count puffs, and perhaps record boasts that "Fanny will whistle 'Dixie' a long time before he ever catches us!"

One of the paddled smokers, Maurice King, told me that decades later he ran into Sandy Williams on a city bus in Dayton, Ohio.
Both had moved there after the war. One day he saw Williams board
the bus, and as he walked up the aisle, King shouted. "Here they are
Mr. Pfanstiel, here they are; come and get 'em, they're all smoking!" Sandy laughed and both of them embraced over what had
become happy memories of a fine superintendent and an excellent
school.

The excellence of education under Pfanstiel and his teachers
speaks for itself. Of some one hundred students in the classes of
1942, 1943 (my class), and 1944, there arose full professors at Tulane,
Berkeley and Dayton; a major Westinghouse executive; a commander
a flotilla of the U.S. North Atlantic submarine fleet; prosperous businessmen, lawyers, farmers, engineers, journalists, and ministers; but
above all, one hundred men and women leading happy and successful lives.

Pfanstiel played a leading role in the difficult task of placing
Carlisle and the county on a wartime footing following Pearl Harbor, a story handled later in this book.

Years later Pfanstiel often recalled his many years as superintendent over coffee with former students at a local restaurant. He worried excessively that he had been too harsh with his students, but we
assured him he had not, that time had changed the system. A man
Pfanstiel admired and may well have known had a similar problem
in justifying past actions with changing times. Albert D. "Ab" Kirwan,
high school administrator, coach, college dean, author, and finally
president of the University of Kentucky, addressed the problem in a
1969 televised speech. I quote from my biography of Kirwan, but I
think it fits Fanny and most schoolmen of his era "to a tee": "Some
25 years or so ago I was the Dean of Students. . . . I would certainly
be classified as a tyrant. I hope I was a benevolent one, but this was
the system. The Dean of Students' authority, insofar as disciplinary
matters were concerned—either on the campus or off, made no difference—was supreme. The Dean said 'come' and the student came.
He said 'go' and the student went. That time, of course, is gone—

long gone—and probably, also, it's well that it has. But there has come in its place a great deal of uncertainty."

Fanny, always a strong Republican volunteer worker, remained at Carlisle High School until his party won the 1944 gubernatorial race. He awarded his last diploma to my pal Nate Young, then moved his family to Frankfort after his appointment as deputy highway commissioner. Resurgent Democrats and the aftereffects of extensive surgery forced him and his family back to Carlisle in 1949. After a lengthy recuperation, he served twelve years as Carlisle's postmaster, retiring in 1967. A stroke felled him in 1980 at age eighty-six. The citizenry was distressed, realizing they had lost the very type of man and leader that comes along only once in a long lifetime.

5

Hammering Catfish
and Other Events

Winter had its charms, in spite of what Lucky said every time he wrestled with the chains on his tires. The upper Ohio Valley has much bitter winter weather and over twenty inches of snow annually. Thirty below zero is Carlisle's temperature record, but several below-zero days usually come to town each year. Coal-burning stoves held winter at bay, but on windless days a light sift of coal soot fell like black snow on hair, skin, shirt, or dress. Kids were warned never to rub or flick it off but always to blow it off. This kept the soot from leaving a black streak on skin or fabric. Nevertheless, slyly rubbing a black streak across someone's back ranked high on the fun list for grade-school boys.

The slickest, longest, steepest place to take a sled was the Christian Church hill. This was the slope where the sled's steel runners talked back at you, with the distinctive clicking rumble that accelerated with the speeding sled. Chestnut Street dropped steeply for almost two blocks before leveling off at Sycamore. Bonfires were built to warm up sledders at the top of the hill. Any contraption that would slide could be seen on the hill: homemade wooden sleds, barrel-stave skis, store-bought Flexible Flyers, and big, flat, rumbling toboggans. These were curved over and back at front and carried seven or eight adults who shouted and screamed as they rushed by. Fred Kendall, later killed on Iwo Jima, usually had the fastest sled on the slope. Although some of Carlisle's churches opposed close-up dancing, no one to my knowledge ever opposed an intermingled stack of boys and girls whooping it up as their sled bounced seductively down a snow-covered street. As I grew older, this sort of sledding became even more exciting than the clicking rumble of the steel runners.

Everything seems to come with a price, including sledding and swinging. I witnessed two bloody accidents on or near school grounds while in grade school. North Street, which ran alongside the school, provided a dangerous double slope. One could coast down the first slope from the school, walk up the other, then coast back down. Sleds were going both ways. One day heavily loaded sleds crashed head-on at the bottom. I was pulling my sled up the opposite hill when it happened but caught a glimpse of tumbling bodies and heard the shouts on all sides. Sledders already coming down the slopes purposely turned their sleds over to avoid hitting the wreck or other sleds. Everyone on the wrecked sleds escaped with bruises except my buddy James "Shimmy" Smoot. Shimmy had taken the front of the opposite sled in his face, losing his front teeth. It was the first time I had seen a bloody injury, but a second one was in store a few months later. Lynn Bowles, a lad from my class, climbed to the top crossbar of one of the swings, hung from the bar by his knees, lost his hold, and fell face first into a chinning bar ten feet below. Again, I saw it happen. He lost his front teeth and was helped crying into the schoolhouse. I became more careful after that, yet I often forgot to remember.

Carlisle did not have the broad waters necessary for ice skating. The waterworks lakes were off limits for swimming or skating, and Brushy Fork creek, which ran through town, was too small and cluttered. But this little creek nevertheless attracted boys for "shoe-soling" across its ice and for "hammering catfish." Spud Marshall, Joe Beatty, Elmer "Popeye" Clark, and I often went "hammering" on icy days. We took a hammer or likely looking rock and looked for little catfish. We could see them lurking in the few inches of frigid water between the ice and the mud bottom. There was no sport to this, for the little fish would seldom move. BANG! the hammer blow resonated through the ice, stunned the fish, and cracked the ice. At first we took the fish home, but our parents stopped this.

"Leave the things alone," they said. "That creek is nothing but an open sewer and those fish are not good for anything." We listened, but we did not obey. We slid on the ice and hammered catfish whenever a cold spell offered us our chance. It seems to me a kid could do worse during hard times than become a hammerer of catfish.

Icicles came in three flavors—water, soot, and bird poop. Licking icicles that had formed around the eaves of soot-covered roofs had a sooty flavor, while those hanging elsewhere usually had a cold and pure water flavor. Not that I really minded. I took my icicles as I found them, soot or no soot. But I was a bit cautious about icicles hanging from roofs frequented by pigeons or with martin boxes above them. Although martins flew south every August, they left an enduring coating of bird poop on roofs. Pigeons did the same. Such icicles had hundreds of tiny specks in them and, although pretty, made one think while licking them.

Snow cream was a winter blessing. We ate all we could hold. Fresh, fluffy snow was best. Mom poured milk, sugar, and vanilla into a snow-crammed pitcher, then spooned it into our cups. We exulted as we ate it, for we lived in frugal times, and its being mostly free struck us as a small but happy victory.

I encountered a zipper for the first time in 1935. After buttons, it seemed magical yet threatening. It looked complicated. Davey Harper showed me his, zipping it up and down on a black mackinaw jacket. These three-dollar jackets came in one style and color. Every boy worried his parents into buying him one or admitting it cost too much. I got one and played with the fascinating zipper until I learned to use it. Another item in great demand was the seventy-five-cent aviator cap. It looked real, with snap-on goggles and ear flaps that fastened under the chin. "Just like Lindbergh!" we thought. Nervous lads peeled away bits of rubberized outer coating to reveal the cotton fabric lining. They were as warm as the woolen mackinaws and ideal for snowball fights, making snow "angels," or hammering catfish.

I paid little attention to weather as a grade-schooler. One kind meant snow and lots of fun, and the other meant swimming and lots of fun. My pals and I had no idea that national heat records were being set during the 1930s—heat and cold alike were acceptable to us as normal for the day in question. The old folks of course knew better, for all-time heat records were set in twenty-five states between 1930 and 1937, and fifteen of these came during the sweltering summer of 1936!

Days of one hundred degrees or more came often that summer. Home air-conditioning was unknown to us. Mom moved the family out to our grassy backyard to sleep on pads and quilts. The entire neighborhood did the same. I suppose heat waves have always forced this response, and I suppose children usually look on it as an adventure akin to camping out. That is the way my brother and I saw it. Streetlights glowed weakly in those days, meaning that nights were dark and skies studded with stars. We lay on our backs with a star chart and learned to identify the dippers, the eagle (Aquila), the Northern Cross (Cygnus), the Scorpion (Scorpius), the North Star, the teapot (Sagittarius), the Milky Way, and much else. In addition, we listened to the sounds of the night: a chorus of bullfrogs bellowing on nearby Brushy Fork, katydids and crickets humming and whirring their songs; the unique gulping sounds of bullbats (night hawks) as they swooped into swarms of insects around street lights; the tuneful bell of the great courthouse clock uptown as it struck the hours; the occasional wrangling of distant dogs; the light scraping sounds of mice chewing holes in the ancient wood of the hoot owl house; the quivering screams of screech owls and the solemn bass notes of the big hoot owls. Energetic roosters crowed in earnest around 3:30 a.m., the first inkling of dawn under "slow time." Somehow, none of these sounds, or the mingling of all of these sounds, ever rose above a few pleasant decibels. They induced sleep. Only the whine of a mosquito now and then ever cluttered the path to sleep.

The incessant summer heat of the mid-1930s deepened the damage done by the Dust Bowl. I could not fully understand, yet I sympathized with the people trapped in it or fleeing from it. Audiences gasped as newsreels showed tremendous clouds of dust rolling along the ground and swallowing farms, villages, and even families scurrying to get out of the way. By the summer of 1936 the finest of the dust overtook us in the East, tinting Ohio Valley sunsets various shades of red, tan, brown, and sometimes even metallic blue. The moon often picked up these hues. But this fine dust was impossible to keep out of houses. The stuff was invisible until it settled on furnishings. It seeped silently through every crack and opening, keeping Mom after it all summer. Even worse, it aggravated respiratory ills.

The dust was mostly a nuisance in the East and also a warning for farmers, but continuing hard times posed a more immediate threat to the nation. While I was still in short pants, the Great Depression seemed on the verge of radically changing America. Carlisle's National Guard Howitzer Company, 149th Infantry Regiment, was ordered south to help stem the violence in the great Kentucky coalfields. The artillerymen boarded their trucks at the warehouse across the street as we in the neighborhood watched. The action and movement excited me, but I had childhood's insulation from the issues at stake. The big brown army trucks snorted and roared as they left town, the soldiers waving good-byes to worried wives, parents, and girlfriends. (Judging from tales brought back each summer about miners' daughters, the girlfriends were the only ones with any real cause to worry!)

Going to the coalfields became almost an annual ritual for Kentucky guard units. And as it became obvious that the guardsmen mostly sided with the miners against the owners, there was little chance of violence against them. But President Hoover was a near universal object of scorn. A poem copied off a coal town sign by a guardsman, and later given to Ed Metcalfe, was bantered about the community and may have been published in the local newspaper. In any event it sticks to my memory. The sign stood by a "honey-hole," a deep pit outside mining company towns where the reeking contents of town privies were dumped after collection:

Here lies Hoover, curse his soul,
In turd in this honey hole,
Hated the poor man, loved the rich
Keep him here, the son of a ———.

My redheaded little brother chased after one of the army trucks as it roared away. The soldiers waved, then gasped as he tripped, falling face down on the street. Frank Sims, operator of a nearby filling station, managed to snatch him out of the path of the following truck, even as the driver skidded his vehicle to a brake-squealing halt. Charles stood glaring at the stunned crowd. He had learned a new word, and now he used it: "Shit," he squeaked, "what's ever' body lookin' at?" But he cried as Mom rushed to pick him up.

Charles Lindsay Mathias Jr. was born in 1928, the year before the stock market crashed. By the time of his run-in with the truck, he was almost six years old and was a typically cute, freckle-faced kid. But he was far from typical in one respect; even at this early age he was capable of pulling his ever ready verbal bowstring against those invading his privacy as well as "dumbhead" acts in general. The year before, he went soundly asleep on our sidewalk. Main Street traffic roared by within three feet of his body. Old Miss Chloe Pimm saw him as she tottered by. She nudged him several times with her foot. "Wake up little boy," she commanded. "Get up in your yard; you'll get hurt down here if you roll into the street. It's too hot to sleep on the sidewalk anyway. Get up, get up, now." Just as Miss Chloe finished her talk, a disdainful little voice came up from below: "Leave me alone, you old pissant!"

Charles picked up a nickname in the fourth grade that became as much a part of his identity as Lucky was for his dad. He had eye trouble, squinting as he read, and he read a lot. Mom took him to see her brother-in-law, Maysville health officer Oliver Morris Goodloe. Dr. Goodloe prescribed calcium tablets and arranged for Charles to be fitted with glasses. When he came home his pals ate up the big chocolate-flavored calcium tablets and made fun of his glasses, calling him "Spectacles," finally, just "Speck." The harder he fought against the name, the tighter it stuck to him, like Br'er Rabbit and the Tar Baby. By the time he entered high school, many had forgotten his real name.

Speck had a complex personality. He was honest, friendly to a fault, intellectually brilliant, perhaps the best dancer in school, and well liked by most, but any who matched wits with him nearly always came out losers. This sometimes soured his relationships with others. The high school principal, Miss Nancy Talbert, evaluated Speck as one who "is seldom satisfied to let sleeping dogs lie for he is always goaded by an overdeveloped sense of justice." This was as accurate an assessment of Speck's basic personality as any I every heard.

Neither Speck nor even the physicians could match wits with the childhood diseases and vermin that attended grade school with us, not to mention much worse ailments afflicting Carlisle's older citizens. There were no antibiotics or other "quick fixes." Speck and I fell victim to the usual ones.

Third grade boys love to wrestle. After a week of recess wrestling, I began to itch and scratch. Mom combed through my hair, and old country girl that she was said, "You've got lice"—using the same tone that she would have announced the time of day. Charles had them too. She rubbed something smelly like coal oil into our hair and boiled all of our clothes and bedclothes. The outbreak at school was soon headed off, mostly with boiling water and simple chemicals. DDT, chlordane, and thousands of other cancer-suspect organochlorines were in the future.

When Miss Helen Gaunce opened her fourth grade classroom door, the "disease of the year," impetigo, came in with the students. By October, most of us had blisterlike boils between our fingers, which oozed pus, hurt, and looked nasty at the same time. Perhaps passing around the ever-present penny pencils, with their cone-shaped rubber erasers, helped spread the infection. The health nurse showed up one day and painted everyone's fingers with a liquid that dyed them purple. My buddies and I had dark brown black walnut stains on our hands, and now we had a new color to be proud of.

Unfortunately, another colorful disease lurked on the autumn of 1934's palette—pinkeye. I escaped this one, but Charles caught it, along with most of the kids in the lower grades. He had red, runny eyes with painful pink eyelids. It soon ran its course, and the remainder of the school year he was free of ailments.

I suffered through mumps, measles, chicken pox, and scarlet fever in grade school; an orange quarantine sign was posted on our front door for each of these. Like the Abe Lincoln tale of the man who was ridden out of town on a rail, I was rather proud to be the recipient of such an honor, but on the whole I would just as soon have missed the whole affair.

Scarlet fever was the worst of my illnesses. Penicillin now cures it in a day or two, but in 1936 it lasted two weeks, and my skin lifted off in sheets the size of this page. Dr. Campbell, silver-haired and portly, might have stepped out of a Norman Rockwell painting to my bedside every three or four days. I loved to talk to this impressive visitor, but he eventually shut me up by pressing my tongue under a wooden Dixie cup-like spatula, peering down my throat, and murmuring, "Hmmmmmmmm, well now, hmmmmmmmmm, yessssss, I seeeee." He always boosted my hopes when he picked up his black bag and left the room; then turned back in the doorway, saying: "Frankie, you are getting along just fine; better than I expected, so keep up the good work!" I knew Dr. Campbell would never tell a lie, so I felt much better the rest of the day.

Dr. Campbell was a practitioner of the "do no harm and let time cure the patient" school of medicine, but Aunt Alma Hines, Mom's sister and a Maysville nurse, did not hold with that easygoing school, at least when it came to tonsils and adenoids: "Anybody ought to have sense enough to have their children's tonsils removed, and I don't doubt but that goes for adenoids too." Such advice to Nannie and other relatives came with extra fervor lest they doubt that she, a familiar family member, might lack medical expertise.

Tonsils were touted as potential cesspools of infection and, unlike today, were removed as a matter of course. Adenoids were often cut out of the throat with tonsils, for swollen ones inhibit breathing. Mom usually took her younger sister's advice on matters medical and turned to another relative, Dr. Winn Hord, to take out my tonsils. He drove over from Maysville to Carlisle's hospital, a converted Elm Street residence, to perform the surgery.

I was a worried six-year-old as I lay on an ordinary but sheet-covered wooden table. A smiling and cooing nurse lowered an ether-sprinkled cloth to my face. The next thing I knew I was awake again with a sore throat. The only blessing connected to my surgery came when Mom excused me from taking my daily teaspoon of cod-liver oil mixed with orange juice. Up-to-date mothers of the Great Depression were sold on this fishy-flavored oil as a health potion, and it probably was a good one. Some, like Aunt Alma, also swore to the magic of graham crackers and zwieback rusk as preservers of childhood health.

There were worse maladies stalking Carlisle's citizens than tonsil trouble. Except for cholera and ague (malaria), the same fearsome disorders causing distress or death in the 1830s were still hanging around one hundred years later: diphtheria, typhoid fever, tuberculosis, syphilis, gonorrhea, dysentery, rabies, diabetes, infantile paralysis (polio), pneumonia, schizophrenia, and smallpox. Vaccination had cut back diphtheria, typhoid, and, especially, smallpox, but the threat was still there. Smallpox scars pocked the faces of some older citizens, and quarantine signs for diphtheria and typhoid appeared in windows now and then.

Then there was "TB." We helplessly threw puns at it and laughed:

TB, or not TB,
That's the congestion,
Consumption be about it?
Of cough!

Lucky laughed for years about what he heard said at a funeral for an old bachelor friend of his. The old-timer had finally died of tuberculosis at age ninety-four. An elderly Irish lady, who still rolled her r's, approached Dad at the funeral. He knew she was a prohibitionist and dead set against "old dog liquor," but her eulogy for the deceased left much to be desired: "Poor-r-r-r old John," she said, shaking her head and lifting her eyes heavenward, "whiskey finally got him!"

I learned about syphilis and clap (gonorrhea) one Saturday morning while playing "fly money" with pals at Simmy's filling station. We had earlier been up in the courthouse yard flying June bugs, each beetle buzzing from twenty feet of fine thread tied to a hind leg. James Hughes directed our attention to the scruffy line of men and women in front of the health officer's clinic. When their

June bugs flew over that way, Spud Marshall and Joe Roundtree approached a man in the line, and Joe asked, "What's goin' on here?"

"Shut up, boy, and mind your own business," the man snarled in reply.

This intrigued us. We now recalled seeing this line most Saturday mornings, and we puzzled about the man getting mad at Joe as we walked the block down to Simmy's to play fly money.

Once there we each laid a penny alongside the filling station wall, and a fast game of fly money got under way. The rules were simple. If a fly lit on your penny first, you won and got everybody else's pennies. It was hard to cheat. We had temporarily banned Davey Harper the day before for baiting his penny with sugar-laden candy-spit. We hopefully watched the flies buzzing over and around the pennies while we argued about the line at the health office and why the man got mad at Joe. A gruff voice from above interrupted: "They're all gettin' their weekly shots for syphilis; some of 'em are gettin' scraped for claps, too." The voice belonged to "Pump," a curmudgeonly but likable old bachelor who loafed around the station. "If you boys think syphilis shots are bad," Pump added, "you don't know nothin'. Get the claps and they stick a silver deal up your pecker, open up the scrapers, and pull out all sorts of stuff."

We forgot about the flies as our imaginations tried to process this frightful news. Pump now sort of let us off the hook. "If you all just stay away from wimmin, you'll catch nary a thing. Wimmin are the cause of all of it," Pump maintained, shaking his bald head for emphasis, "and that's a fact!"

Nicholas County had most of the big name diseases, but it also hosted a lesser known but serious ailment. Rabbits were the cause. As the county lost farm population, much of the land went into briars. Untold thousands of rabbits eventually sheltered and multiplied in these extensive blackberry briar thickets. They provided good hunting, tasty meat, and profitable fur. Numerous hunters came to town each autumn, bringing tourist dollars with them. Dad's German-speaking city cousins were always among this crowd, dressed in fancy knickered hunting outfits and sporting fine twelve-gauge shotguns. They stayed at our house and at Uncle Joe's, filling their country cousins in on family news from Cincinnati, Covington, and Chillicothe. We thoroughly enjoyed their visits, for they were a jolly bunch.

Lucky was a fisherman, not a hunter. Although we ate plenty of rabbit—spitting out the embedded buckshot as our teeth struck it—we usually bought ours from Jim Barlow's small grocery a half-block away. Jim paid hunters fifteen cents per rabbit. He gutted, skinned, and lined them up for sale on his sidewalk during cold weather. Some boys took advantage of this by gutting and skinning a tomcat and slipping it into the line. Barlow innocently sold it to some poor soul who ate some "god-awful rabbit" for supper! The joke was on Barlow and of course spread all over town. He was known ever after as "Jim-cat" Barlow, but what happened next moved rabbits out of joking range.

Around 1935 skinned rabbits often displayed a freckling of dark red spots all over their normally pink flesh. People began showing up in doctors' offices with fever, aches, and swollen lymph glands. They were soon diagnosed as having highly infectious tularemia, a deadly disease for rabbits and a painful one for humans. The word went out in record time: "Hands off rabbits!" Dad had cleaned a rabbit a few days before he heard of the disease. It had spots on its flesh and he poked at them and wondered out loud about them. I was puzzled as he mumbled, then dumped the rabbit into the garbage can. His early experience picking chickens at Matt Ruddell's produce house made him cautious when he saw those unusual spots. In any event, we and our Main Street neighbors escaped the disease, leaving Nicholas County's million or so rabbits to fend for themselves.

Kentucky's tularemia outbreak came the year Ethiopian Emperor Haile Selassie emerged as an antifascist hero when Mussolini's modern legions crunched uninvited into Selassie's ancient but "backward" African land, which they occupied until kicked out by the British in 1941. Fascism had, in this 1935 venture, achieved a threatening, bullying status, a position quickly enlarged by Hitler in Germany and Stalin in the USSR as they locked horns in their intervention into the "tune-up" for World War II, the extremely bloody Spanish Civil War, 1936–39. And the actions of Japan only added to the fearsome shadow looming ever larger over the world's democracies. Western leaders hoped and prayed somehow to escape another such catastrophe as the Great War of 1914–18. Unfortunately, they failed.

We the people of the 1930s were conscious of living in the shadow of fearsome trends, but we had to live it out day by day, with no analysis of coming events such as that above. And concerning Ethiopia, we of the GI Generation not only learned some African geography but added Selassie to a long list of generational heroes— to the point of placing him in a popular swing version of "Shantytown":

> I'll be just as sassy as Haile Selassie
> If I were king, wouldn't mean a thing,
> Keep my boots on call,
> Read th' writin' on th' wall
> And it wouldn't mean a thing
> Not a doggone thing. . . .

We can hope that Selassie never puzzled himself trying to translate that verse, but the fact of his presence in a swing hit of the era indicates fully his acceptance as a hero of the GI Generation. Most were not included in songs, but a listing of some of them indicates the type of men and women my generation tried to emulate: Eddie Rickenbacker, John J. Pershing, Benny Goodman, Will Rogers, Richard E. Byrd, J. Edgar Hoover, Charles Lindbergh, Frank Buck, Knute Rockne, Marie Curie, Helen Keller, Walt Disney, Amelia Earhart, Margaret Mitchell, Babe Ruth, FDR, and of course various religious figures and leaders. "Tell me with whom you associate and I will tell you what you are."

6

The Uncommon Cold and the Specialty Man

There was no cure for the "uncommon cold" until Smith Brothers shipped three cases of their cough drops to our home. One of the joys of being the son of a wholesale grocery salesman was the arrival of edible, chewable, or suckable promotion samples. Lucky handed out samples along his route, often making a sale of the same brand. As nearly as I can remember, the cough drops came in menthol, lemon, cherry, and horehound flavors. Speck and I begged a few packets and found them almost as good as candy—good enough to swipe, in other words. Dad soon used all he needed along his routes, leaving two cases bulging with several hundred packets. Mom moved them into a corner of our pantry. "You two stay out of these," she said, leaving Speck and me to wonder if she really meant it.

We guessed correctly that she did not really mean it and started handing out packets to our pals. The word spread like a virus. There came an urgent knock on our door. Mom answered to find a tiny girl asking if she might have some cough drops. "I need some real bad, Mrs. Mathias," she said hoarsely, followed by a hacking cough.

"Why you certainly may, honey," Mom said, her voice full of sympathy. "I'll get you a pack right now. How long have you had such a bad cold?" The child mumbled something as she left, skipping down the sidewalk to spread the good news.

During the Depression, when many kids never saw a penny or a nickel for weeks on end, a gift packet of cherry-flavored cough drops had an appeal hard to imagine by today's sugar-saturated kids.

Mom soon caught on and moved the cough drops out of the pantry to the front door. By this time boys and girls were coming to the door coughing, snorting, and swooning to prove their need. Mom gave each a packet. Soon, however, the cough drops took on the aura of a natural right: "Mrs. Mathias, I don't want this old pack of horehound cough drops; give me lemon ones like you gave my little brother."

Or trickery: One girl disguised herself in various dresses and hats and finally in boys' clothes to siphon off five packs in each flavor before Mom wised up.

Or unbelievable ignorance: "Mrs. Mathias, you know those nice cough drops you gave out to the sick last week, well Ma'm, I was down with the croup and never heard tell of them until just today. Might I have a pack?

Mom finally handed out the last of the cough drops. "Cough drop week," she later laughed, "had me thinking I might join those patent medicine Indians uptown!"

Hot summer Saturday afternoons often found one or two swarthy-skinned men hawking "Old Mohawk Medicine" in a vacant lot behind C.C. Cole's Men's Store. They may or may not have been Indians, but they dressed that way, with head feathers, beaded jackets, leggings, and moccasins. A knife was buried to the hilt in one's lower arm, the blade protruding on the other side. We kids soon discovered the trick—a small metal offset circled his arm hidden under a red bandana. We tried to tell the circle of farmers gawking and buying from the Indians that the knife was a trick. In short order one of the Indians stepped over: "Get the hell out of here right now," he growled, "and we don't mean maybe!" He said this in a non-Mohawkian language known as plain English.

Depression issues of the *Mercury* reveal that although patent medicines might not have cured much, their advertisements point to the more common ailments of the era. The Indians ran an ad for their medicine, selling "two big bottles for only 95¢," and prescribed for "all systems that are full of poisons due to constipation. . . . You people need a good cleaning out every now and then." If Old Mohawk failed to do the job, there was Fletcher's Castoria (3 percent alcohol) to "regulate constipation and diarrhoea," apparently both at once! Frey's vermifuge, spooned into any kid with worms, was guaranteed to make the pests move on. Backache? Dodd's Kidney Pills and Swamp-Root vied for your business. Acne, boils, and bumps? Cuticura soap vowed to "clear your skin while you sleep." But there was one well-advertised medicine we kids never managed to figure out—Lydia E. Pinkham's Vegetable Compound for Middle Aged Women. It never promised to do anything.

By far the best medicine of the year for Nicholas County's citizens was Christmas. It was a joyful season, devoid of most of the post–World War II commercial hustle. Christ's birthday was the center of attention with beloved old carols extolling the biblical facts of his birth. Churches, schools, homes, and streets were decorated with cedar trees or cuttings. Cedars grew wild all over the county, and their fragrant smell meant Christmas to every kid in town. Tinsel, lead-foil icicles, and popcorn strung on thread decorated most trees. A string or two of colorful lights usually flickered on them, always with a "Star of Bethlehem" shining on the treetop. But tree lights were come and go, for if one burned out it darkened every light on the string. About half the time, the best decoration of all stole silently into town—fresh fallen snow.

My first indication that Christmas was on its way always walked in our back door in the person of Andrew Metcalfe. He was welcome anytime of the year, but in early December I knew he was going to draft me into helping him make the superb candy he used as gifts. My job was to stir the boiling pots, pull certain types of cooling candy as it hardened, and serve as "gopher" anytime Andy needed more supplies from his dad's grocery. I was privileged, of course, to sample his work as we went along.

Andy took great pride in his equipment. He had light and heavy metal pots, each used for making specific candy concoctions. A cooking thermometer told him exactly when a batch was done and ready to cool. But he was proudest of a big marble tabletop, I think, for when this was buttered up, he poured out his cream candy for cooling and pulling. Although he got supplies from his dad's store, he often took me with him into the October woods, where we collected and cured a heaping pile of black walnuts, hickory nuts, and butternuts. He used these along with dried and candied fruits as he unfurled his recipes. He specialized in walnut loaded fudge, caramel rolls, divinity, and various types of cream candy. And he had special concoctions of his own which he named after the people receiving his gift. His gifts, as most, were wrapped either in red, green, or white tissue paper, for the more costly paper designs of later decades had not arrived. We never missed what we did not have.

My most immemorial Christmas came when I made my first Communion at midnight mass. I was seven years old and walked down the church's center aisle with Frances Holland, a second-grade classmate. Everyone said we looked like a bride and groom, she in her lacy white outfit and me in my black suit. The church was packed full of Protestants for that one colorful mass. I was thoroughly frightened and mad. A roaring sound filled my head as I went through the motions. For all I knew, I really would be married when the thing was over. I found out later that my "bride" enjoyed the whole thing immensely. People crowded around after mass and told Frances and me what a lovely couple we made. I wanted to kick their shins or run and hide; confusion between the two wishes kept me in place. Frances and I had been dropped in the middle of a big show for adults. All enjoyed it but me, yet I forgave all upon returning home to find Santa had left toys and a sled under our tree.

Christmas week was the best week of my year, but there were other eagerly awaited times: Halloween, Easter, July 4, May Day, and the arrival of Harvey. Harvey? Harold Harvey was a "specialty man" for Sauer's Extracts. Specialty men promoted only one product, unlike Lucky who promoted and sold hundreds of items for Lexington's Bryan-Hunt Wholesale Grocery Company. Harvey was a native of Newport News, Virginia—which he pronounced "Nupote"—and worked from there by train and bus over parts of Virginia, West Virginia, and Kentucky. Good roads and motels lay in the future, so specialty men stayed for a workweek at the homes of general salesmen, like Lucky, accompanying them on their route and promoting their product as they went. They paid a small fee, and like Dad, most got by on "a shoeshine and a smile."

Everyone called him Harvey, his last name, except Speck and I of course, who added "Mr." to it. He was about Dad's age but taller and a mite overweight. Every April a letter, followed by a shipment of his samples and promotional material, preceded his arrival. There was also a heavy box of candy "for Nannie" and "presents for the boys." His presents were always up to the minute, whether Flash Gordon "ray guns" or the latest Big Little Books.

Harold Harvey arrived by train and Dad drove him home. For Speck and me the fun started immediately after the greetings. We always asked the same question: "Mr. Harvey can you say there's a mouse about the house?"

"What a silly question," he exclaimed. "Why anyone who speaks the language can say there's a moose aboot the hoose!" His strong Chesapeake Bay accent broke Speck and me up, sending us into fits of laughter. It did the same for our pals.

Harvey was a fountain of new jokes for Dad to use on his route, and they also exchanged tall tales. He asked Lucky if he had caught any notable fish since his last visit.

"Well, Harvey, nothing really to brag about, but I did catch a bass last June down on Licking that measured five feet, eleven and one-half inches."

"Lucky," Harvey replied, shaking his head, "that's a powerful lot of fish; are you sure you measured his length right?"

"Why, Harvey, I was only telling you what he measured between the eyes. I could have said 'six feet,' but I wouldn't lie for half an inch!"

Harvey was up to the challenge when Dad let him into the game: "Anything interesting happen to you since last year, Harvey?"

"Folks," he said seriously, "I want you to look at this gold pocket watch of mine. I value it highly but I lost it last October, then got it back in a most miraculous manner." All of us perked up as he continued. "I was visiting a farmer friend and he bet that I couldn't milk a quart in five minutes. He wasn't joking. Now that was an insult for sure; he didn't think I knew how to milk at all. I pulled out my watch, noted the time, then laid it down on the feed box. As I started to milk, the watch tumbled into the feed and that doggone cow gobbled it down with a mouthful of feed."

Then, Harold Harvey, consummate actor that he was, embraced

his story personally: "I was heartbroken, folks, plain old heartbroken; that watch was a wedding gift from my wife and it meant the world to me. I lost it for a day or two during our honeymoon at Niagara Falls and she cried the night away."

Speck and I by this time were caught up completely in his tale; we thought he was going to cry and that the story was over. But Harvey continued.

"My farmer friend stuck with me, checking that cow month after month, but the watch never did come out. Then whadda you know, my friend called me last month and said he was going to kill that cow—she had Bang's disease. He said I ought to drop by and see if the two of us couldn't find that watch inside her. I'm telling you I got there in ten minutes. After he killed her he opened up the four stomachs, one by one. By golly, do you know that watch was in the fourth stomach, the one that keeps moving all the time as a cow chews its cud. I pulled it out and it was still ticking as loud as ever. The constant movement of that cow's stomach had kept it wound all winter. And do you know something else? It had kept perfect time. It was showing five o'clock exactly as the *Five O'Clock News* started on the farmer's radio."

We all laughed and applauded, then Dad said: "Harvey, I believe your cow and my fish have a lot in common!"

Harvey's story reminded me to warn him about staying over at Uncle Joe's house in what had been Grandma Mathias's room. I told him that I could not be sure, but there was probably a "death clock" in the wall. It had been heard ticking the day she died; I had not heard it, I admitted, but others had. Mom explained it to him, pooh-poohing as she went. Finally, Mr. Harvey looked me in the eye: "Frankie," he grinned, "if that death clock gets straight time and has never been in a cow's stomach, I believe I can handle it!" I was never again afraid to visit Granny's room, at least not in the daytime.

Only one grocer, I think, ever got one up on Harvey. Sometime during the mid-1930s Uncle Ed Metcalfe bought himself a "poo-poo cushion." This flat little rubber pad, when slightly inflated, was hidden under an ordinary seat cushion. When someone sat on it, a metallic reed emitted a rather delicate but very authentic farting sound. Ed occasionally placed it in one of several seats comfortably located in the rear of his store. Customers loved to go back and "sit a spell," for once there, Ed was usually up to joking with them or telling tales of his days in the Yukon, Montana, or the AEF in France. He caught Mom once. She heard the awful sound and later said she was sure "one had slipped out." Whenever this happened, Ed always cleared his throat, coughed a bit, changed the conversation condescendingly, and made a very obvious point of never looking at the embarrassed victim.

Dad and Harvey stopped by Metcalfe's Grocery one afternoon. Harvey asked if he might put up an easel and some shelf tape advertising Sauer's Extracts. He gave Ed some samples and exchanged a few jokes. Lucky suggested that they sit down and rest a while, making sure that Harvey got the doctored chair. Harvey settled down on the cushion, talking all the time, and then there came the p-p-f-f-f-t-t-t-t. Ed went into his routine as Harvey suddenly went silent. He looked so flustered that Ed finally had pity on him and told him what had happened. Harvey pulled the little rubber pad out, looked it over, and grinned. "What a relief!" he cried. "I have a touch of diarrhea and thought for sure I had blown the whole afternoon!"

Unfortunately for Ed, the show was not over. While Lucky and Harvey sat chuckling and planning their afternoon calls, Ed spied Betty Sue McKell, one of his son's girlfriends, bent over and pinching her ruinous way through a basket of peaches. He liked her and knew she was a good-natured girl as well as one who had played some tricks on him in the past. Since she had her back to him he slipped up behind her to teach her a lesson, using a light orange crate slat for a paddle.

WHACK! The figure exploded to full height, whirled around to face him, and seemed ready to froth at the mouth. He was horrified to find himself face to face with Miss Priscilla Grimmshaw, Carlisle's most persnickety "old maid!" Ed immediately started backing and filling, begging her to believe that he had though she was "pretty Betty McKell," that she had "looked like Betty from the rear." This of course only made matters much worse as Miss Priscilla lectured him up one aisle and down the other. Finally she stomped loudly out of the store.

Lucky and Harvey had enjoyed the affair from seats in the back of the store. They pretended sorrow for the distraught grocer. "Ed," Lucky suggested, "if you'll get that poo-poo cushion ready again, I'll entice Miss Prissy to come back in, sit down, and apologize for the way she sassed you."

"Lucky, you do that and I'll kill you!" But all three of them laughed uproariously at the very thought of it.

Basketball and football offered welcome relief for Carlisle's citizens throughout the Depression. The year I entered the fifth grade, 1935, Carlisle High School hosted a basketball tournament and became the second-best football team in the Central Kentucky Conference (CKC). I became a lifelong sports fan that year.

The late winter tournament was eagerly awaited by everyone. It brought interesting visitors and prestige with it. Carlisle was one of the smallest towns in the CKC and had very limited hotel space, thus citizens volunteered room and board for visiting coaches and their teams. Lucky and Nannie volunteered the usual bedroom at Uncle Joe's, the one with the death clock in the wall. Two tall athletes slept there and ate breakfast with us, neither reporting any suspicious ticking sounds. They were likable lads who quickly swung my fickle allegiance from CHS to Stanford. During the games my pals and I hung around outside the gym, for few kids had money for tickets.

Carlisle had a first-class gymnasium, typical of a style popular in its day. It had been built in the late 1920s and cost a whopping $50,000, enough money then to have bought 125 Chevrolet sedans! A fine hardwood playing floor was bordered lengthwise by four rows of benches, and a balcony with similar seating surrounded the entire gym. A stylish front wall area of glass blocks combined with big windows and screened ceiling lights to illuminate the main floor. Adequate dressing, shower, and office space lay under the front balcony. In short, it was a gym worthy of tournament consideration.

The gym had something to offer everybody. The important May Day festival was an annual event. Exercise classes let girls as well as all boys in on the action. The Junior-Senior Prom, with big dance bands and "belly-to-belly" dancing, which upset several church groups, was an annual affair. Banquets, meetings of all sorts, and much else took place in the gym. But the tournaments were special. In 1935 Carlisle bowed out early, but this would be forgotten when its football team won its way through the best season the little school would ever have.

I suppose most towns have fielded a football team that "wins them all" and gains legendary status. The 1935 Musketeers set a local record never equaled before or since.

Home games were played on Jackson Field, several acres of bottomland cow pasture just west of town. It was bordered by railroad tracks, Brushy Fork, and a sloping entrance area to park cars, buggies, and wagons. The men's "pissoir" was inside two massive but hollow sycamores alongside the railroad embankment. Women, of course, were expected to hold out in a ladylike way until they returned home. The morning before a game the field was picked clean of animal dung, mowed, lined off, livestock penned up, and the worn wooden goalposts checked for strength and alignment. There were no lights; all games were played on Friday afternoons.

By game time several hundred fans milled around the sidelines. There were few seats. Many came by auto, but some arrived riding fine saddle horses. Kids like me walked in on the tracks. The half-pint bottle was in vogue—it was cheap and easy to conceal—and filled many a young man's pocket. Powerful one-hundred-proof bourbon filled these slim bottles, and once it was inside drinkers, fights broke out, usually around the sycamore tree "restrooms" where drinking was the heaviest. Drunks lurching onto the field quickly earned laughs by wobbling after rabbits zigzagging through the end zone. My gang and I, keyed up by the excitement, ran wildly with others like us all over the place. The entire scene was always permeated with the neutral scent of new-mown bluegrass in cool, autumn air.

When the two teams trotted onto the field, competing cheerleaders turned cartwheels and led cheers. Cheers were free of all poetic limitations, such as this one composed by cheerleader Betty Dollins:

Boom chicka boom
Boom chicka boom
Boom chicka ricka chicka
Boom boom boom
Zip zip la
Zip zip la
Carlisle! Carlisle!
Rah! Rah! Rah!

As the cheering continued, coaches gave final instructions to their teams. Carlisle probably had the best football coach in its history in Chester Shearer. He was a scholarly, football playing product of Danville's Centre College, a small Kentucky school that had whipped mighty Harvard in a David and Goliath game in the 1920s. Shearer knew the game, but above all he was able to pass it on to his boys. The 1935 record speaks for itself.

Carlisle's green-and-white-clad Musketeers played eight games, each one against a larger school. Shearer, in his calm and competent way, kept his players' emotions directed on the game instead of on themselves. His plays worked beautifully. It was the era of the single wing attack, and when Reynolds "Bugs" Green and blockers led by Malcolm "Army" Armstrong swept around left end, big gains were nearly inevitable. Before season's end it became apparent to many that Carlisle had come up with a once-in-a-long-lifetime-team. The *Mercury* of November 21 summed up the season in one sentence: "The team was so good it scored 258 points to only 18 by its eight opponents!" Carlisle should have been Central Kentucky Conference champions, but owing to a weird rating system, Somerset won that honor with a lesser record of six wins, no losses, and one tie. But Green and Armstrong were named to the All Conference Eleven, and a bit later Armstrong was named an end on the All Kentucky Team.

Six years later these boys as well as we hero-worshiping kids were jolted by news of Pearl Harbor. One of the sturdy 1935 linemen, Jack Cassidy, had joined the navy, surviving the attack on the battleship *West Virginia* even though Japanese torpedoes had sent her to the bottom. Jack had been the team favorite of most of us little boys, partially because he was friendly, but also because rumor held that he spit tobacco juice in the eyes of opposing linemen. How I would have liked to have been on Jack's team! My wish was answered in an unexpected way.

Ten years later, on a January morning in 1945, my infantry outfit splashed ashore on Luzon's Lingayan Gulf beaches. My Higgins Boat churned past the rear of a battleship. It squatted on its haunches as its sixteen-inch guns flamed and thundered, turning the sea red as it hurled giant shells toward enemy positions. Suddenly I saw its name in big gold letters standing proudly across its stern: *WEST VIRGINIA*. It had been resurrected to deadly new life. I thought of Jack Cassidy. We were now on the same team.

7

Major and Minor

My schoolboy daydreams fancied a genie swirling out of a bottle to grant my wishes. The football prowess of Jack Cassidy and "Bugs" Green was mine. The girls all admired me and I soundly thrashed every bully in town. No genie showed up; I was tightly stuck in place as a physical "late bloomer," not reaching "keeper size" until my senior year. Unknowingly, I was already unraveling my predicament.

Schoolboys need an identity beyond their home folks. Some find it in athletics or scholarship, others in acting silly or even in bullying. I found mine in music. My genie had always been there, just waiting to be called out of the bottle. Music became my first true connection with the outside world.

There was little musical talent on my father's side but plenty on my mother's. Samuel Bramel Jr. (1800–1881), my great-great-uncle, is Rosemary Clooney's great-great-great-grandfather. He and his wife, Mary Jane Taylor, are buried in rural Mason County's Mount Gilead Cemetery. As musical talent came down the family tree it left Clooney, a truly great jazz and ballad singer, sitting on by far the biggest branch, yet there was still enough left to go around. All of Nannie's sisters played instruments and were ready to vocalize at the drop of a chord. By the time I could recite the *Vater Unser* with Granny Mathias, I could also sing "The Wearing of the Green" with Mom. The steady beat of the wringer washing machine dasher nearly always got Nannie going on "How Fickle Women Are" (*La Donna è Mobile*). It was just the right tempo. She whistled or hummed the barcarole as she hung the wet clothes on the line. Sitting at her sewing machine somehow evoked memories of teaching days in Colorado, leading her to sing and pump the treadle in time with "Springtime in the Rockies." Nannie played her mandolin with zest and precision, giving her best efforts to "Sorrento," "Prisionero del Mar," and "O Sole Mio." She played everything by ear.

I was not above making music at church. I discovered on Palm Sunday that a long strand from a palm leaf could be held between my teeth and left hand, then plucked with my right to sound like one of Mom's mandolin strings. I was playing along with the gospel when Dad reached over and snatched it, slapping my hand in the process. Mom glared at me along with several parishioners seated near us. Speck snickered, with a holier-than-thou smirk on his face. When we left church I gave him a hard push. He cried and Dad grabbed me by the ear, pulling me whimpering and crablike behind the church. He said he was surprised to find that I did not have any gumption at all. I told him that I would do better. He said he hoped so but insisted that I apologize to Speck. Telling a smirking brother that I was sorry put considerable strain on my gumption supply.

Subtle changes were overtaking American popular music in the early 1930s. Most of this music's loose ends were coming together to emerge as "swing," a jazz-based style which became the most widely popular American music of all time. Records, radios, and jukeboxes spread it into every corner of the nation. Benny Goodman's theme, "Let's Dance," could be heard on jukeboxes in the most isolated spots in the country, or one could hear the "King of Swing" himself playing it in the nation's best ballrooms or in the White House. Swing was simply everywhere. It was part of a cultural unity that carried us successfully through World War II. It was *the* music of the GI Generation.

Country music was called "hillbilly" and had a large following in Nicholas County, a following it would share yet keep during the swing onslaught after 1935. My musical memory goes back to four itinerant fiddlers and guitar pickers singing "Brown's Ferry Blues" in the courthouse yard, probably on a Saturday afternoon around

1930. Listeners were putting coins in a hat. I liked that, and I was impressed enough to memorize the first line, mistaking "ferry" for "berry"—"Lord, Lord, I've got them brown berry blues!"

I sang this line over and over with childish enthusiasm. People laughed to hear a child singing such a lugubrious and ungrammatical lyric, but Mom soon got fed up. Nannie had little use for most hillbilly music, and my singing it may have heightened her consistently expressed desire to move the family to Colorado (Lucky was never to carry out his prenuptial agreement to do so). As she might have expected, another hillbilly classic, "Boil Them Cabbage Down," shoved "brown berry" aside until it too gave way to a new favorite.

There was plenty of live country music in Carlisle. The courthouse courtroom's main floor and balcony seats several hundred people. Every month or so during winter a country music show performed there. This was before records and radio fastened a tiresome pattern on such shows. Each one lasted about two hours and cost twenty-five cents for adults and fifteen cents for kids. Dad, Speck, and I always favored the balcony seats; Mom always stayed at home.

We saw musicians later to win country music fame, such as the Carter Family, but my strongest attachment was to Uncle Henry and His Original Kentucky Mountaineers. They offered skits and comedy but mostly played folk and hoe-down numbers as well as recent "hits." A good string band, like this one, generated a surprising amount of power, needing no electrical pickups except for announcements or jokes. Uncle Henry's crew left us with a verse to "Old Joe Clark" that even made Nannie laugh:

Old Joe had a daughter, boys,
And she was mighty sly,
She'd blow her nose in yellow cornbread
And call it punkin' pie!

Nannie admired instrumental expertise in good string bands and loved hearing the folk songs she had known and played most of her life. But she was dead set against the sound-alike hillbilly "hits" infesting the airwaves. These were usually sung by off-key, nasal, twangy-voiced singers. "He sounds like a dying calf in a thunderstorm," was her comment as she turned off the radio or changed stations. She held the rash of "cowboy" yodelers in equal contempt, rolling her eyes when my buddies and I tried to imitate them. Ever the teacher, she was determined to expand my musical tastes, and her assumption that selected radio programs would do most of the job for her was a correct one. Andrew Metcalfe, as will be seen, would do the rest.

One of the best folk and country music singers of the era was Bradley Kincaid, of Berea, Kentucky. Kincaid offered a children's program each Saturday morning. Speck and I were quickly hooked. He enchanted us with such rollicking songs as "Froggy Went a Courtin'" and "The Green Grass Grows All Around." His guitar and voice added new meaning to "Comin' Round the Mountain" and enhanced the beauty of great old folk songs such as "Greensleeves" and "Barbara Allen." Above all, he took time to explain to his young listeners what he was doing.

Kincaid's program was followed by the concert orchestra of Walter Damrousch playing music attractive to young listeners. Later in the day, Dr. Frank Simon's renowned ARMCO (American Rolling Mills Company) Band of Middletown, Ohio, was usually scheduled to play concerts of stirring band music featuring great soloists. It was here I first heard "Willow Echoes," a famous Simon composition and trumpet solo I was destined to hear and admire at every regional and state music contest I ever entered.

Mom told often of hearing John Phillip Sousa's band play a concert in Maysville before World War I. I was unimpressed until I heard his marches played over the radio by the Damrousch Orchestra and Simon's band. Nannie marched Speck and me around the room, giving us a feel for the pounding rhythms generated by the music. But like any kid, I had to learn some things the hard way. Sousa's title "Washington Post" puzzled me briefly until I was laughingly told it referred to a newspaper, and not, as I assumed, to part of a fence on General Washington's farm. Even as late as high school I heard some say that it was written in honor of the Washington, D.C., post office, or maybe the marines' Washington military post.

In any event, Sousa might better have named it "*Toledo Blade*" or even "*Carlisle Mercury!*"

Uncle Joe had a stack of records dating back to 1900, when they were cut on one side only. My favorites were "La Paloma" and "La Golondrina," which I played often on his big hand-cranked Victrola. When I heard Damrousch play these two songs, no one had to tell me there was a vast difference in quality. Again, Simon and Damrousch played country music standards such as "Golden Slippers" in a way far different from familiar courthouse string bands, in this case not better, but different. I was learning that musicians had many ways to present the same song. In short, by the time I was in the sixth grade I had learned to like several kinds of music. It was no longer true that "the only song that I can sing is boil them cabbage down." Then along came swing.

Andy Metcalfe introduced me to swing, showing me the way as usual. He was one of the best friends I ever had. Andy was five years older than I, a good-looking lad of average size who pompadoured his black hair in the fashion of the day. His two greatest assets were a keen sense of humor and a genuine love of people, no matter their station in life. Organized sports such as football and basketball meant little to him, and, self-contained soul that he was, Andy ignored formidable peer pressure to play them. In other words, life as he lived it was sport enough for him. Many of the boys and even some of their parents labeled him as a "sissy," but his many girlfriends knew better, as did I and my pals. It made us mad to hear it. But Andrew was to prove himself as one of the finest of the GI Generation.

A decade later, on April 22, 1945, S/Sgt. Andrew B. Metcalfe, 349th Infantry, 88th Division, single-handedly attacked two Nazi machine-gun nests with rifle and grenades in the Italian mountains. The German gunners had pinned down his platoon. Metcalfe knocked both guns out but not before the second one shot his life away. He freely gave all he had to save the men of his platoon and was posthumously awarded one of his nation's highest honors—the Silver Star. Some "sissy!"

When swing and the big bands took command of America's

musical tastes in 1935, Andrew was of course ahead of the pack. Metcalfe's Monarch Grocery took telephone orders which Andy delivered after school. His dad paid him twenty-five cents an hour, which he saved to buy a tiny tabletop record player. The thing was no bigger than a loaf of bread, but it worked. He soon had a stack of the most up-to-date records, and flocks of girls began showing up to plot out and practice the steps and movements to a new dance called the jitterbug. None of this made any impression on Bummie, his grandmother, who complained to Nannie that "the stuff he plays on that thing is just about to drive me up the wall!"

Andy did not object, so I hung around the Metcalfe house listening to the music and watching the dancers. So many girls were named Jane, and Andy dated or knew so many of them, I often got their last names mixed up. This always caused a laugh, and before long I fitted in with these older kids, sort of like a mascot. I was too young to want any contact with girls, but I knew I liked that music Andy played. Before long, big bands were broadcasting over the radio and my brotherly neighbor let me in on this, telling me the stations and the times.

When Kay Kyser's *College of Musical Knowledge* hit the airwaves, Mom was quick to recall her days as his typing teacher in Rocky Mount. We seldom missed his show. Kyser used singing song titles to introduce each number. I soon knew what to expect from vocalists Harry Babbit and Ginny Sims, and Kyser's soft Carolina accent won equal billing with his musicians. Trumpeter "Ishkabibble" (Merwyn Bogue) and saxist Sully Mason got laughs from all of us. Radio exerted a lure that only television would overpower.

Another weekly program we never missed was *Your Lucky Strike Hit Parade*. Attention was centered on songs rather than bands. A studio orchestra played the top ten songs of the week as determined by the "Lucky Strike Survey." Until gathering war clouds dictated a more serious or patriotic approach, these were mostly Depression-era fare: love songs and ballads with "pack up your troubles in your old kit bag" type lyrics. Suspense mounted as the announcer guided the band up the rating toward the number one spot. With much fanfare, this came at the program's end, and I joined others in feeling my musical tastes in good shape whenever my favorite song emerged on top. I learned new songs this way every week. The radio and Andy had swung me solidly behind swing. If I ever learned to play a dance band instrument, I would be able to take a more active part. Meanwhile, I followed the bands and the songs, learning the music as I listened.

In the mid-1930s the Carlisle school board hired a part-time bandmaster. Cleary Fightmaster, Paris High School music director, traveled twice weekly to CHS to give instrumental lessons and form a concert and marching band. He had studied at the Cincinnati Conservatory, was young and personable, and his band soon won favorable comment. When the bass drummer quit, I "auditioned" for a chair no one else wanted. Fightmaster had little choice but to use me, yet I was so small I could neither see over the bass drum on its stand nor be seen behind it. At the next concert whispers ran through the audience concerning the bodiless, ghostly drumstick beating the drum. When I stepped out from behind the drum after the first number, I was greeted with stares, scattered applause, and loud laughter. "They were laughing *with* you, not *at* you," Dad said later, thinking I was upset.

"Either way's okay with me, Dad," I said, knowing my world of musical daydreams had ended. I was finally making music in a real band with real people.

An evergreen musician's joke starts with this question: "What do you call a person who hangs around musicians a lot?" The answer: "A drummer!" The joke of course ignores the all-important role of rhythm while bowing to those playing solo or melody instruments. I had never heard the joke, but I soon wanted to switch from bass drum to trumpet. Fightmaster was willing for me to do so but said he needed a saxophone player more than a trumpeter. "All those sax keys scare me," I told him; "I don't think I could ever figure them all out."

"Look at it this way, Frank," he replied. "You'll have to play all of the notes on just three trumpet keys, but on a sax you'll have a key or fingering for each note. Besides," he added significantly, "I know of a saxophone your parents can borrow for you to learn on. If things go well they might want to buy you one later."

I still leaned toward a trumpet, but the realities of hard times dictated that I start on the free C-melody saxophone to see what I could do. And that is how I became what big band musicians call a "reed man," even though only a seventy-five-pound one.

Fightmaster was a good teacher, and Mom goaded me along with her musical "connections": Kyser and Willson. I did not need much goading for I could see my progress. Music's best-kept secret, until rock and roll came along, was that it offers no place to hide. Consistent and patient practice, combined with talent, produces easily recognized results. The proof comes out of the musician's instrument for all to hear.

My small size served as a goad to my music making. By the eighth grade I was excluded from most of the pickup sports boys organize in fields and vacant lots. I had two pals also trapped in a slow growth cycle, but, even better, I had Andrew. He and I were chatting one afternoon when he noticed that I was down in the dumps. I had been mumbling and paying little attention as he talked. "Andy," I finally admitted, "I just feel plumb bad."

"What's eating on you?" he inquired.

"Girls will never like me," I replied. "I'm going to be a runt all my life. They only go for athletes and big guys. I feel awful," I said, with tear in my eyes.

Andy laid a hand on my shoulder. "Do I play football or basketball?" he asked.

"No," I said.

"Do girls like me?"

"They sure do," I said, sniffling as I began to see his point.

"Girls like lots of things besides sports. They like to dance, for example. I hear you practicing your sax all the time. Dancing and music go together. Girls love that. You'll be in a dance band someday, and by then you'll have grown up as big as your dad. You'll have plenty of dates. Say, I wish I could toot a horn like you!"

Although I lacked Andy's faith in my growth, he had convinced me that girls could like me for reasons other than sports—he was living proof of that. Above all, he suggested a goal I knew I could live with—music. High school was coming up next year, and before it was over I would turn my sympathetic neighbor into a prophet.

Few things have ever impressed themselves on my memory as much as what came out of an "imitation alligator hide" case one April afternoon as I walked in from school. "Go open that box," Mom said, smiling and pointing to a shipping box on the front room floor. I was interested yet puzzled until I saw the alligator hide case inside. My heart surged; it had to be what I had dreamed of for years. I laid the case on its side and popped open the two spring-powered latches. I opened it. Swirling emotions moistened my eyes as I gazed at it—a shimmeringly shiny gold-lacquered King Zephyr alto saxophone nestled in "red crushed plush."

I cried for joy and so did she. I danced her around the room, thanking her in every way I could think of as we whirled. She had cashed her World War I Liberty Bonds for the $120 purchase price.

"It's a doozy!" I cried, as I put it together while wetting a reed in my mouth. I knew it was a name-brand sax, one often seen in movie shorts and photos of big band sax sections. That meant a lot to me. I spent the remainder of the afternoon playing it, marveling at its tone, its easy "lay" for my fingers, and the silent response of its keys. The old borrowed sax lay alone in its case like a discarded lover.

My playing improved immediately, not only because of the superior mechanics of the sax but also because Mom's love had led her to give up a lot of money in my behalf. That and the new sax led me to a deeper and more realistic dedication to music. Mom would never again have to goad me along with references to Willson and Kyser. The new sax was above this, for it did not allow excuses. There were no leaky pads, bent rods, loose springs, or anything else to interfere with playing scales or practice assignments. And pride in my new possession soared every time I saw one like it in movies or photos of the bands of Benny Goodman, Duke Ellington, Xavier Cugat, and many others. "When I grow up," I said to myself many times, "I'm going to play in a big dance band." And I did, in more than a dozen.

Mom's love for me multiplied in an unexpected but crucial way. Just seven years after opening my new sax, I was a scared rifleman in G Company, 145th Infantry, 37th Division, on Bougainville, an embattled South Pacific island. I was cannon fodder and I knew it. A reorganization of the division's musical units brought me to the attention of the bandmaster, and I was transferred to division headquarters and the band. Although HQ suffered some combat deaths and wounds, two-thirds of G Company's soldiers were killed or wounded during savage combat on Luzon the next year. Would I have been one of them? Who knows? But I wrote Mom at the time that "I probably owe my life to those music lessons and that sax you bought me back in 1937."

The Carlisle band often played concerts at schools in nearby counties. One of happy memory was at Tollesboro High School. At this time I was trying to hang around girls, not really knowing what to do, just hanging around them and hoping I would attract favorable attention. I liked several girls in the band and managed to sit with them in a booth at a tiny café near the high school. Putting a nickel in the jukebox was a rite of passage, so I punched the number of a record I had never heard before, hoping for the best. We sat there as "The Beer Barrel Polka" entered our lives. The response was immediate—we loved it! They "wished" they could hear it again, so I blew another nickel, no mean feat for a kid with a quarter to eat on. The girls thought I had known all about this new song and had played it just for them: "Frank," one said, "you just know so much about good music, and you played that wonderful song with the Andrews Sisters singing it, just for us!" Who was I to deny such a happy thought!

Soon after this the band got impressive new green and white uniforms, and we proudly played in them at the Ewing Fair. Ewing was a village fifteen miles north of Carlisle boasting a large agricultural-based fair each summer. Livestock, poultry, machinery, put-up fruits and vegetables, jams, pies, cakes, and household arts and crafts vied for blue ribbons. We played as massive Clydesdales and Percherons engaged in well-attended horse pulling contests (modern tractor pulls are simply silly by comparison). Amid all of this, as well as the unmistakable smells of straw, popcorn, hot dogs, and manure, the band played on.

Volunteers drove band members to the fair. Drummer Bobby

Cunningham and I rode with John D. Power, a young man who had graduated and gone to work. John had a sense of humor, never talked down to kids, and told us to meet him at the Ferris wheel at eight o'clock for the drive home. I had a quarter, and I doubt that Bobby had much more. Within five minutes we lost all we had in a midway "fishing game." We were outraged but hungry. Marion "Steamboat" Evans loaned us twenty cents to get two hot dogs. I lifted mine for a bite and the wiener slipped out of the bun, plopping into a fresh cow pie. What to do? I fished it out, took it to a water truck faucet, and shined it up like new. I stuck it triumphantly back in my bun, slapped some mustard on it, and ate it. Bobby and Steamboat watched with approval, seeing no room for adverse comment.

It was dark when John picked us up. Bobby told him of the hot dog in the cowpie. "I thought I saw a few more flies than usual hovering around Frankie's head," he chuckled as he headed his Chevy coupe for Carlisle.

The ride home impressed me deeply. The Chevy departed the high ridgeline north of Pleasant Valley and began winding steeply down into a deep lowland carved eons ago by the Licking River. A stunning scene filled the windows. Wispy tendrils of fog drifted across the extensive valley floor below us. They reflected the greenish white moonlight, matching it in color. High bluffs along the valley's sides framed the scene, as if put there to emphasize its beauty. I had never been over this road on such a night; the unearthly beauty enchanted me. Little I had seen in movies and magazines was any lovelier. I saw that my homeland could be as pretty as anyplace, when dressed for the occasion. It made me rethink Dad's determination to live his life in Nicholas County. Perhaps he was smarter than I thought.

8

The Forces of Nature

Lucky Mathias was always at ease with the forces of nature, and I did my best to follow in his often muddy footsteps. Profit, however, united with Mother Nature's forces during my seventh-grade autumn when I discovered that money lay thickly among the October leaves under black walnut and hickory trees. Vivian Scott's produce house paid seventy-five cents a bushel for hulled walnuts or hickory nuts. Although Andrew and I had picked a peck or two for his candy gifts, this small annual harvest was nothing compared to what Speck and I gathered between 1937 and 1943, the year I entered the army.

Many afternoons after school from late September through October, my brother and I hiked to various "secret" groves of walnut and hickory trees. These trees are seemingly ordained to lose their leaves earlier than most, thus revealing nuts hanging from bare branches—for the benefit of mankind and squirreldom alike. We climbed to the treetops, gleefully shaking limbs along the way to make nuts cascade down, all thumping with the sound of money as they hit the ground. We liked seeing our hands stained an ever darker, indelible brown as we scooped walnuts into burlap sacks after stomping them out of soft, juicy, pungent husks. Nut-heavy shagbark hickory trees were also raided, but walnuts came first because they were bigger and filled a sack sooner. A bushel was our limit for any afternoon, enough to fill our wagon for the trip of a mile or so to the produce house. We averaged about seven dollars annually for nuts and two dollars for medicinal yellow-root.

Yellow-root grew along railroad cuts and similar slopes beside country lanes and creek banks. Speck and I once struck it rich under a rural railroad bridge. Masses of the root grew in and out of the fertile, soft banks alongside the tracks. Our eyes turned dollar-bill green as we pulled out twenty- and thirty-foot lengths of it. The plant looks like a thick yellow clothesline with leafy attachments. The three dollars we earned would have bought sixty loaves of bread or twelve haircuts!

It was never profit alone that lured me into the autumn woods, because, as William Wordsworth said in *Nutting*, "There is a spirit in the woods." Nicholas County's flaming fall forests had yet to be dulled through cutting of so many star performers—the great hardwoods. Dad, Charles, and I often hiked through them to favorite fishing spots alongside lakes and streams. He knew the trees and reviewed their names, appearances, and uses according to the season. He always stopped us to exclaim at the blazing autumn maples, ashes, sumacs, and hackberries, especially when they doubled their beauty by reflecting up from the dark mirror of deep, still lake water. Kentucky has more tree varieties than any state save Pennsylvania, and when frosty winds color them, they are second to none in beauty. But I neither needed nor wanted Lucky or other company when I wandered alone through autumn woodlands, gazing in poetic ownership at banks of red and yellow maples, golden ashes, kingly maroon oaks, multicolored sweet gums, persimmons and sassafrases, and giant tawny-leaved sycamores with spotted white trunks glaring boldly along riverbanks as their leaves sifted down. I was impressed with the sovereign importance of 130-foot-high tulip poplars bulking pale yellow above distant ridge lines. Interspersed with these scenes of leafy death and destruction were the cedars and pines, each a green testament that life was still triumphant in the forest and would return next spring. These unspoken feelings were put into words when Miss Thelma Linville had my seventh grade class memorize parts of Percy Shelley's great *Ode to the West Wind*:

O Wild West Wind, thou breath of Autumn's being
Thou from whose unseen presence the dead leaves
Are driven like ghosts from an enchanter fleeing,

Yellow, and black, and pale, and hectic red,
Pestilence-stricken multitudes!

The poem closes with a statement of near perfect optimism: "Oh Wind, if Winter comes, can Spring be far behind?"

Autumn's many facets were fulfilling, but Chautauqua was a tent full of unautumnlike excitement. A large tent with stage and dressing rooms was raised each summer behind the courthouse. It seated perhaps four hundred customers and was part of the nationwide Chautauqua circuit. Chautauquas were traveling tent shows providing cultural and educational entertainment to twelve thousand Chautauqua towns and allied societies.

The program began in Chautauqua, New York, in 1874 as a training camp for Sunday school teachers, but someone later packaged the program and took it on the road. Many others followed suit. Carlisle became a Chautauqua town after the Great War and was served each summer by Redpath Chautauquas. A *Mercury* editorial of June 6, 1925, observed that "Carlisle is one of the few Kentucky towns that supports the full 7 day circuit of Redpath Chautauqua." One could buy a season ticket for three dollars, certainly a bargain in the 1920s and arguably one during the Depression.

Each show started with local talent—singers, comedians, dancers—to warm up the audience. Professionals then took over. "Living History Under a Tent," for example, featured actors dressed as historical characters, each giving a speech pertinent to the assigned role. Also popular nationally were black groups known as "jubilee singers" who sang gospel and plantation work songs. This evidently fit white ideas of black status or "place." Jazz was too lowbrow to include. Experienced politicians spoke on recent trends such as Prohibition and the New Deal. The *Mercury* reported that North Dakota governor R.A. Nestos spoke on leadership at Carlisle's 1925 Chautauqua. There was always music: "Ruth Ford, noted mezzo-soprano; college singing girls who dress to match each tune, whether Japanese, Scotch, Hawaiian. . . . Bachman's Million Dollar Band, formerly the 'Sunset Division Army Band,'" and much else. Chautauqua was high-quality entertainment and in no way identified with circus midways or carnivals.

The "bee man" was a memorable part of Carlisle's Chautauqua. As he stood on the stage, thousands of honey bees swarmed over his head and upper body. He lectured on bees for a few minutes to a wide-eyed crowd, noting that as long as he washed himself thoroughly, the bees never stung him. Mom, always clean to a fault, never let Charles and me forget this, bees or no bees.

With the advent of radio and sound movies, Chautauqua faced deadly competition. The Depression delivered the final blow. Carlisle's love affair with it ended in the late 1930s, and nationally it fizzled out around 1940, in spite of a rousing appearance that year by Eleanor Roosevelt.

The greatest show of my youth was performed not by a Chautauqua but by the Ohio River in January 1937. Christmas vacation had hardly ended before there was talk of high water at Maysville. Heavy rains on the Ohio Valley snowpack followed. The soaked earth sped further rains straight into the drainage system. To make matters worse, most forests of this hilly valley had been clear-cut, adding silt and brush to water plunging down overburdened tributaries. One of the greatest floods and display of nature's forces in American history was under way.

Carlisle was not on the Ohio, but nearby Licking River set records not broken until 1997 as it flooded parts of Pleasant Valley and blocked most roads to the north. Concern increased when the radio reported that Portsmouth, Ohio, had opened its flood wall to allow controlled penetration by the rising river instead of waiting for the inevitable smashing overflow. The river was setting a new record every day. Floodstage at Cincinnati is fifty-two feet. The river climbed into the sixties early in the game, but this was not unusual; it happened every few years. Before long, measuring gauges read seventy feet and climbing. River watchers now knew that an unprecedented flood was in the making. They were right. By January 20, the mighty Ohio was hovering at just under eighty feet! Large areas of downtown Cincinnati and Louisville were underwater.

Meanwhile, we in Carlisle followed the news and pondered the situation. Roads were blocked north of us into river towns. Food, clothing, and bedding were collected for flood relief and delivered by National Guardsmen. Our antique fire engine—the one Uncle Joe had commanded as fire chief—was loaded on a flatcar and sent to Louisville as a pumper to fight fires in that flooded city. To our dismay, the Louisvillians neither acknowledged nor returned our unique engine. But much worse, from a student's point of view, painful typhoid shots were administered to everyone in school. Three shots, each flowing through a two-inch needle, were spaced over several days for each fearful student. The playground seemed full of baseball pitchers as kids tried to ease sore arms and shoulders by swinging them up, down, and around. To us, the flood had been just an exciting distant event, but those shots united us to the more painful aspects of such happenings.

Complications arose. Grandpa Furlong had been ailing since the autumn of 1936. It was not just one thing but a mix of old-age ailments. Grandma phoned us on January 22 that he was dying. Police and guardsmen blocked all passable roads to Maysville. Mom's dentist brother-in-law Dr. Walter Hines—"Uncle Doc" we called him—had enough "pull" as commander of Maysville's American Legion post to get us through the police cordon if—and it was a big if—we could get to Maysville.

Dad packed us and a week's luggage into our Model A Ford. His traveling salesman's knowledge of back roads, creek beds, and shortcuts paid off that day. He was able to guess where water would cover the more traveled roads, bouncing us cross-country over muddy country lanes and rocky wagon roads along ridgelines. We finally came across Jersey Ridge Road to join US 68 at the top of the Maysville Hill. Dad drove our mud-spattered Ford up to the police barricade and asked if Doc Hines had told them about us.

"Who's he?" they asked, laughing, watching our faces fall. "Sure he did," they added. "Go on through; give our sympathy to Mrs. Furlong." They opened the gate and we soon saw what a true disaster looked like.

A corkscrew stretch of highway drops steeply down to the town and river. In pioneer days it took draymen and six-horse teams nearly a day to climb up this heavy grade. As we started down, the town and river came into view through winter-stricken roadside trees. Dad stopped the car as the view struck us silent, a silence soon broken by murmurs and gasps. I first thought that everything had changed: "Is this really Maysville?" But the reality was there for anyone to see. Muddy yellowish-brown water now covered and swirled on three-fourths of Maysville and Aberdeen, Ohio. Both ends of the great suspension bridge were in deep water. Houses, barns, huge trees, storage tanks, and wreckage of all descriptions rotated and bobbed in the river's rushing center current. Looking upriver one saw a vast debris-dotted lake that blended with, then lost itself in, the cold, gray mist.

When our little Ford chugged in at Grandma's, Speck and I were delighted to see many of our Mason County cousins waiting for us. The Clarksons had ventured in from their farm as sightseers, but Uncle Doc Hines and his family were there as refugees. Their nice East Second Street home had water up to its second floor. But we on Fifth Street were far above the flood. From our perch we beheld the awesome scene below, with stricken homes sitting stolidly in the water as if resigned to their new surroundings. We climbed up Strawberry Alley to Sixth Street for a completely unobstructed view of the widespread watery wasteland.

That evening fire rose out of the water to threaten Maysville. We stared wide-eyed as a huge gasoline storage tank blazed furiously, spouting flames hundreds of feet into the humid, starless night as it tilted and slowly spun in the river's main current. It had floated free from its foundation at some upstream "tank farm," ignited by an errant spark. Desperate but courageous men in small motor craft had intercepted it and were visible in the flickering light and reflections. They hoped to keep it from turning shoreward and getting in among the town's buildings. Fortunately, they did not have to attempt the impossible. The current carried it rapidly downstream, and we watched it drift out of sight, still blazing and heading for Ripley. I sensed that there were things in life even beyond the control of adults.

Grandpa John B. Furlong died Tuesday morning, January 25, 1937, the day the flood crested at a formerly unbelievable height of near eighty feet. "Daddy was always able to pick exactly the wrong time to stage a big event!" his daughter Alma commented brightly, even if a bit irreverently. Following the funeral, we boarded the Model A, and its puckety-puckety little engine pulled me away from the most memorable adventure of my young life.

Years later I told University of Kentucky dean Albert D. Kirwan about my experiences during the great Maysville flood of 1937. Kirwan, a Louisvillian, whose father's lumber business washed away in the great Ohio River flood of 1913, said whenever flood talk came up it reminded him of the old fellow who bored everyone to death telling about the great Johnstown flood of 1889. "Have you heard about him?" the dean asked, a typical twinkle in his eye.

"No sir," I replied.

"Well, Frank, the old fellow died and stood before the Pearly Gates. He immediately started telling Saint Peter about the great Johnstown flood. But Saint Peter stopped him and said, 'Look, it's OK to tell me about this, but if I were you I would tone it down a little when I got back in there, because Noah is in the crowd!'"

I became a Boy Scout the year of the flood for the usual reasons plus two: Camp Black Hawk and Salt Peter Cave. These attractions were positioned on the east flank of a mile-long ridge rising three hundred feet above Licking River as it carves out the southwest border of Pleasant Valley. L&N tracks notch the nearly clifflike side of this ridge lengthwise, the trains crossing the river over a high bridge at the far north end. A few minutes' walk down the tracks from a county access road are two natural coves, both running back into the ridge from track level. The first is Salt Peter Cave, not a cave so much as an accessible, weatherproof, 150-foot-deep gouge into and under a layered, rimrock overhang. It is a fascinating, lonely place. Hummingbirds pause in midsummer air to sip from the slight stream of spring water tumbling down from the rimrock.

Indians and pioneers used the cave to break journeys on Licking River. Saltpeter (potassium nitrate) was dug and mixed with sulfur and powdered charcoal to make gunpowder, thus the cave's name. The most famous pioneer of all, Daniel Boone, used this cave. He later made his home in Nicholas County from 1795 to 1797, and his cabin is still within a three-hour hike from the cave. The very thought that Daniel Boone had slept and made gunpowder in Salt Peter Cave was more than enough recommendation to any boy or girl of my generation.

Black Hawk is 500 yards farther down the track. As a U-shaped hollow, it thrusts 200 feet into the ridge, with a 150-foot frontage along the tracks. High on the cove's steep but tree-clad slopes is Coon Cave, a walk-in cavern from which permanent spring water trickles down to the cove floor and from there a steep 150 feet down to the river. The river here has a smooth, solid rock bottom, gradually deepening from 2 to 10 feet, a near perfect "swimmin' hole." If there ever was a choice spot for a Boy Scout camp, this was it.

Carlisle's American Legionnaires realized its potential, leased the land, and installed several barracks, a kitchen, cistern, and office in the mid-1920s. It was named for Chief Black Hawk, a noted Sauk war leader. Enthusiastic scouts took up where the Legion left off, hammering and cementing over one hundred stone steps down to the river. Giant trees soon supported rope swings dangling from high branches above the cove and the river, each with a happy boy aboard. The camp soon became the prime summer recreation area not only for Boy Scouts but for Nicholas County's citizens between the wars. All admired the newly formed Legion for such praiseworthy projects.

Although the camp buildings were for scouts or their guests, the river was open to swimmers, boaters, and onlookers. "Let's go to the river" meant a trip to swim and be seen at Black Hawk. There was no nearer or cheaper place to relax and cool off on a hot summer afternoon. All piled into a flivver and headed north on the Flemingsburg Road. If the car was blessed with "freewheeling" apparatus, the driver could save gas by coasting four of the seven miles, or three without it. Friends and neighbors met and chatted after parking and walking the tracks to the camp. Older citizens sometimes laughed about secret card games in Salt Peter Cave as they walked by. Heads bobbed knowingly, for the cave had earlier served as a gambling hideout for the usual refugees from the massive crowds attending religious activities at nearby Parks Hill Protestant camp meetings.

Ugly, itchy, woolen one-piece bathing suits covering the torso were donned by adults inside the camp barracks, but children were allowed to wear skimpier and more suitable swimsuits. It was an adventure in itself to hurry eagerly down the one hundred steps to the river, and once there, frayed emotions and sweaty bodies were soothed and cooled in the clean river water.

One hot summer afternoon in 1930 Uncle Ed Metcalfe crammed Andrew, me, and several other boys and girls into his old Chevy sedan for swimming lessons at Black Hawk. I was enthralled by what I saw. Daring boys dropped or turned flips off the soaring rope swings into the river. Others dived from a diving board built into the opposite bank. Water-slickened mud slides sent others careening down thirty-foot slopes, splashing butt first into the river. The gentle current removed the muddy water in preparation for the next slider. Somehow, in the midst of all this, Uncle Ed patiently hung on, his weekly lessons producing enthusiastic swimmers by summer's end. Black Hawk was the place to be from that time on.

Scoutmaster David Worth Sapp spent each summer in the "Hawk's Nest," the camp's office shed. He was in his fifties in 1937, the first year I stayed overnight at Black Hawk. Sapp not only directed the scouts but hosted several church youth groups for a week each summer. In addition, poor children from Louisville claimed a week of his time during the late 1930s. A *Mercury* editorial of May 1929 held that "no man in Carlisle has done more or had a more wholesome influence on the life of boys of the community than Mr. Sapp."

Sapp's greatest secret in handling campers was never to overorganize things, let them roam rather freely, but warn them and teach them to look out for each other. Until I later spent a week at highly structured Camp Friedlander in Ohio, I never fully appreciated Sapp's technique or his pleasantly eccentric personality. He could be strict, however, when one of his cardinal rules was broken. Fighting earned a quick trip back to Carlisle. Any scout sent to Cameron's store over on the highway to get him a ten-cent sack of roll-your-own Bull Durham tobacco had better bring back Bull Durham. Any other brand got a grumpy reception and a repeat of the one-mile trip. His usual comment on scout failures: "If you can't listen to instructions, what can you listen to?"

He was listened to. During his years as scoutmaster there were no serious injuries, drownings, or other problems. Black Hawk's isolation gave him and his boys and guests practical ownership of a mile-long section of ridge and cliff, a normally placid river of sparkling riffles and biting fish, a railroad track with a challenging high bridge to climb, and a teeming cross section of Kentucky's flora and fauna. Above all, this was a place a boy could do a lot of growing up, of coming of age with other boys. Our scoutmaster was wise enough to let nature take its course.

When it came time to spend my first week at Black Hawk, I got two sacks ready. In one, I put a toothbrush and mixture of soda and salt to clean my teeth, a bar of soap, a bathing suit and towel, an extra pair of pants, and two long-sleeved shirts (sleeves were rolled up to make "short-sleeved shirts," and older boys sometimes hid cigarette "makings" in the rolls). The second sack carried my food.

Mom gave me seventy-five cents for food. I paid five cents for a loaf of bread, five cents for a twenty-ounce package of pancake flour, twenty cents for four cans of pork and beans, twenty cents for a pound slab of bacon, five cents for some apples and a dime for a jar of peanut butter, which took hard stirring to mix butter and oil. This left me with a dime to buy candy or pop at a concession stand Sapp ran for swimmers and drop-ins. In addition, I took salt and pepper mixed, brown sugar to make syrup, and potatoes from home. The sixty-five cents worth of groceries, a sack of clothes, a blanket, and a dime easily got me through a week at Black Hawk.

As often as not I took the train to camp, waiting impatiently as the small engine and two cars swayed down the tracks, gliding to a huffing, steamy stop at the station. Uncle Joe was there, of course, and usually paid my fifteen-cent fare for the six-mile trip. The little train was often ridiculed as the "Ragweed Special," or the "Carlisle Cannonball," but it was nice to have it available for trips to Black Hawk or for connections with mainline trains in Maysville or Paris. Again, it stopped to pick up passengers or deliver items all along the line. Sapp used it to bring hundred-pound blocks of ice from Carlisle every day or so for the camp icebox and soft drink stand.

While waiting for the train, several boys and I began aping the laughable Hitler and his Nazis as seen on newsreels. We goose-stepped across the station platform, giving stiff-armed "Heil Hitlers" while holding black combs or paper on our lips in imitation of the Fuhrer's dinky mustache. We had done this elsewhere, and as usual adults gave us a big laugh. Behind such laughter lay a tacit hope that the world's fears were misplaced after all and that it was hard to take the antics of the Nazis all that seriously. Who could have envisioned the coming Holocaust in the mid-1930s? A few years later the laugh was on us.

When I got off the train for my first week at camp I was welcomed by several pals who had come by car as well as older scouts already there. Sapp took us beginners aside, standing by a large water barrel under a barracks gutter. "Boys," he said, "you know you're welcome; now I have a few rules I want you to follow. First, there's no fighting at any time, any place, or any how at this camp. Is that understood?" We nodded appreciatively, for we were the smallest fellows around.

Sapp liked our attitude and continued. "Another thing you'll have to do is take a morning dip. Nobody eats breakfast here until everybody, including me, goes down to the river and spends a few minutes in the water. Starts the day off right. Understand?" Again we nodded that we did.

The scoutmaster now stared into the eyes of each lad, as if to see through him. "Now, boys," he said slowly and pointedly, "there's nary a thing in the camp, or in the river, or along the tracks, or on the ridge that will hurt you if you don't hurt it first." We gasped, then jumped back when he suddenly scooped up a big wolf spider that had been lurking on the splintered rim of the water barrel. The hairy spider sat calmly in the palm of his large hand, its shiny multiple eyes staring at us. Sapp deftly but gently switched the creature from hand to hand, then carefully let it run back to the barrel rim. "See what I mean?" he asked, looking each of us in the eye.

Indeed we did! We talked about his feat all afternoon, but when we tried to imitate him with other big spiders, the beasts stared us down every time.

Sapp concluded his introductory talk by telling us to remember the all-important difference between "city dirt" and "country dirt." "Out here with Mother Nature," he said, "we have good clean country dirt. City dirt is different because it's what I call 'dirty dirt.' It comes from spit in the gutters, open sewers, germs in the air, cigarette butts, and who knows what all. See what I mean?"

We nodded vigorously, glad now to have rid ourselves of Carlisle and its "dirty dirt" and full of hope that we might be able to spend more than just one clean week with Scoutmaster Sapp.

Ralph Shearer, an older scout, guided us to our bunks in the rear barrack. On the way he took us inside a small shed housing the Delco light plant. A local citizen had donated it. Banks of big glass batteries with pea-sized red and green balls floating here and there had the appearance of Flash Gordon's movie serial space station power plant. Suddenly a small putt-putt motor cut in and we stepped back. "The little motor switches on automatically now and then to keep the batteries charged," Ralph said. Camp Black Hawk had electric lights several years before the REA (Rural Electrification Administration) brought them to most Kentucky farms.

We also had occasional interesting but no-nonsense river men fishing for food or passing through on the river. Most were as long, lean, and weatherbeaten as their sixteen-foot, homemade, wooden johnboats. We scouts were tolerated by them as a cross between "city dudes" and "playboys," as nearly as I can define it. They were friendly, however, unless too many questions were asked because they were shy by nature but also because jugs of homemade whiskey often lurked half-hidden in the boats. Well-oiled and polished rifles were always in full view, somehow serving as "answers" before "too many damned questions" were asked!

My introduction to Black Hawk might well have had a sad ending. When Bobby Cunningham and I finished filling straw ticks for our cots, we decided to skip rocks on the river. But we stopped to pick blackberries along the sunny tracks before racing down the hundred stone steps to the rocky river beach. Bobby spotted the big snake first, as it flexed its coils in the fork of a giant sycamore leaning steeply over the river beach. We threw rock after rock before knocking it senseless to the ground. It was a handsome creature, with brown and black hourglass markings and a head as shiny as a penny.

We hit it several more times, then I took its tail, held it out a bit from my body, and both of us ran up the steps to show it around camp. We felt like heroes.

As we crossed the tracks, Shearer walked by, and I proudly held out the snake. Ralph stopped cold in his tracks; the big snake had regained its senses and was curling its body like a corkscrew. "Drop it, Frank, drop it now," the older scout said in a serious but calm voice. I dropped it, wondering what was up. Ralph's next words struck Bobby and me with the force of simple but unrecognized truth: "That's a big and dangerous copperhead!" he exclaimed as he clubbed the writhing pit viper to death.

The scoutmaster now happened into the action as he walked out of the nearby Hawk's Nest office shed. Shearer had no choice but to tell him what had happened, lifting the four-foot serpent on the end of a stick. Sapp stared at Bobby and me and turned grumpy, but he took it mostly out on me because I was identified as the one who had carried the copperhead. "Boy," he grumbled, "you don't learn very fast, do you. What did I tell you last Sunday when you came here?"

"Well, sir, you said there wasn't nuthin' would hurt us if we didn't hurt it first." I said this apologetically, knowing he had me dead to rights.

Sapp bent over and looked me straight in the eye: "Did that snake hurt you first or did you hurt that snake first?"

"I hurt the snake first," I said, with eyes on the ground. "Bobby and I did," I added, glancing at my silent, wide-eyed pal.

"Boys, that snake was only tryin' to get hisself some birds' eggs; that's all he had on his mind 'til you two came along. Copperheads like him now and then float down outa th' mountains on driftwood durin' a flood. Don't ever fool with one but come tell me, and that goes for ever' scout down here." Other scouts had sidled up to listen. "Either one of you could've gotten bit real bad. If you two had followed my rule, you and the snake both would be a lot happier. If you can't listen to instructions, what can you listen to? Take that snake now and drop him down the privy. Boys, have you learned anything?"

"Yes, sir!" Bobby and I said together. "We sure have." And we meant what we said.

Lucky was due on Saturday to drive Bill Hopkins, Popeye Clark, Bobby, Davey Harper, and me home. "Don't tell Dad about the snake," I warned, "or they'll all get scared and keep us from coming back down here." I also told them that Lucky never went straight home once he saw the river. "He always has to go over to the riffle and fish a while." And that is what happened.

We kept quiet about the copperhead when Dad picked us up at the Parks Hill parking area. "Say," he said as he revved up the motor, "if you boys can spare a few minutes I'd like to wet my line over at the riffle." We agreed but smiled knowingly at each other, pleased that we had predicted an adult's actions.

The riffle is a sparkling five-hundred-foot stretch of fast-flowing river water. It dashes across fossil-encrusted limestone rocks and until recently bathed extensive mussel beds. These fell victim to the Japanese cultured pearl industry. Oysters form the most perfect pearls around bits of inserted freshwater mussel shell. Scrubgrass Creek enters Licking River at the head of the riffle, where Dad parked. Jokers as usual had rubbed the GR off the highway sign naming the creek. The whine of buzz saws biting into wood came from the sawmill several hundred feet up the river.

We descended to the riffle, skidding and thrashing through a thicket of head-high horseweeds. Dad cut several of these as he passed through. We watched him look for holes in sections of the segmented stalks, then cut those sections out. We knew that inside each of those sections was a horseweed worm, and once on a hook it would attract channel catfish like few other baits. I knew now that Dad would be sitting along the riffle fishing for channel cats. I also knew what we would be having for supper.

Sure enough he found a likely spot along the riffle, told us to be careful, then lost himself matching wits with the big channel cats that prowl these swift waters. We swam a few minutes in the still, deep river above the riffle, then struck out for a huge sawdust stack sloping steeply from the mill to the river, some thirty feet below. The river nibbled daily at the ever-growing pile of woody waste until high water came to gobble it all up.

We followed each other up the steep clay and rock bank, using tough bushes for handholds, then stood atop the sawdust stack with a feeling that the world was ours. One by one we rolled, twisted, whooped, and careened downward into the cool, deep river. We did it over and over. Millhands watched in envy, thinking back a few years to a time they too had been sawdust sliders. We hated to see Dad beckoning us from the riffle as he proudly held up a string of fish. Sunburned, happy, and hungry, we piled into the old Model A.

Dad let my pals off before driving on home. Mom met us with a quizzical look, one that aroused my suspicion. She gave me a hug, listened as I enthused about the week at camp, then bumped boldly into my secret world: "Tell me about the snake," she demanded.

"Snake? Snake? What snake?" I asked, trying to buy time enough to conceive an innocent sounding answer.

"You know what snake. Cute little Mary Ellen Pumphrey told Mrs. Metcalfe about it up at the grocery. Ben Henry—you call him Pokey—anyway, her brother was down at camp with you and told Mary Ellen that you and Bobby nearly got bitten by a copperhead. And Mrs. Metcalfe said Mr. Sapp gave you two a good talking-to. Is that right?"

"Aw, Mom, it was just a little snake," I lied. "Ralph wasn't even sure what kind of snake it was," I again lied. "And Mr. Sapp, who's kind and gentle to all bugs and snakes, said we shouldn't kill anything, even a snake. We dropped the little dead snake down the privy for him."

I felt better now but was mad at Mary Ellen. I thought maybe she was the keenest girl in class, but this just proved girls could not be trusted with anything important. And as for her brother Pokey, I would have felt much better about him had a genie told me he was destined to fly some thirty B-29 missions over Japan.

"I hope you haven't lied to me," Mom replied, letting me down easy. "I don't want you running around down at the river if poisonous snakes are there. I'll have Dad ask Mr. Sapp about this next time he goes down." To my disgust, Speck was standing by, nodding his red head in complete, grinning agreement.

She had dented my returning optimism, but Dad did not fish at Black Hawk, thus he seldom saw Sapp. The matter self-destructed as time went by. That night for supper we had a superb meal of catfish fillets and hush puppies. I could tell from the way Dad looked at me that everything was all right. I knew I loved that old fisherman.

9

They Called Him Lucky

Mom called him Charlie, his sisters called him Charles, his sons called him Dad, but everyone else in his world called him Lucky. He signed Lucky to his checks and letters. Mail to him from acquaintances was always addressed to Lucky Mathias. Few people in town knew his real name. He liked it that way; I never once heard him complain.

He did not remember how he picked up his nickname but assumed with everyone else that fishing had something to do with it. Few would argue that he was not the best fisherman in the county. Some held that A.R. "Tickie" Fisher, or Hicel Asbury, or Stan Hutchings, or even Superintendent Pfanstiel—all of them fast friends of his—could hold their own with him. That was probably true on a given day, but week in and week out Lucky had no peers. He fished in every season of every year in every body of water available in Nicholas and surrounding counties. And unlike most others he had plenty of time to fish, for he was completely divorced from any temptation to allow his sales job to take on time-clock dimensions.

Lucky was known everywhere and warmly welcomed to ponds and lakes the owners stoutly denied to most fishermen. He was known as a sportsman who had no intention of "fishing the place out." A few "keepers," usually bass, newlight (crappie), or bream, satisfied him; he carefully dehooked and threw back smaller fish. His disgust with "fish hogs" carrying a string of forty or fifty tiny fish was total. He despised even more the illegal methods some used to get fish.

"Dynamiting" was one method, the stunned fish scooped up by the poacher. Another was to get down in the water and "feel them off the nest." This got the fish but kept next year's crop from hatching. Yet another was called "telegraphing." This required a car battery with two pokers, one wired to the positive and the other to the negative pole. When stuck into the water, the electricity stunned nearby fish, and they could be scooped up as they floated to the surface.

Lucky was seldom a sit-down fisherman. He usually walked as he fished, especially if he was after bass. He had a good casting rod with a well-oiled Pfluger reel. He called his casts like a pool hustler calling his pockets: "There's a big bass under that root over there just waiting for me," and with a flick of his wrist the plug invariably lit softly within inches of his target. He seldom lost plug or bait since he nearly always hit where he aimed. Lucky made it look so easy.

Following Lucky as he walked and casted along Licking, Hinkston, Stoner, and other streams was a chore for Speck and me. He was as much at home in this element as a bullfrog or shykpoke (heron). Lucky confidently attacked all obstacles head-on, whether briars, fallen trees with grapevine tangles, overgrown water gaps, collapsed banks, swamps, snakes, farmers' dogs, and the unexpected stuff that came up each trip. His one object was the stream and its fish; all else was secondary, and this sometimes included Speck and me!

We struggled along after him, catching up when he stopped to cast to "a likely spot over by that stump." We had been with him many times on rough-and-tumble hikes. We knew what to expect. He always headed to his favorite stretches of a stream where he stopped and spent several leisurely hours strolling and casting. But he often got there the hard way, fishing his way through thickets so as not to "miss that big bass I nearly hooked here the last time." Once at his favorite spot, however, he settled down. If it was noontime we had a picnic of sardines, Vienna sausage, and crackers. Speck and I did not think it got much better than that!

Dad's favorite spots were cherished swimming holes for Speck and me, not that we swam near him. On South Licking, for example, an old brick gristmill had tumbled into the river near the village of Berry. Dad fished on the downstream side and we swam above it. The clear water revealed the brick-clad bottom through our fifty-cent water goggles, our early version of snorkeling. When on Fleming Creek, the "blue hole" held our attention on hot summer afternoons. Hinkston and Fox Creek had exciting stretches of smooth water dappled with sun and shade, and both offered lovely covered bridges to play in and initial and date with our pen knives.

Then there was the johnboat at Millersburg dam. A grocer owned this long, lean, homemade rowboat and let Dad use it whenever he wanted. It took us ten minutes to row upstream to Dad's favorite spot. For some reason he nearly always rinsed off his false teeth on this trip, pulling them out, swishing them in the river, snapping them at us, then putting them back in his mouth. We always tied the johnboat to the same easy-to-get-to tree. The river here was deep, with steep banks and no shallow spots for swimmers to rest. The place always bored my brother and me after fifteen minutes of paddling around.

One afternoon, when Lucky was pole fishing for newlights, I eased from the boat with my goggles, swam underwater twenty feet, tugged his bait hard, then swam underwater back to the boat. He was a study in concentration, mumbling something about either a big turtle or water dog grabbing his line. The next time I did it I had to come up for air before reaching the boat. "I knew it was a water dog," he laughed, throwing a handful of clods splashing about me.

Water dogs deserve mention. They are tailed amphibians with toothy dog-shaped heads and four small legs. They can reach a foot and a half in length and weigh around two pounds. Trot line fishermen hate them because they bite chunks out of hooked fish. But they often hook themselves when they do this. Every fisherman of my generation knew what had to be done with a caught water dog. Tradition held that the only way one of these baleful looking creatures could be killed was to pound a wooden stake through its heart, pinning it helplessly to the bank. We who did this sensed that we were taking part in a mystery rather than acting foolish. Then came the night several pals and I shuddered through a movie at the Lyric titled *Dracula*. We used much longer and sharper stakes on water dogs after that, often looking over our shoulders as we did so.

Lucky knew the denizens of Kentucky's lakes and streams as well as Ed Metcalfe knew his cattle when he was a Montana cowboy. He was at home there and wanted his sons to be the same. We were, up to a point, but that point was reached when it came to "feeling for turtles." He had done this often, he said, when he was a boy, and he was determined to show us how it was done.

Turtles hang around half-submerged brush piles and overgrown water gaps. They sun themselves on protruding brush or branches. Dad decided to show us how to catch them one afternoon. He peeled down to his BVDs and started feeling his way along a brush-burdened water gap. Water gaps are gatelike affairs of fencing and boards hung across small streams to keep livestock in their assigned fields. Lucky talked as he slowly moved, keeping his hands underwater to feel for a turtle among the morass of sticks and brush.

"You will always know when you touch something alive," he advised. "Always feel your way around the top edge of the turtle's shell until you get to his tail; a snapper can give you a bad bite if you grab his head instead of his tail."

As he talked he felt the tail of something alive. In one quick splashy motion he sent a big water snake flipping through the air, just missing Speck and me. We ducked but saw no room for comment; we had swum with plenty of water snakes. They were a nasty-tempered lot, compared with field snakes, but we knew that the only dangerous ones, cottonmouth water moccasins, did not live in the Bluegrass.

We thanked Dad for showing us how to feel out turtles—he found none at this gap—but we secretly drew the line at water gaps and soggy brush piles. Down in that sunless morass there was bound to be a grabbing, grasping, biting something or others we would be better off to leave strictly alone!

Lucky was pragmatic when it came to bait—he would use anything that worked. A frugal soul, he never bought every touted new plug that hit the market. When he found one that worked, he stuck with it until it did not work. He experimented constantly with older plugs, finding that some of them were back in style with the fish. His live bait ran the gamut of minnows, worms, crawdads, and the fierce-looking larvae of dobson flies, called hellgrammites. In season, he used tadpoles, horseweed worms, grubs, and much else. He knew where to get bait and often started a fishing trip with a seine and minnow bucket at a favorite creek. I never knew him to buy bait, nor did I ever see any for sale in Nicholas County between the wars. Why pay hard-earned money for something you could dig up in a field or yard or seine in a creek?

Dad was fishing at the Carlisle reservoir one afternoon when a woman walked up and asked him how come he caught so many fish, what was his secret? "Ma'am," he replied, "you just have to have more sense than the fish." She took his reply personally, feeling slightly insulted, but Lucky meant exactly what he said. He respected fish, believing they were smarter than most folks thought. He convinced me of this one afternoon at the Flemingsburg reservoir. He fished there every time he worked the town—calling on the grocers in the morning and the fish in the afternoon. "Come over here," he shouted, "and I'll introduce you to some fish that know me."

I thought he was going to pull a joke on me, but I ran over. He tapped two rocks together underwater. Three or four bass immediately glided up to the water's edge and hung there expectantly. He pinched a squirming worm between his thumb and index finger, then held it underwater. Each time he did this, one of the bass struck it and flashed out of sight, leaving a small whirlpool behind. When I tried, I could get them to the waterline by clicking the rocks, but when my hand touched the water they sped away. In fact, they often swam away when I got within four or five feet of the water. On later visits, Mom and Speck were also flunked by the fish, yet they always came and ate at Dad's calling.

From a fishy viewpoint, however, Lucky should have been avoided as the most dangerous guy on the lake, so perhaps this tale proves that fish are dumbbells after all, but I like to think that he and the fish knew something the rest of us missed.

Mercury editor Warren Fisher published a little fish story back between the wars that I often heard but have yet to locate in his paper. Lucky was fishing one spring afternoon at the Carlisle reservoir when his hook snagged something on the bottom. It slowly loosened and he reeled it in. It was a minnow bucket full of live minnows, and he was flabbergasted to find his friend Stanley Hutchings's name on it. He called Stan, hinting that he might have some news concerning the minnow bucket "you whined so much about losing last autumn." Hutchings doubted that, saying that it had rolled down the bank and sunk into water too deep for anyone to get at. But it was his turn to be flabbergasted when Lucky told him he had retrieved the bucket and, lo and behold, the minnows had made it through the winter not only alive but healthy! He and Dad concluded that the minnows had eaten well from the small stuff that filtered in through the bucket's screening. Nevertheless, both of them endured sly grins and foolish questions about their "miraculous minnows" for several months.

The Carlisle reservoir makes a cozy corner where its right bank meets the dam. Lucky loved to sit here under a small sycamore shade tree on hot days and fish for bream and newlights. Often he brought a sack of dead houseflies, sprinkling them abundantly on the water to attract fish. Once a feeding frenzy developed, he dropped his bait in and quickly caught whatever was biting.

No one between the wars ever wondered where Lucky got his flies. Flies were everywhere, breeding abundantly in manure on the streets and in the fields or in backyard privies. Although houses and businesses had screening, flies made their way in through open doors and faulty screens. In fact, one of the first lessons of life came with this warning: "Keep that screen door closed or you'll let the flies in . . . where d'ya think you live, on a hillside?"

Flies, of course, were already in. Curled strips of sticky flypaper hung from ceiling thumbtacks in kitchens, restaurants, and groceries, flies dotting the gluey sides like nasty raisins. And just outside the back doors of homeowners and grocers stood big, two-gallon-sized screen flytraps. Since no one had figured out how to sell dead flies, Lucky had his pick of every flytrap in Carlisle!

Dad almost always asked Speck and me if we wanted to go fishing with him; it was up to us to figure out if he *really* meant it. He often did not mean it if he had his casting rod and plugs, for we got in his way as he walked banks and overgrown paths, casting as he went. He usually meant if it he had minnows and light tackle, and he always meant it when showed up with worms and crawdads, telling us with a nod of his head to get our cane poles ready. We knew we would be sitting with him at some farm pond or Hinkston Creek. We also knew he would do a lot of talking and we would enjoy listening.

"Let's see if they are biting down on Hinkston," he told me one day. Summer vacation had just started and I felt like I owned the world and everything in it. I stuck my cane pole through the car's side window. The hook still had dried worm on it from the last time. We drove five or six miles to a favorite spot along Hinkston, a meandering stream of riffles, shallows, and occasional deep pools. Our spot was a deep pool down from a covered bridge. It was May, and dogwoods, violets, and redbuds were still in bloom along the banks, reflecting colorfully in the still, dark water. The white trunks of giant sycamores peeked through the startling springtime green of willows downstream. Birdsong and buzzing insects added vibrancy to the scene. It was altogether a very pleasant place. Dad and I fished here quite often, but this time he had something on his mind besides bluegills. "Your teacher tells me that you and some boys got into a fistfight at school last week. Is that right?" He waited patiently for me to devise an answer.

"Yes, sir," I said, feeling anger again, "but it wasn't my fault. Scoop Mercer butted into our marble game. He hunched out across the shooting line to hit our marbles, then when the recess bell rang he shouted 'GRABS'!"

"Is that all? What did you do?"

"Well, he tried to run off with our marbles so I knocked them out of his hand and shoved him real hard. He hit me and everybody jumped into it. We were all on the ground when Mr. Burgess [the janitor] made us stop."

"Did you get your marbles back?"

"I got all but my shootin' taw. Pat Conley and Doug Roberts picked up most of the marbles."

Dad patted me on the knee. "Boy, you had a right to be mad," he advised, "but not a right to haul off and hit him. Pfanstiel could've gotten those marbles back for you all. The thing to do is to walk away, then work things out. A huncher always outhunches himself. You're bound to run into a few hunchers as you go along. Scoop's dad has been one all his life. Some hold he got that way only in the last few years, but they're wrong. I've known him from the time he was born."

Dad was now hooked on "hunchers" and kept running out the line, like a bass with a tasty minnow. "Hunchers always try to get something for nothing," he explained, "and usually at the expense of other folks. You'll even see them at church, 'thumping their craws' and praying loudly as they try to hunch up to the Lord before the rest of us. Hunchers come up to where I'm fishing sometimes, sit right down beside me, drop their line alongside mine, and then look at me like it's my fault if they don't catch anything. They didn't know enough to catch anything anyway; they were just afraid somebody else was getting ahead of 'em. There are even salesmen hunchers, boy, who hunch into my territory spreading all sorts of rumors about prices and products and honesty. Now then, is there anything else you'd like to know?"

"Yeah, Dad," I risked asking, "did you ever do any hunchin' when you were younger?"

"Shut up, boy, and mind your line; you've let two good bites get away from you already!"

I never fully understood that Dad often aimed his talks at some recent failing of mine, such as "hunching" musicians up to some imagined higher status in life. But whenever I made fun of or talked down other religions, blacks, or who Mom called "the looney old characters that walk Carlisle's streets," he stopped me in my tracks, looked me in the eye, and reverted to his oft-repeated philosophy: "Boy, never forget that one man is as good as another man if he *is* as good."

He meant that race, sex, politics, religion, money or no money, poor health, or other afflictions should never keep any man (or woman) from being considered as good as any other man if he *was* as good. Dad failed at times, but he tried hard to believe that every person he met was as good as or better than he was until that person might prove otherwise. And unlike most, he was able to hope that

his long-lost and unknown relatives in Germany would not perse-
cute the Jews; "After all," he said, "Jesus was a Jew."

Lucky never reminisced about his school days, which ended
with the eighth grade in 1893. Judging from my grade-school subjects, I was puzzled to find that he had read a bit of Shakespeare,
Irving, Whittier, Ben Franklin, and other authors I had never then
heard of: Byron, Pope, Addison, Milton, and Thackeray. Years later
I discovered the well-worn textbooks the Mathias children had used
stored in Uncle Joe's bookcase. As I paged through *McGuffey's Eclec-
tic Reader* for the sixth grade and *Swinton's Classic English Reader*,
I was astonished at the contents. Only the best of British and American poets, authors, and political writers were quoted. The *Maury-
Simonds Physical Geography* was interestingly written and left no doubt
as to the location and interplay of our planet's nations and physical
features. These books were plainly meant to present the best our
civilization had to offer. They challenged the students.

I reviewed these books again as I prepared this book. I felt that
testing had probably been "second-rate" in Dad's era of "unen-
lightened teaching methods" and that he had mostly educated himself later. I was in for a surprise. As if in answer to my biased doubts,
my local newspaper carried an article in which the columnist Mona
Charen quoted from an eighth-grade test recently discovered in
Kansas: "It required farmers' sons and daughters to find the interest
on an 8 percent note for $900 running two years, two months, six
days; to write an essay on the works of Thomas Jefferson; to give the
meanings for the words zenith, deviated, misconception, panegyric,
Spartan, and talisman; to name three important rivers in each of the
five continents; and to write 200 words on the evil affects of alco-
holic beverages." I conclude that Dad's grade school education gave
him a more-than-adequate preparation for his life thereafter.

Another spot Speck and I loved to bank-fish with Dad was the
lake formed behind Stoner Creek dam in Paris. We sat on a flat
concrete deck at one end of the small dam. The narrow lake usually
had enough water in it to make pleasant sounds as it piddled over
the dam, splashing harmlessly on the rocks and gurgling through a
wide expanse of river weeds and willow saplings. Speck and I often

got a nickel to buy and split a cold Ale-Eight-One, a locally bottled pop with a pun for a brand name—"A Late One."

At most places, Dad started fishing as soon as he reached the water, but not here. Stoner Creek exerted a soothing influence on him. He approached fishing slowly here, first cutting himself a piece of twist tobacco and a slice of "sweetner"; only then did he carefully bait his hook and settle down to his avocation. Sweetner is cake tobacco. He liked Brown's Mule but would take Star if he had to. He chewed every day and smoked several pipeloads of Golden Grain. Mom detested his chewing, especially when he spit on his car door window after she had washed it. On the other hand, when he drove with it rolled down, anyone in the backseat was at risk.

But fishing and chewing went together admirably once Dad wet his line in Stoner Creek. Since Speck and I looked forward to the day when we too could chew, there was no one to criticize him when he spit rusty red streams of tobacco juice into the water. Life, however, is seldom as simple as we wish it to be. Unknown to Dad, he was being watched by a competitor. Many years later a traveling salesman for Sistrunk Grocery Company recalled fondly that whenever he worked Paris, he first checked Stoner Creek dam: "If Lucky was there I knew I had the town to myself!"

10

A Shoeshine and a Smile

Lucky Mathias supported his family as a wholesale grocery salesman. It was an uncomplicated job and an era in which a salesman could get by on little more than a "shoeshine and a smile." He worked for Lexington's Bryan-Hunt and Company, calling on grocers and restaurants in Nicholas, Fleming, Robertson, Bourbon, and Harrison Counties. The largest communities were Paris and Cynthiana, with populations of six thousand and four thousand respectively. Village and country grocers held most of the purchasing power. Supermarkets lay in the future, but small Kroger and A&P stores were in three of the county seat towns. "I hate those two chains like the devil hates holy water!" Lucky sometimes complained. Although he said it with a smile, the "devil" gradually won out. By eliminating the middleman the chains sold cheaper, driving wholesalers like Bryan-Hunt out of business. But this did not happen during Dad's lifetime.

Lucky worked on commission—the more he sold the more he made. He averaged around $85 a month, equivalent to about $1,000 in 1999 purchasing power. The most he ever made was $180 one month when a new grocery bought its entire stock from him. He made the mistake of taking Charles and me with him when he wrote the order. We kept running up to the counter asking, "How much have you made by now, Dad?"

Finally, he grabbed both of us by the ear and hustled us out to the car: "Sit there in the backseat and keep your mouths shut 'til I'm finished or I'll give you both a spanking!" But when we left he gave us a Kokomo Bar, often called "ku-klux-klandy" because Kokomo, Indiana, had hosted a notorious KKK "Konklave" in 1923.

The family earned several hundred additional dollars annually. Lucky cured and sold over one hundred hams annually, refurbished concrete walls with an invention of his own, and grew bushels of early tomatoes each spring for sale. We also killed a hog each autumn and bought most of our groceries wholesale. Nannie added to our income by substitute teaching at CHS. I suppose I should add the obvious: we paid not one cent for first-class fish suppers at least once a week throughout the year!

Lucky's five-county territory took in 1,250 square miles. There were a few paved roads in the late 1920s, but he usually drove across dirt, gravel, and even creek beds at this time. Rapid improvement came only after politicians linked the gasoline tax with highway construction. By then I was old enough to go on some of dad's routes with him, experiencing not only the joys but also some of the hazards, a major one being flat tires.

Weak natural-rubber tires and tubes, rather than road conditions, caused most of the many flats. A wobbly thumping combination of sound and movement announced a flat tire. No one took time to complain. Each had an assignment. Dad took out his tools and jacked up the car. He removed the wheel, took off the tire, and pulled the deflated inner tube out, reinflated it a bit, and handed it to me. I ran it to the nearest water—creek, pond, or puddle—which in Kentucky is seldom far away. I dunked the tube until I saw a stream of bubbles, then marked the hole. Dad scraped the hole dry with his knife, smeared glue on the area, and set it afire for a second to cure the glue. A pre-cut rubber patch was stuck on it. He ran his hand inside the tire for a nail or other damage or to make sure a boot was in the right spot. Boots were oblong rubber reinforcements to protect tubes from holes or weak spots. He now stuffed the deflated tube inside the tire, making certain the tube's valve stem came through its hole in the steel wheel. With a bit of the same spirit Lucky showed when he landed a big bass, he screwed his pump hose onto the valve stem and inflated the tire. By the time I weighed in at sixty-five pounds, I was manning the pump. After the wheel was bolted back in place we chugged away, seldom losing more than fifteen minutes. Chains complicated the job in winter, a time he was by himself.

For unusual or humorous village names, no county in Lucky's territory could touch Nicholas; in fact, one might have to go all the way to Texas to find its equal. True, the county has plenty of ordinary village monikers, but it also has these: Headquarters, Barefoot, Buzzard Roost, Sprout, Hog Jaw, Shakerag, Morning Glory, Bucktown, Frog Town, Licking, Mexico, and Dog Walk. It has an East Union even though the nearest West Union is an hour's drive north in Ohio, while South Union is 201 miles west in Logan County. But one thing each of these villages had in common was a country store, most them called on regularly by Lucky.

Country groceries had a general mood or atmosphere all their own. Each one was much like the other, yet, paradoxically, they were all different. The differences arose from location, of course, but much more from the likes, dislikes, and personality of each owner. Successful salesmen, like my father, instinctively understood this; those that did not were soon looking for other jobs. He could as easily discuss the ever more ominous situation in Europe and Japan as he could the price tobacco might bring in the fall or swap jokes on even terms anywhere.

The country stores Lucky worked were mostly located at or near road junctions or river bridges, but some seemingly isolated ones served populous neighborhoods. Typically, there were two hand-operated gasoline pumps in front of a roofed-over porch. Steaming piles of horse manure and a hitching rail proved that "hay burners" still competed with "gas burners." Wooden benches and some chairs sat on the worn wooden porch floor, and a few equally worn old-timers and loafers sat on these.

Flies buzzed in and out of the scene, as did wasps going to and from mud or paper nests under the eaves. Clucking chickens wandered here and there scratching at the dirt while greedy sparrows pecked at undigested corn kernels shining yellow in the horse manure. Somewhere on the shady porch lay a sleepy-eyed hound, flicking his ears and tail when the flies got too thick. A cat was somewhere inside, its presence a minor threat to hungry rats and mice. A salesman entering the store was greeted in one way or another by all of these beings, either personally by words of the loafers and a raising of the dog's eyes to tell you he knew you were there, or impersonally by the scatter of the sparrows and the slinking away of the indifferent cat.

But no one entered a country store of this era without encountering the "artwork" tacked in a riot of color to porch posts, store siding, sheds, and doors. There were metal and fiber signs put up by sales promotion men. Financially hard-pressed grocers sometimes used them to cut down on paint and roofing costs. Tobacco signs were the most prominent: Prince Albert pipe tobacco, Beechnut and Red Man chewing tobacco, Bruton's snuff, and all the cigarettes: Domino, Marvel, Twenty Grand, Avalon, Sensation—the ten-cent brands—and the much more "respectable" twenty-cent ones such as Camel ("I'd walk a mile for a Camel"); Old Gold ("Not a cough in a carload"; Phillip Morris ("Call for Phillip M-o-r-r-i-s!"); Lucky Strike ("Lucky Strike green has gone to war!"); and Chesterfield ("While a Chesterfield burns . . ."). Filter cigarettes, such as Kent, were far in the future.

Patent medicine signs abounded, with Anacin, Black Draught, and Swamp Root leading the pack. And every front screen door in Dad's territory had a long, metal, horizontal handle advertising either Honey Crust or Baby Bear bread.

The most noticed signs of all were the huge fiber Bull Durham tobacco signs tacked across store and barn sides. On these a life-sized bull stood full length with his mighty horned head toward the viewer. Almost every lounger and grocer was in on a joke about these signs that I puzzled over but never understood until I grew up some more.

"Lucky," a grocer asked, "do you know what life's greatest disappointment is?"

Dad, good salesman that he was, guessed a few things but gave up quickly.

"Didn't think you'd get it, Lucky," the grocer might say, then slyly offer the punch line while winking at his all-male audience: "Life's greatest disappointment, Lucky, is when a cow backs up to a Bull Durham sign!" The size of his laugh determined how big an order Dad was going to write in that store that day.

A well-kept country store blended odors in a wonderful way. They crept up barrels of sun-dried apples, peaches, and prunes; from pickles and sow belly; and also from casks of white and brown sugar, baskets of cabbages, a thick round of cheddar cheese, hard crackers in a barrel, and other barrels of salt and beans. There was usually a big vinegar barrel with a built-in pump that gave built-in trouble to tinkering kids.

Hanging on the walls or from ceiling beams were horse collars and harness, coiled ropes, coal oil lanterns, buckets, slop jars, and, on display tables, various items connected to dairying, cattle, sheep, and swine, as well as a big stack of work gloves. Rifle bullets of .22 caliber were a penny apiece. A long counter for "women folk" had the ubiquitous red-glass lamps, big white washbowls with colored bands around them, and pitchers to serve them. In season were several sizes of Ball jars to can berries, beans, and much else. Any woman wishing to change cheaply her family's wardrobe could choose from a dozen colors of packaged dye. These were offered on a rack with a background painting of revolutionary general Israel Putnam charging down a long flight of steps. I envied this cavalryman for years, gazing at him often when with Dad on his calls.

Speck and I ranked grocers according to gift pop. Henry Barlow ran a first-class country grocery at Headquarters and ranked near the top, for he always asked the same question as he handed us an Indian River grape: "Do you two dare drink this stuff?"

"We sure do, Mr. Barlow!" we gushed, running with the bottle out to the storefront hitching posts where each took a measured swig of the liquid, worriedly watching the other to prevent "hunching."

One day Barlow was out, so we got no pop, but Dad was always on his route to Cynthiana when he stopped here and promised to buy each of us a pop when we got there. We went to Biancke's Restaurant and ordered Pepsi Colas. The waitress set two oversized Pepsi bottles in front of us.

"Hey," I said nervously, "I never saw any like these before; we only have enough money for the nickel size."

She smiled a waitresslike smile at us as she said, "This *is* the nickel size; you get twice as much as you used to."

This was for us one of capitalism's most momentous advances. Six-ounce Cokes and 7–Ups were out. Kids now parroted the Pepsi jingle heard on every radio:

Pepsi Cola hits the spot,
Twelve full ounces, that's a lot,
Twice as much for a nickel too,
Pepsi Cola is the drink for you!
Nickel, Nickel, Nickel, Nickel(fade out)
Trickle, Trickle, Trickle. . . .

Whenever Dad worked Cynthiana he either spent the afternoons fishing in the South Fork of Licking before driving home or drove another fifteen miles to work Berry, a village in northern Harrison County. When he did this he always spent the night at the home of Newt Dunn, a Berry grocer and one of his best friends. Dunn and his wife kept a room to rent to traveling men, providing supper as well as "bed and breakfast" for around a dollar.

I think Dad viewed his stay at Dunn's as a short vacation. He had no paid vacation in the modern sense and, except for an occasional night at Dunn's, was at home nearly every night during the eighteen years I lived with him. He loved it at Dunn's and with good reason. They were a gentle and interesting couple, and they liked him. Moreover, there was a challenging fishing spot along Licking's South Fork which I have mentioned earlier—a place where an old mill had collapsed into the river, spilling its bricks all over the bottom. And in addition, Berry had an added attraction that enhanced Lucky's true love for all things mechanical. The L&N's big Baldwin and Lima locomotives that highballed passenger and freight trains through little Berry always brought gasps of admiration from him.

Although Dad took me over most of his route at one time or another, no trip equaled that to Berry and Newt Dunn's house. Dad looked me over one summer morning, then said with a wink: "How about you and me going over to the Dunns' today to spend the night?"

I ran to Mom, chattering all the way: "Mom, Mom, we're going to the Dunns'; get out my toothbrush and my clothes for tomorrow!" I put these in the Model A's backseat with Dad's samples. I listened politely as Mom combed my hair and offered the usual advice: "Behave yourself and be polite. Say 'mister' and 'missus' and 'thank you' to Mr. and Mrs. Dunn. Brush your teeth and don't pick your nose and do what Dad tells you. Now give me a big kiss."

We usually arrived in Berry around midafternoon, a quiet time of cooped chicken sounds and buzzing insects but occasionally a time ripped asunder when a train roared through. The village's main street was crossed by the shiny, heavy-gauge tracks of the Louisville and Nashville Railroad. I knew from Uncle Joe's lectures the difference in weight per foot of main line as opposed to the light branch line track running through Carlisle. I felt proud of Berry and Maysville for their being on the main line. In addition, I of course picked up Dad's favorable opinion of Berry and its friendly citizens.

Dad and I entered Dunn's Grocery and exchanged greetings with the owner. The two joked and talked business until I impatiently pulled on Dad's finger to get his attention. "I know what you're after; go on out and watch for a train, but stand way back. Remember what Mr. Dunn told you last time we were here." How could I forget! Dunn told of a boy who got sucked under a fast L&N freight train. Speeding trains, he explained, sometimes create a great suction, and the helpless lad was pulled under the train as if by a giant hand. I shuddered when I thought of it.

The suction story was bad enough, but Dunn's tale of the boy whose boot got caught in a switch was more dramatic. While he was walking the track, his foot slipped into the narrow hollow between switching rails and got stuck fast. He screamed for help when a fast freight rounded a curve a mile down the track. Men working nearby rushed to his assistance but could neither unravel nor cut his knotted boot string. By this time the engineer had tied his whistle down and was desperately sanding the tracks for braking traction, but momentum drove the big freight forward. Two men grabbed the boy's body and pulled him back as far as they could to spare as much of his leg as possible when the onrushing engine's wheels severed his foot and ankle. As the engine pounded by, the two men and the boy abruptly tumbled backward. Horror gripped the crowd of on-lookers. They shared a single thought: "The poor kid's leg is smashed!" But suddenly the boy jumped to his feet—both feet! "Praise be to God!" one man yelled. "It's a miracle!" and all agreed, staring at the boy in awe.

Perhaps what happened should rank close to a miracle. The heavy engine spread the switch just enough to release the boot and dump the men and boy backward in time to turn a certain tragedy into overwhelming joy!

I never had to wait long for a train to come through Berry. Seven or eight fast passenger trains sped by each day and probably as many or more lengthy freights. I liked the passenger trains best, but the rumbling freight trains carried a special attraction. Hoboes, mostly victims of the Depression, sat with their feet dangling out of open boxcar doors. I waved at them and they often waved back. Dad said that every autumn he saw ten times as many going south as north and just the opposite in the spring. We even had a few hoboes on Carlisle's little "Ragweed Special," but nothing like the numbers seen on the main-line tracks at Berry and Maysville. Mom always gave canned goods to any hobo or beggar who knocked at our door.

Any loafer along the Berry tracks could tell me when the Southland was due. I listened for the whistle, or its echo, announcing that the famous passenger train was coming in, though still out of sight. I looked up the tracks. An exciting sparkle of light appeared at the distant point where the tracks seemed to converge. The headlight grew in size and the whistle in volume as the swift Florida-bound train descended upon Berry. The Southland carried some sixteen cars, including club and dining cars, Pullmans, and the usual coaches, baggage, and mail cars. It even had a hostess at the service of passengers.

As it approached, I could feel the locomotive's six great drivers pounding the track and see the engineer looking from his cabin. I stood back, completely enthralled, as the great train literally blew through Berry in a seventy-five-mile-per-hour clatter of sound, dust, and flicker of windows. Silence quickly descended as the train rushed on, leaving an unexplainable vacuum in my soul. Often, I turned back to Dunn's Grocery to find that Dad had been standing behind me watching the Southland just like me. And just like me, he often had moist eyes.

After calling on several Berry grocers, Dad walked down to the river to wet his line. He quickly caught a sunfish or two, cut them up for bait, and announced, "We'll soon have a nice mess of fish to take out to Dunn's."

I waded in the shallows, pinning water snakes with a Y stick, then letting them go. Or I handed him bait while he fished. I hoped he would not catch any fish for supper; I had eaten enough fish to last me a lifetime. Besides, Mrs. Dunn was a great cook and always had stuff better than fish to eat. But hoping that Lucky would not catch fish was like hoping the Depression would end tomorrow. I watched in resignation as he "snaked in" a nice string of newlights. Then we headed out to Dunn's.

I thought of the Dunns in the same way I thought of my uncles and aunts. They lived in a one-story frame farmhouse along Route 36, several miles west of Berry. A "dogtrot" linked the living area of the old house with its kitchen. Seasonal shrubs, flowers, and herbs enhanced the scene. There was a memorable solitude about the place and its surrounding fields, as if poet William Butler Yeats had visited here before writing of Inisfree and its "bee loud glade."

Mrs. Dunn always gave me a big hug when I arrived, then I told her what I had seen that day: the stop at Henry Barlow's, the Southland, and Dad's catching her some fish. I added, "By the way, Mrs. Dunn, what might you be serving for supper?" This always got a chuckle out of her. Greetings over, I ran outside, scattering the chickens as I raced with Soapy the dog down the long field fronting the house. Soapy and I explored things until the dinner bell rang, my signal to come in, wash up in well water, and sit down for supper.

By the time I got washed up, the Dunns had lit several brass-based table lamps for light. These were unlike coal oil lamps, burning a different fuel and producing much more light. They had neither wicks nor chimneys; a kitchen match set the two mantles aglow. A small pump was pushed to produce pressure for the gasolinelike fuel to hiss from a tiny hole and supply the mantles. At least that is how I remember it. A glass shade covered the lamp. They looked like modern electric lamps as they sat there, but they would be replaced forever when the New Deal's rural electrification program (REA) reached the Dunns.

Fried chicken was a special treat during the 1930s and was often on the menu at the Dunn's, with milk gravy, ham-flavored green beans, homegrown vegetables, and homemade pies. After Newt and Lucky smoked a pipe or two, it was the well-earned time to go to bed. Night fell by eight o'clock under the "slow time" of Depression-era summers. I pulled up a bucket of well water and Dad and I washed up a bit before heading to the big bedroom. A large four-poster feather bed beckoned us. I got to know that bed well during my school days, and after a while it made me sleepy just to look at it. It was somehow more than just comfortable, and it tuned me in to the lyrics of a hillbilly song: "If I had done what mama said, I'd be sleepin' in a feather bed!"

And later in life, when I heard labor unions accused of "featherbedding," I knew what management was trying to get across.

Climbing into its soft, protective depth was an adventure for a small boy and his dad, both soon to lose a busy day to sleep over at Newt Dunn's between the wars.

11

Burma Shave and
Buzzard Roost

Lucky believed Dunn's the best place to spend a night in his territory, but he ranked the Stewart Girls' house in the Fleming County crossroads village of Elizaville as the best place to eat. Five sisters cooked and served dinners (the noon meal) that were works of art. They conducted their business in a handsome frame home near the crossroads. Drummers (traveling salesmen) were always in a majority, yet they were not there only for the superb meals or the silver, china, and linen table settings but also to exchange gossip, pass on useful information, and renew acquaintances. All knew Lucky and, when Speck and I were along, made much pleasant ado over "Lucky's two boys." There was little money in the crowd, but a happier and more jovial crew of drummers hardly existed than those found enjoying the food and company on and around the tables at the Stewart Girls' dinners.

These frequent Fleming County sales trips produced checker playing and tall-tale-telling buddies my age at each village grocery, such as Arthur Evans's at Jabetown, Oscar "Duck" Farris's Poplar Plains store, and Minor Denton's Hillsboro grocery. But I had a favorite in Franklin Sousely, who lived near and hung out at Neal's Hilltop grocery. There was only four months difference in our ages, and we became friends over the years. I was drafted into the army, but Sousely volunteered for the marines, landing with the Fifth Marine Division on Iwo Jima. On February 23, 1945, Franklin and five of his comrades proudly raised the Stars and Stripes atop Mount

Suribachi just as photographer Joe Rosenthal snapped his shutter, becoming perhaps the most recognized subjects in photographic history. Franklin was killed in action near Kitano Point on March 21 and rests in an impressive tomb in Elizaville Cemetery.

Going with Dad was adventure enough for Speck and me. Auto air conditioners were unknown, but it was probably better without them. Meandering Bluegrass country roads smelled as good as they looked. Wildflowers turned shoulders and fencerows into riots of color. Electric blue cornflowers and white Queen Anne's lace intermingled all summer, while every few weeks different trees, shrubs, and flowers had their day, whether it was June roses, dogwood, and violets early in the season, or black-eyed Susans, ironweed, thistle, and hollyhocks as September and school bells beckoned. I could offer little more than childish appreciation of such surroundings, but I absorbed them into my being, and later in life, as Wordsworth held, "They flash upon that inward eye, which is the bliss of solitude."

A form of manmade "scenery," far removed from cornflowers, violets, and hollyhocks, were the Burma Shave signs seen along the more traveled roads. I doubt that any roadside advertising has ever matched these signs in consumer acceptance. Each of six small signs, tacked to six-foot poles and spaced some twenty feet apart, carried three or four words of a poem meant to make the reader remember Burma Shave brushless shaving cream, which, in the 1930s, came in a bottle or in a tube like toothpaste. Nearly everyone could recite several of these catchy poems. Dad often swapped them with grocers, and challenges were met to see who could recite the most poems. Kids committed them to memory; the following have weathered some sixty years in my mind:

Life Is Sweet
But Oh!
How Bitter
To Love A Gal
And Then Not Gitter!
Burma Shave

Within This Vale
Of Toil
And Sin
Your Head Grows Bald
But Not Your Chin!
Burma Shave

Let's Make Hitler
And Hirohito
Look As Sick
As Old Benito!
Buy Defense Bonds
Burma Shave

Lucky was always on the lookout for humor to put his customers in a happy mood. Ed Metcalfe gave him a poem that worked wonders throughout every county in Lucky's territory. *The Romance of Rex*, by an anonymous author, tells of a country dog who comes to town and easily outpiddles every know-it-all city dog he meets. This of course set well with Dad and his rural friends and grocers:

A farmer's dog came into town,
His Christian name was Rex,
A noble pedigree had he
Unusual was his text.
And as he trotted down the street
'Twas beautiful to see
His work on every corner—
His work on every tree.

The city curs look on amazed
With deep and jealous rage
To see a simple country dog
The piddler of the age.

Then just to show the whole shebang
He didn't give a damn
He trotted in a grocery store
And piddled on a ham.

He piddled in a mackerel keg—
He piddled on the floor,
And when the grocer kicked him out
He piddled through the door.

And all the time this country dog
Did never wink or grin,
But piddled blithely out of town
As he had piddled in.

Lucky also saved a clipping cut from the *Mercury* of November 14, 1935. He used it for laughs along his route, acting out the story reported in the clipping. A Cynthiana wood chopper had missed the log and chopped off his big toe. His dog immediately swallowed the toe—"urp"—and stood hoping for more. Lucky worked this into his job by limping noticeably into stores. Someone always asked him what was wrong.

"My dog ate my big toe," he whined, soon attracting a gathering to hear the rest of his story. He carefully repeated the clipping story, almost verbatim, and always with a big "urp," as reported in the paper.

"We're on to you, Lucky," someone usually said. "You're telling another one of your tales; what *really* happened to you?"

This was his cue to take out the *Mercury* clipping, all the while criticizing his audience for "an awful lack of faith in me and my tales." His reading of the clipping invariably brought a chorus of "Well, I'll be damned!" And his act often brought a better-than-usual order for Bryan-Hunt. Lucky may not always have had shiny shoes, but he knew all about smiles.

Lucky had another trick of which grocers never tired. He reeled off a rapid-fire string of nonsense nouns to answer this invariable customer question: "What specials do you have for me this week, Lucky?"

"W-e-l-l n-o-w," he said slowly, getting bystanders' attention, "I have: [rapid fire]

Dogs, logs, pigs, and hogs
Big ship, little ship, small ship, and battleship
Butter beans, navy beans, green beans, and jelly beans
Stifles, trifles, and rusty rifles
Bananas, pandas, and Alf M. Landon
. . . .
Just tell me what in th' hell you want and I've got it!

My memory of his spiel ends with the above; the entire thing would perhaps take forty lines and a minute or two to chant. I never heard anything like it until much later when the Jack Benny show featured a "Mr. Kitzel" doing exactly the same thing. Dad never wrote any of it down, so far as I know, but added lines to his memory as the years went by. One grocer composed several lines for him.

Butler Ritchie, a Nicholas County grocer, admired Dad's spiel so much he tried to think up lines for Dad to use, and Dad adopted some of them. Ritchie's grocery was at tiny Barterville, near Carlisle. Speck and I judged Ritchie among the best, for he always came up with licorice sticks. We chewed the licorice, then went out front and spit with the tobacco-chewing loafers and checker players on the porch.

Ritchie always hit Dad with two questions as soon as he stepped in the door, the first one: "What specials do you have for me this time, Lucky?" Dad was always ready for him, going all out with the full forty or so lines of his spiel. By this time, the loungers and checker players had sidled in from the porch to hear what all of them had heard many times before, but never mind, they whistled and stomped and patted Lucky on the back as if it was all brand new. "I'll be damned if I've ever heered ary thang like that afore!" was a typical comment. "He's a good'un ain't he?" was another.

Ritchie's second question came as the loafers filed back outside to their benches and checkerboards and was always the same:

"Whatcha got on H&E, Lucky?" H&E was a sugar brand, and asking the price was his signal to get down to business. He and Lucky loved to dicker back and forth and put one over on the other, even if it never came to more than pennies won or lost. Ritchie's usual tactic was to tell Lucky that his competitor, "that straight-talkin' Sistrunk feller," had dropped by a few days before and quoted a lower price than Bryan-Hunt on the item in question. Lucky of course anticipated this by jacking up his asking price a few cents. Now, he lowered it.

"Why, Butler, Bryan-Hunt will meet Sistrunk head-on anytime," he boasted, offering a price the same as or lower than the competitor's. Similar dickering over many items might continue for half an hour or until an unusual rush of business claimed the grocer's attention. As Lucky walked out the front door, both of them were looking forward to another session several weeks down the road.

Butler Ritchie and nearly every grocer in Lucky's territory learned the hard way that Lucky had a "floating kidney." It was frightening. He would be standing at the counter, doing business with the grocer. In the wink of an eye he was on the floor, kicking, thrashing, and groaning! Just as suddenly he leaped back to his feet as everyone in the place was rushing to his aid. All were relieved to see this, but an explanation was demanded.

"I'm sorry for all this," he apologized, brushing himself off, "but I've got a floating kidney." He knew few had ever heard of one, so he tried his best to explain it to the wide-eyed crowd. "Years ago old Doc Kash in Carlisle punched around on me and told me what was wrong. He said I didn't have enough fat in the right spot to keep one of my kidneys in place. Whenever it decides to slide a little, it kinks the big tube that drains it. That really hurts and knocks me to the floor, but this gets the kink out. After that I'm fine as frog hair split in the middle and rarin' to go!" He might have added that this unplanned but frightening performance usually resulted in increased sales to sympathetic grocers. My brother and I hated to see it happen, believing as we did that our dad ought to be near perfect. The attacks left him by the time he turned sixty.

Anyone might think Lucky got enough fish to eat at home, but that would be wrong. He usually ate a can of sardines for his noon meal on the road. When Speck and I were along we invariably had a picnic of pop, Vienna sausage, sardines, "rat cheese" (grocery store cheddar), and hard, round crackers called "cow crackers." Whenever Lucky chose a shallow ford along a creek for our picnic, my brother and I knew we were in for a car wash. "After we eat I'll park out in the ford and you two can wash the car while I seine for minnows and crawdads." Just as we predicted.

There was money to be made in places like this, so after giving the car a lick and a promise, my little brother and I busily turned over rocks and deadwood looking for hellgrammites. Dad paid a penny apiece for them, depending on his mood. If we had been "fighting and yowling" he took the things and paid nothing, and we knew why without asking. Instead, we silently glared at each other, assigning blame for the pennies lost. Our anger of course faded as the day wore on. Around five o'clock the Model A chugged up our steep driveway. Mom was nearly always standing there to meet us, just outside her kitchen, welcoming us with smiles, kisses, and sometimes critiques: "I see you two have slopped down the car again," she laughed, inspecting the crisscross of streaks on the Ford's finish. She sure was a hard one to fool!

"How's your wife and kidneys?" was a greeting that had nothing to do with Lucky's kidney problem. It was a feeble attempt at humor among men during prohibition. All organs, but especially kidneys, took a beating from the "rotgut" liquor pouring out of Kentucky's illegal stills—"moonshine." At its worst, it damaged nerves, producing a rocking, stumbling walk in its victims. "He's got 'jake-leg,'" Dad said, whenever I pointed to such a man on the street.

Prohibition might have worked if Congress had not limited alcohol content of beverages to less than one-half of 1 percent in the Volstead Act. Millions of wine and beer drinkers had voted against hundred-proof "old-dog liquor" but now found their low percentage drinks included. These millions justly felt betrayed and either ignored or openly opposed the law.

Repeal came in 1933; counties could now exercise "local option." The counties in Lucky's territory rocked back and forth, voting "wet" in one election, and "dry" in the next. This supported bootlegging, for booze and beer were smuggled—bootlegged—from wet into dry counties. Moreover, moonshiners continued making the stuff since they sold cheaper than legal distillers.

Dad knew where moonshining was going on in each county he worked. It was easy to pin down. A small grocery suddenly ordering several thousand pounds of malt and sugar was selling to "shiners." Malt is made from water-softened barley sprouts and is mixed with other grains to distill into whiskey. Adding sugar along the way quickens the process but produces fitly named "bust-head" liquor. Dad knew the score, but he dared not do anything about it. In fact, B.F. Reynolds, a beloved family physician in Carlisle, drove an easily identified auto—the "blue goose"—for many years. He was thus immune to hostile action by moonshiners when he drove up country lanes to deliver babies or treat illness and accident. In short, selling to the honest majority of grocers—men like Tom Abraham, for example—was not only more rewarding in orders but a lot safer.

"Let's go see Tom Abraham," Lucky said one summer morning. I was elated and jabbered about Abraham and his Mount Olivet store all through breakfast. We were soon driving through tiny Robertson County, which, with one hundred square miles of land and barely two thousand people, is the smallest of Kentucky's 120 counties. It is also one of the loveliest, a bucolic setting of lush valley farms interspersed amid hills thick with cedar and hardwoods. After some twenty miles we entered Mount Olivet, adding ourselves to its five hundred citizens. A covered sidewalk ran the length of Abraham's store. There were benches occupied by the usual loafers, one of whom shouted: "Welcome to Hell's Half Acre, Lucky!" proving he knew a trifling pioneer name for the pretty little county seat.

When we entered the store, Abraham rushed over and caught Dad up in a bear hug, and Dad hugged him back. American men seldom hugged each other, but I liked this big sign of friendship. I knew Tom Abraham was an immigrant and spoke with an accent, so I assumed he must have brought the hugging notion from Syria. I was not sure where Syria was, but I knew from Bible studies that it was in or near the Holy Land.

Abraham came to America around 1900 and walked Robertson County's roads peddling pots, pans, and utensils. Dad and his brother Frank, both traveling men, gave him a ride whenever they saw him. They became close friends and fellow parishioners, for he regularly attended Carlisle's Catholic church. Abraham gradually saved enough money to bring his wife and daughter to America. He quit walking the roads and opened a store in the county seat. He was a man of obvious integrity and attractive personality, and his venture expanded in size and stock to become one of the largest in the county.

Tom and Lucky talked business while Mrs. Abraham quizzed me about any goings on at church or school, loosening my tongue with doses of cold pop. I delighted her by romantic embellishments of what I thought was important news or big events.

After one of our stops in Mount Olivet, Dad left the village on a fishing expedition and got lost, of all things! He intended to go to Augusta and take the Ohio River ferry over to nearby White Oak Creek. This stream empties its clear burden into the big river at tiny Higginsport, and he had enjoyed memorable fishing in its racing riffles and deep pools as it erratically drops from the interior plateau down to its union with the Ohio. Since it flows alongside rustic Ohio Route 221 for several miles, it allows easy access to numerous fishing spots. Lucky always went by way of Maysville, but this time he tried a much shorter route over unknown roads outside his sales territory. He had studied out a route from a map drawn by one of the loafers at Abraham's store.

Lucky soon sensed he was off course, so we pulled up to a run-down Bracken County grocery to ask directions. We went in, walking over to the cash register and grocer through a dusty clutter of barrels, baskets, and hardware. Five or six men of varying ages were playing checkers or dominos or just sitting and staring near a cold, pot-bellied stove. The stove's four legs punched solidly into a shallow square of boxed-in gravel. It protected against fire but had done nothing to stop the daily spurts of tobacco juice spit into the gravel, staining it a shiny brown.

Lucky introduced himself, allowing that although he worked bordering Robertson County for Bryan-Hunt, he was not familiar with Bracken and needed directions down to the Augusta ferry. His audience squinted up at him as he continued. "What I have to do, I think, is follow 875 to Germantown. Then I believe I take a right on 10 for a few miles. After that I take a left on 435 to Minerva, bearing right on 1235 and on into Augusta and the ferry. Is that right, boys?" Had he paid attention to the grins and sly looks crossing their faces he might have guessed that he was wrong.

The grocer came out from behind the counter. "Well, sir," he began, "you can, if you're a mind to, follow 875 to Germantown. Then you can take a right on 10 for a few miles. Next, as you say, take a left on 435 plumb into Minerva and bear right on 1235. That will take you right down to the Ohio River at Dover," he said, emphasizing Dover. "But they ain't no ferry there, is they, boys?"

Everyone laughed and mumbled a lot of words meaning "They ain't no ferry there!"

I sort of expected Dad to get mad, for Mom was right in claiming he never had the patience of Job, but old Lucky hung on.

The grocer, his fat face shining, tongued a chaw of Beechnut from one jaw to the other, stretched his galluses with his thumbs, and bored in. "Now, sir, if'n I was you I'd follow 875 to Germantown for sure, but I'd take a left on 10 instead of a right. After a coupla miles, turn right on 1011 which leads to 19. Bear right on 19 and it'll run you smack down to Augusta and the river. And they is a ferry there, ain't they, boys?" All of the boys, young and old, nodded their heads in happy agreement.

Dad thanked them, and we left a crowd happy that they had finally gotten the best of a traveling salesman. We had made their day and perhaps the next week to boot. The directions were perfect. We enjoyed the ferry ride across the broad river and the fishing that followed. Lucky, however, drove home by way of the Maysville bridge. He had had enough of ferries for one day.

One of the nicer trips out of Carlisle is the ten-mile drive to Buzzard Roost. This tiny crossroads village straddles the pioneer Buffalo Trace drawn on Kentucky's earliest maps. For the last five miles one drives alongside Cassidy Creek, a clear brook tumbling over limestone ledges and often through shady tunnels of giant sycamores. Swinging bridges cross over the creek to paths leading to hillside farmhouses. (The incursions of bulldozers to widen and straighten the creek have destroyed no little of this between-the-wars beauty.)

Buzzard Roost picked up its unlovely and unlikely name by accident. The first settler opened a grog shop, peddling rum and "bust-head" whiskey. Sickened drunks staggered and lay outside, puking and dirtying the place. A passing stranger observed that the vomit and other droppings on the ground reminded him of the mess around a buzzard roost. He was disgusted, but his listeners were not. Since the place had no name, why not call it Buzzard Roost, which they did. Decades later, when a U.S. post office was installed, a much less exciting name was chosen: Sprout.

Each summer Uncle Joe and our family joined the Metcalfes for a picnic with their relatives, the Gills, near tiny Buzzard Roost. We of course had no idea we were living in a "between-the-wars" era but were lost in our own small, happily peaceful picnic of a world. But while we frolicked so innocently each August at Allie Gill's home, the Japanese army was killing millions of Chinese, Spaniards were slaughtering a million of their own people in a bloody civil war, Italian fascists were slaying Ethiopians wholesale, Joseph Stalin was killing off hosts of Russian "spies," and the Nazis were preparing to kill off all the "racially unfit" in Europe and any place else they might conquer.

We knew in a vague way that all was not well elsewhere, but it was a big world with big oceans to protect us. As always, we lived our lives optimistically day by day. Nuclear bombs and the continuation of World War I, now called World War II, were just around the corner, but we could not know that. Mercifully, also, we could not know that Andrew Metcalfe, so much fun at the picnics, would die at the age of twenty-five of Nazi bullets. In short, anyone willing to ponder world history between the wars and learn a bit about the goings-on in such classy cities as Berlin, Madrid, Tokyo, Rome, and Moscow is almost certain to conclude that, by comparison, a helluva lot can be said in favor of Buzzard Roost!

12

Foo-fighters and Kinniconick

Superstitions floated like jack-o'-lanterns in the mists and foggy hollows of the Ohio Valley. I heard many when on the road with Dad, and since Mom pooh-poohed them with such disdain, I believed a few in self-defense.

Cats were nightmarish creatures to some folks. Mom was disgusted to find that Dad "sort of" believed leaving a sleeping baby unguarded was to invite a cat in to suck its breath and kill it. Several grocers held that cats usually hunkered around a house where a funeral was in progress, hoping to leap up on the corpse and gnaw its face. A Flemingsburg grocer admitted that he postponed trips a day if a black cat passed in front of his car. All kids shuddered with knowledge that black cats rode witches' broomsticks, especially noticeable when silhouetted against a Halloween moon.

Snakes probably equaled cats in arcane powers. Nicholas County had no dangerous snakes other than the rarely seen copperhead, but we thought we did. The fantastic hoop snake had a poisonous tooth in its tail. Coiled into a hoop, with its tail in its mouth, it rolled swiftly downhill after its victim, jabbing the poor soul with its deadly tooth. Another bad one was the hair snake. Shaped like a long black hair, it was often seen wriggling in watering troughs. Whatever the thing was was not important to a true believer: "You just better not swallow one if you want to live!" Cowsuckers were not that bad; they simply reared their "soft-lipped viper heads" up to cows' udders and sucked out milk. Superstitious farmers often blamed them whenever a cow's milk was below par in quantity or taste. Rattlesnakes were no longer in the county, but that did not end the danger. A widely believed story told of a man changing a flat tire. He pricked his finger on a sharp object inside the tire and died shortly after, for a rattler had struck the tire earlier in the day, leaving a poison-filled fang behind. The car and driver had been in the rattlesnake-infested Kentucky mountains.

"Surely you have enough gumption to scoff at numbskulls!" Mom huffed anytime Speck or I asked about such superstitions. Nevertheless, we kept an uneasy eye out for black cats, hoop snakes, hair snakes, and cowsuckers—better safe than sorry!

Ghosts and their ghastly allies occupied the top spot in any ranking of superstitions. The Third Person of the Trinity—the Holy Ghost—added to my confusion despite explanations. Moreover, I had vivid memories of death clocks and banshees—topped by tales of ghostly doings nightly amid the tombs in the Carlisle cemetery. But my brother and I relished ghost stories if told or read in a snugly familiar setting. One of our favorites, whether read by our parents or us to our pals, was "Little Orphant Annie," by Hoosier poet James Whitcomb Riley. It and its "great big Black Things" had considerable clout for any kid, even though it preached good behavior. The Hoosier dialect is close to that spoken by Nicholas County kids of my generation; after all, Indiana is "jist up th' road a piece."

> An' one time a little girl 'ud allus laugh
>   an' grin,
> An' make fun of ever one, an' all her
>   blood-an'-kin;
> An' wunst when they was "company,"
>   an' ole folks was there,
> She mocked 'em and shocked 'em, an'
>   said she didn't care!
> An' thist as she kicked her heels, an'
>   turn't to run and hide,
> They wuz two great big Black Things

a-standin' by her side,
An' they snatched her through the ceilin'
'fore she knowed what she's about!
An' the Gobble-uns'll get you
Ef you
Don't
Watch
Out!

As a sixth grader I changed Riley's last line to read: "An' the FOO'll git you ef you don't watch out!" More about "FOO" below, but I inserted this nonsense word because silliness is synonymous with sixth graders—as in trying to say rapidly five time: BUMPY RUBBER BUGGY BUMPER. Icky puns, riddles, and word games fortified lives leaving childhood's certainties. For my classmates and me, a password bridging this generational gap was "FOO."

FOO was a nonsense word coined by Smoky Stover, a loony but saucy comic-strip firefighter. He often mocked adult adages: "Where there's smoke there's FOO"; or oft-cited proverbs: "A FOO saved is a FOO earned." We loved his word games. A painting on his firehouse wall showed two people clinging desperately to a huge icicle. The legend read: "On an icicle built for FOO." Another strip portrayed a well-known Chinese literary character stroking his droopy mustache, saying: "Many men smoke, but FOO-men-chu." Translating this into sixth-grade life gave me the courage to approach girls: "Will you FOO me in December as you FOO me in the May?" If she were an addict of Smoky Stover, she might reply, "FOO to you too," or write it either as "FOO too you too," or "FOO 2 U 2." Others of course simply stared and pondered my sanity.

Lucky fell in the latter group, especially when I doctored his oft-repeated maxim: "One FOO is as good as another FOO if he is as good." Nannie of course expected such grade school silliness, matching me FOO for FOO.

During World War II I discovered that Smoky and I had been ahead of the crowd all along. Scores of American fighter pilots spoke of mysterious unidentified flying objects—possibly extraterrestrial vehicles–that accompanied them at high altitudes. They were discussed widely in newspaper and magazine articles and taken under scientific study elsewhere. They were called "Foo-fighters," a name Smoky and I and my GI Generation could easily understand and live with!

Lucky was something of a FOO himself when it came to treating us to trips outside his territory. He was not alone in this, for extended family travel was difficult. Many links were missing in the nation's road network, and tourist homes and restaurants were hit-and-miss propositions. Small-town speed traps were endemic, and money for travel ranked low in Depression-era budgets. Labor unions had yet to win "guaranteed paid vacations" for members and, by this example, for most other workers. Vacations, such as they were, were spent relaxing at home rather than in a fruitless search for the "curative powers" of some well-advertised beach or mountain chalet. If a family did take a long trip, the ideal way to go was by train. Dad planned to go this way in his one futile stab at extracting himself from familiar surroundings and taking the family on a long vacation—to Florida!

Lucky's sister Anna, the wife of a wealthy Ohio industrialist, owned a winter home in Palm Beach. She suggested that Dad take the family there for an off-season vacation and made suitable arrangements when he agreed. Tickets were bought on the Flamingo, a famous L&N Florida passenger train. Ed Metcalfe agreed to drive us to Paris, where we could board the train early in the day. Charles and I were excused from classes for the duration of the trip.

Dad seemed to relish the idea, for he had never seen an ocean. He joked about the sharks and whales he was likely to catch. Mom fussed over our luggage, packing and repacking it several times, but eventually got it all in place amidst mounting excitement. Speck and I finally got to sleep, but Mom awakened us next morning with disastrous news: "I'm terribly sorry, you two, but Dad is sick and we won't be going to Florida."

We were utterly crushed. But great disappointment turned to disgust and anger when Lucky made a miraculous recovery that afternoon and set off for the reservoir to "wet his line." Mom, Speck, and I were the ones who stayed sick for many weeks thereafter.

I never heard what Aunt Anna thought of her brother's illness and somewhat fishy recovery, but she cannot be faulted for trying to give us a Florida vacation. Hers is an interesting story in its own right. Following a stint of teaching in Nicholas County's Taylor's Creek grade school, she accepted a better position in Coldwater, Ohio. She fell in love there and married a local lad, Ted Oppenheim, in 1920. His father, Joseph, was a schoolteacher blessed with a streak of mechanical genius. One afternoon in 1900 he idly watched schoolboys playing with flat bats, knocking balls in wild patterns from the angled wood. His mind suddenly opened to a new possibility. He went to a shop and transferred what he had seen into inventing a much needed farm machine, the modern manure spreader. Out of this grew the New Idea Spreader Company, a major producer of farm machinery. Interestingly, New Idea at the time of our visits in the 1930s was selling and shipping trainloads of farm equipment to the Soviet Union as part of several "Five-Year Plans." The peasants, however, saw this as a job threat and let most of the machinery rust in the fields.

Dad took us several times to Coldwater to visit the Oppenheims. These 190-mile trips were the longest he would ever make with the family. The wealthy Oppenheims had a fine summer home on Grand Lake-Saint Mary's. We swam and fished and enjoyed being with our cousins. We were enthralled when Uncle Ted took us on a guided tour through the huge factory, an exciting experience for rural folk like ourselves. And we laughed long and loud at one of his jokes, an old one for him but new to us: "Did you know that the manure spreader is the only invention the inventor refused to stand behind?" Charles laughed with the rest of us, then suddenly stopped with a puzzled look on his face when he realized he did not understand what he was laughing at. "Did he ever, ever stand behind it, Uncle Ted?" the eight-year-old asked earnestly.

"Well, Charles," Ted replied thoughtfully, "if he did the paddles threw manure all over him!"

"You sure have some dumb relatives, Uncle Ted," Charles sighed, giving his uncle and the rest of us another loud laugh.

Lucky managed to talk himself into taking the family on two

other trips. The first one was a failed effort to visit historic Bardstown and Lincoln's birthplace in Hodgenville. Somewhere near Bardstown, he said he had had enough and turned back. Mom had tears in her eyes and my brother and I were grumbling as we pull in to eat at a roadside diner. We ate the first chile con carne of our lives here, later saying it was the highlight of the trip.

After we ate, Dad drove off thinking he was heading east on Route 62; instead we pulled into Springfield, some twenty miles southeast of Bardstown. It was getting late and we were ninety miles from home, so we paid $1.50 and checked in at a tourist home.

Before long Dad and the owner were on friendly terms, and when he introduced Mom as his "Maysville gal," the owner smiled broadly: "I'll bet you know a good friend of mine there, an old army buddy named Doc Hines."

"Well, my lands, I should know him," Mom exclaimed. "He married my sister Alma!"

The owner said that he and Doc had grown up in Somerset and served together in the Great War and that they met annually at American Legion conventions. He and his wife invited us to eat breakfast with them the next morning, which we did.

Years later, an avant-garde traveler asked me if I had ever stayed at a bed and breakfast.

"Sure," I replied, "back in 1938 I stayed in the first one ever invented, in Springfield, Kentucky—four of us for a dollar and a half!"

Another family trip ventured by Dad was right down his alley. The year I was born, 1925, Dix River Dam was completed twenty-five miles southwest of Lexington by Kentucky Utilities Company. The hydroelectric dam is 270 feet high, 700 feet thick at the base, and 920 feet long and impounds 2,335-acre Herrington Lake. At this time, it was the largest rock-filled dam in existence, and it attracted attention throughout the Ohio Valley. For a number of years, "Tickie" Fisher and Hicel Asbury had tantalized Lucky with glowing and perhaps exaggerated reports of their success with bass and crappie in Herrington Lake. "Lucky, you'll just have to kick off the traces and come with us," Hicel told him. "It's so good down there you've got to get behind a tree to bait your hook!"

Dad was itching to go and Mom knew it, suggesting an all-day trip and picnic at the dam. He took the bait, running the line out as he talked about the fishing reports he had heard and of what an engineering feat the dam was. Montgomery County relatives, the King family, accepted an invitation to join us at the dam.

We left early in the day for the sixty-mile drive to Dix Dam. A flat tire sidelined us at lovely Elmendorf Horse Farm on Route 68, just a few miles east of Lexington. I dunked the inner tube in Elkhorn Creek, Dad patched the hole, and on we went. The Kings were awaiting us in the parking area. Charles and I romped with our cousins, then joined the old folks to see the vast spillway.

A crowd of onlookers was oohing and ahing as they looked with awe at the thousands of square feet of concrete in the spillway. Somewhere there, beyond my recall, was a lengthy, well-engineered swinging bridge, perhaps across part of the spillway. It was narrow, and when Charles gingerly wobbled out on it he got scared, whimpering as he clung tightly to it, refusing to budge. But he got mad when strangers tried to help him, clinging desperately to the side cables. "The little shitass bit me," one man grumbled as he rubbed toothmarks on his arm and fled the scene.

Dad finally got to him and walked him off the bridge on his shoulders. With that excitement out of the way, it struck us that once seen, a dam just sits there being a dam. The lake was pretty, but our interest soon faded, especially after Dad found that there was no fishing allowed in the dam area. We picnicked and enjoyed a nice get-together with the Kings, then headed home.

Although Dad was short on long family trips, he made up for it with many short ones, such as a memorable one to Kinniconick Creek. This Lewis County stream, named after a tobacco and herb mixture smoked at Shawnee Indian ceremonies, empties into the Ohio some twenty mile upriver from Maysville. It is a clean stream of extraordinary beauty, and, Lucky knew from many reports, marvelous waters to fish.

We were spending a summer weekend in Maysville when it was decided to drive over to Kinniconick for a picnic. We arrived at a likely spot about noon, parked beside an isolated and ramshackle grocery not much larger than a school bus, and spread a tablecloth on a grassy area above the stream. Nannie was carrying the picnic box around the tablecloth when the bank gave way, dropping her and the boxed picnic into a friendly four feet of water!

Dad jumped in to rescue her, and Speck and I followed suit. The four of us soon stood laughing loudly in the water as pieces of our picnic drifted slowly down the stream. After wringing out our clothes in some woods, we entered the small grocery, clothing damp, hair stringy, and hungry. We told the gray-haired grocer what had happened as he sliced a cheddar cheese and a "stalk of baloney" for us.

"Well, I'll be switched," he exclaimed. "I've hardly ever heered of the like! Good thang for th' missus that ole Kinniconick waren't up and floodin'."

We agreed as we happily ate our unexpectedly simple fare. Dad of course was soon on good terms with the grocer, who began to call him Charlie, just as Mom did.

"Charlie," he said in a slightly worried way, "you can see I've got a bad roof by lookin' up at the daylight comin' through them little holes in it. Would you feel put out to stick one of these broom straws up through each hole while I get up on the roof and nail cigarette signs over them? I hate to ask you but I ain't got nary a soul to help me here."

Dad was "proud to help," standing on counters and chairs to fix each straw in a spark of light. The grocer had taken down a host of signs and hammered one in place wherever he saw a straw. When they were finished, he and Dad agreed that the old tar paper roof was mostly waterproof and colorful too, thanks to metal signs by Old Gold, Anacin, Swamp Root, Nehi, 666, Grapette, Camel, and others.

Dad and Mom fished together after the roof job while Charles and I played nearby. We arrived back at Grandma Furlong's in time for supper. "I'd sure like to go on another picnic like that!" Charles shouted as he jumped out of our Model A. We all agreed.

It was more than a picnic on Kinniconick that attracted the Mathias family at summer's end each year. All of us looked forward to going with Dad to Lexington for the annual "September Saturday Sales Meeting" at Bryan-Hunt's. Lucky's brother Frank lived and sold in Lexington for the firm, so Mom was left off at Aunt Woodsie's to chat and go shopping for school supplies. Uncle Frank, Dad, Charles, and I went on down to Bryan-Hunt's big brick wholesale storage and office building.

The five-story structure was built into a slope separating High and Vine Streets, with its business entrance on High and loading platform on Vine. It was downtown and just a few blocks east of Sistrunk, its major competitor. Boxy-looking yellow trucks carried its name and products throughout the Bluegrass. Likable "Old Man Al Bryan" and associates employed several hundred people, supporting the enterprise from profits made from buying commodities from producers and selling them for higher prices to retailers.

Wandering freely through the five floors of Bryan-Hunt amid a blend of enticing sights and smells became a happy annual adventure for my brother and me. Each year Dad reintroduced Charles and me—"My, Lucky, how they've grown!"—to friendly secretaries working in the expansive front office area. He joked a few minutes with the loaders he knew working out on the main floor, then turned to us: "I've got to go to the meeting now, so I'm turning you two loose. Do what the loaders tell you and stay out of the way. I'll meet you at the usual time here in the office."

Speck and I always began our two-hour adventure by boarding one of the large freight elevators, riding to the top floor with a friendly loader. Once there we darted back and forth, stopping to sniff up exotic smells and ogle the impressive heaps and stacks of items creating a maze of passageways on each floor. Genial loaders always came up with goodies from a broken container—cookies, peanuts, candy, licorice sticks. But one clue alone would have told us, even if blindfolded, that we were at Bryan-Hunt's, and that was the unique blend of odors and aromas.

Sophisticated packaging with sheets of plastic and aluminum foil was unheard-of back in the glory days of the grocery wholesalers. Pleasant or pungent food and related odors escaped wooden and pasteboard—now called cardboard—casks, boxes, and vented metal containers. Other scents, sweet and sour, blended together over the years when damaged barrels and cans and broken bottles spilled their contents on the floor. Moreover, the sheer volume of coffee, tea, and tobacco handled by a big wholesaler produced aromas permeating the storage slots. Areas stacked high with meal, flour, and dried fruits also identified themselves. Great stacks of poultry feed gave its corner of the floor a musty odor. Sparrows and finches fed there, flitting and chirping their way through the building while pigeons cooed on window ledges. These sounds blended with the laughs of workmen and the rattle of the big open-sided elevators. My little brother and I were always reluctant to leave this inner world and return to Carlisle and our real world for another year.

13

Making Do with the Great Depression

That word, *Depression,* was to me a designated way of life, like Democrat, Republican, town, country, Catholic, or Protestant. I had no memory of life without it; it was happening, so what? Since food, shelter, and clothing—love—came my way, typical boyhood concerns were all that really mattered until Pearl Harbor awakened me to larger issues. I think my generation generally took a casual view of the Depression, dismissing it whenever possible, like certain disagreeable aspects of school and religion. Perhaps we were too young to do otherwise.

Lucky and Nannie had no childish quibbles but met the Depression head-on. As true Victorians, they were invigorated by this setback. Although the nation's pockets suddenly held pennies instead of dollars, this was seen as a challenge. The less the nation's wealth, the harder the achievement, but the grander would be success. Even if defeat awaited, it would be honorable and not derive from a timid lack of effort. Moreover, they correctly sensed that the economic situation was not nearly as catastrophic as hysteria made it out to be, often offering vocal support to Will Rogers's statement that we were "the only nation that ever went to the poorhouse in a Cadillac!" My pals and I debated this, for Nicholas County had a poorhouse but never a Cadillac in sight there or in Carlisle.

Their Victorian optimism might have withered considerably had Nicholas County's economy been based on industry instead of agriculture. Millions of America's idled factory hands and miners, who had owned nothing but their jobs, stretched optimism to its limits. Nicholas, like other rural counties, faced no propertyless masses, and its simple agricultural economy provided ample food, shelter, and clothing for its citizens.

By the time Franklin D. Roosevelt's New Deal had taken hold in 1935, I was in the fifth grade. Each afternoon an NYA girl (National Youth Administration) washed the blackboards, sprinkled oiled sawdust on the floors to sop us dust, and swept it out. Her father might well have been at work for the WPA (Works Projects Administration), building the town's new post office or armory or replacing several bumpy tar and chip streets with concrete. I became used to seeing the NRA signs (National Recovery Administration) propped in business windows. A blue eagle centered the signs with the legend "We Do Our Part" at the bottom. When the Supreme Court struck down the NRA, citizens joked that the blue eagle had become a sick chicken. Schoolkids made a game of identifying as many New Deal "alphabet soup" agencies as possible. Most Nicholas Countians strongly supported FDR and the New Deal. With childhood's unerring instinct, I sensed that life was gradually improving and public confidence growing as I lived the years down through the 1930s.

Carlisle found itself host to an alphabet soup agency in 1935. One of the best ideas of Roosevelt's "Brain Trust" was the Civilian Conservation Corps. The CCC was dedicated to restoring natural resources as well as providing work for single young men, thereby opening jobs for married men supporting families. Eventually this agency employed some three million young men, each earning thirty dollars a month, twenty-five of which was sent to parents or guardians. CCC boys planted over a billion trees, constructed roads, fences, walls, fire towers, dams, culverts, and much else. They undertook projects such as stump clearing and the deepening and cleaning of creeks.

A CCC camp was built on a ten-acre lot along Carlisle's western border during the summer of 1935. Four tar paper and wood barracks held fifty men each. Also built were a mess hall, supply room, garage, kitchen, and headquarters. These buildings were valued at twenty thousand dollars. A regular army captain and his lieutenant ran the camp, assisted by a CCC enrollee assigned as first sergeant.

The two hundred young men gradually won acceptance in Carlisle. They wore civvies into town for dates or movies instead of their rugged olive drab and ill-fitting uniforms left over from World War I. They were hard workers. I watched them trucking to work in their baggy, blue denim fatigues, wearing floppy, round denim hats. Shortly, they were part of the scenery, playing basketball or baseball against local teams. And others led local girls down the aisle in marriage. Although they lacked military training, it was believed by many that they would be the first to go if the European war spread to America. And that is what happened. The camp closed shortly after Pearl Harbor, but the boys left Nicholas County with a much healthier environment and a satisfying legacy of friendship.

Although too young to have buddied with the Carlisle CCC boys, I had an unforgettable meeting with one two years after the camp closed. I was hanging on the rail of a troopship sailing up New Guinea's mountainous north coast and admiring the magnificent scenery when a soldier sidled up and started a conversation. He asked where I was from.

"A little Kentucky town nobody's ever heard of," I replied.

"Where's that?" he asked.

"Carlisle," I said.

"How's old 'Prissy Pants'; is she still taking them on at two bucks a throw?"

"Good Lord!" I stammered. "How did you ever hear of her? She's a whore, you know." Hearing her name here in the South Pacific amazed me. "How come you know her?" I asked quickly.

He smiled a knowing smile. "I spent two years at the CCC camp on the west end of town. Remember that place?" By this time we were laughing and slapping each other on the back as we recalled names and places we had in common. Both of us justifiably feared the future, but common memories of a Bluegrass village conquered our fears for that day, even though the village now seemed as inaccessible as the moon. I never saw the lad again but thought of our joyous encounter as a "delayed action" contribution of Roosevelt's Civilian Conservation Corps. Both of us sorely needed it at that time and place.

Roosevelt's New Deal programs seemed "God-sent" to many citizens, or so they stated. This mixture of theology and politics was examined by Carlisle's Presbyterian minister, the Reverend Cecil V. Crabbe, in his book *The Individual in Our Present Day World* (1939). A *Louisville Times* reviewer called it "a Christian Philosophy of individualism." Jesus was concerned "not with politics but with principles; not with programs but with personalities, and through them to make a point of contact with the social order." According to the *Mercury* editor, Crabbe made these points to counter Depression ideas that Christ perhaps backed "contemporary" economic or social programs, whether of the New Deal, Tiberias, or many others throughout history.

I was greatly impressed to think we had an author in town, holding Brother Crabbe in awe whenever I saw him. He may have had trouble convincing his flock, however, that the Lord did not back the New Deal, for Nicholas County was a Democratic stronghold, solidly supporting Roosevelt's entire program. Republican was almost a dirty word for my pals and me. I could hardly understand how Uncle Ed and Aunt Elsie Metcalfe voted that way. Most adult sentiment probably paralleled an old political quip: "When I'm alone in that voting booth with my Lord and my conscience, I simply have to vote the straight Democratic ticket!"

Lucky and Nannie started the Depression with a great advantage—their new home was paid off and Dad's sales job guaranteed a steady income. Instead of sitting on this money, they bought a filling station in 1931 for eighteen hundred dollars, letting the rent pay it off. Several years later an old rooming house and restaurant were added, the rent nearly equaling their bank payments. As income mounted, they bought a building across the street from the rooming house. A dry cleaner rented the bottom floor while a bar held forth upstairs when the town was "wet" but gave way to an apartment when it was "dry." When Carlisle's last blacksmith, John

Lawrence, closed shop, Dad bought his building and turned it into rental rooms and a doctor's office.

By the late 1930s, Lucky and Nannie were collecting about $250 a month in rent. They bought a large Main Street building housing the Square Deal Grocery, selling it a year or so later for a profit they used to pay off other property, and from then on they were in the clear. When the draft took our filling station renter, Dad manned the gas pumps himself. By this time he was able to quit Bryan-Hunt because likable "old man Al Bryan" had died and been replaced by a "pushy fellow" disagreeable to Dad. When Lucky died in 1958, he left Nannie with a monthly rental income of around $600. I doubt any retirement plan could have done much better than that. Victorians somehow got the job done!

My parents carried neither fire nor life insurance. When the fire bell rang, Lucky was up and running. Mom stood waiting, fiddling with her fingers. We listened for the deep rumble of the fire engine motor. If it went north, east, or west, our property was safe, but if it ventured south or stayed uptown, we became anxious. Dad quickly located the fire, returning to tell us all was well.

Lucky delivered a singular but serious message to Speck and me after every fire bell scare: "I want to repeat to you two that whatever you do, never and I mean never, offend the 'Firebug' in any way. I surely don't have to harp on it because you know what I mean." We knew full well what he meant. The "Firebug" was a man rumored to be the arsonist who had set several big fires owing to real or imagined insults or other conflicts with property owners. Although guilt was never proved against him, whenever the "Firebug" was present, the Mathias boys were on their strictest best behavior.

Lucky and Nannie were in debt during the 1930s from buying property, so they were forced to attack the Depression on all possible fronts: animal, vegetable, and mineral. The animal front had to do with "Old Colonel Hams." Few meats taste better than Kentucky country ham. Before refrigeration, hams and other meats were preserved with salt and smoke, but recipes evolved using sugar and various spices to produce rather standard-flavored Kentucky hams. Our family bought, cured, and sold over one hundred country hams each year, adding a good many dollars to the till.

Every spring a big truck pulled up our driveway and unloaded our hams. We first trimmed the hams, then inserted heavy wire hooks in the hocks. Sugar, salt, and various spices were rubbed into each ham, then Dad injected a spice, salt, and sugar solution deep inside the meat. The hams were now ready to smoke and were hung from beams and studs in our backyard garage. We kept a hickory fire smoldering day and night on the garage floor for most of a week, yet neighbors never complained of the smoke, probably accepting it as one of the inevitable parts of making a living. After the hams were smoked, we enclosed each one in a paper sack with two or three inches of sawdust in its bottom. The hams were then hung in our attic where summer heat sweated them and sawdust absorbed the drippings. The impenetrable paper sacks kept "skippers" and other insects from ruining the meat. After a year or more they were cured and ready for sale.

We turned out good hams. A postcard portraying a Kentucky colonel sipping his "rock and rye" and a quote of the poem "In Kentucky" was mailed with each ham or sent to prospective customers. But our most notable success came in supplying a dozen hams annually to Egypt's King Farouk. What this Muslim king was doing with pork poses an unanswered question. In any event, an order for hams arrived one day from the king's chef. Lucky and Nannie were flabbergasted—could it be a joke? But everything was in order, so the hams were shipped. A bit later we learned how we had obtained our royal customer.

A missionary from Carlisle had bought a ham from Dad and taken it to his post in Egypt. The ham made a hit with all who sampled it, including Farouk's chef. He obtained Dad's address from the missionary and we thereafter received an annual order for a dozen "Old Colonel Hams."

We ate country ham at home as often as some people ate hamburger. It showed up at breakfast with eggs and homemade biscuits, at noon as tender, crumbly baked slices on bread or beaten biscuits, or served fried at supper with red-eye gravy, green bean and corn succotash, and various breads. My brother and I paid no more attention to this unique repast than we did to the delightfully cooked fillets of fresh bass and crappie Dad continually brought in from lakes and streams. Familiarity bred contempt. We thought much better of Bill Henry's split frankfurter slathered with Dijon mustard at his Little House with the Big Eats uptown. Even better was the nickel hamburger mashed together at Maysville's first fast-food restaurant, the White Spot on Third Street. H.L. Mencken was on the right track when he said that children, before the age of eighteen, "should be kept in a barrel and fed through the bunghole."

Lucky's porcine successes on the animal front led him to overreach himself by including a cow in his fight against hard times. Down through the years a farmer delivered two bottles of milk to our porch every morning. It was neither homogenized nor pasteurized. Several inches of thick cream hovered on top of the milk, and in freezing weather a tube of creamy ice pushed up from the bottle, the cardboard cap perched on top. We trusted the farmer for cleanliness, but our trust was misplaced.

As I poured a glass of milk one morning, I was startled to see a dollar bill swirling around in the glass. My amazement turned to joy—this was big money! It was like getting a pink center and thus a free candy bar at Gatewood's Confectionery and better than winning fly money games for a week at Simmy's Gulf station. I rushed into the kitchen, shouting as I went: "Mom! Mom! Look what the farmer put in our bottle! We won the prize!" By this time I had fished the dripping bill out and waved it in her face, but I was puzzled at the disgusted and angry look Mom gave it. "What's wrong, Mom," I asked. "Isn't it real money?"

"I'll say it's real money!" she exclaimed. "Good and dirty real money."

"Well, what are you mad about, Mom?" I asked, completely puzzled by now.

"You just don't understand, do you. Somebody left that bill as pay in the bottle, and the old boy refilled the bottle without washing it. If he'd washed it he'd found his money. If this doesn't beat all; we'll have to get our milk someplace else."

When Dad heard about it he decided to buy a cow. He allowed that he had always had a "bent" toward farming, and the dangers of the dirty milk convinced him that his time had come. "Besides," he said, "think of the money to be saved." With time and instruction

The author's grandfather, State Representative John Benedict Furlong (1862–1937), in 1912. (Unless noted otherwise, photographs are from the author's collection.)

Elizabeth Browning Furlong (1868–1950), the author's grandmother, in front of her Maysville home at 122 E. Fifth Street.

Charles "Lucky" Mathias and Nancy "Nannie" Furlong during their courting days in 1923, ages forty-one and thirty-five, respectively. Taken along Moransburg Road, Mason County, Kentucky.

Lucky and Nannie and son Frank just after moving into their new bungalow in 1926.

Frank Mathias in 1926.

Author's watercolor of his Carlisle home, the Jazz Age bungalow at 371 East Main Street.

Meiner grossmutter and her son Uncle Joe during a visit to Covington, Kentucky, in the mid-1920s.

Frank Mathias, three years old, poses for a picture on the running board of Lucky's Model T Ford in 1928.

Charles Mathias, age two in 1930, rides between Uncle Joe's house and his own, with the "hoot owl house" looming in the background.

(Above) Carlisle's pride and joy, her Victorian buildings along the south side of Courthouse Square.

(Left) Carlisle's railroad station is long past its glory days when Uncle Joe met eight passenger trains a day here.

(Below) Simmy's Gulf Station, home of "fly money" betting.

(Above) Carlisle High School, Carlisle, Kentucky.
(Courtesy of Nicholas County Library)

(Left) Everett Earl "Fanny" Pfanstiel, much admired superintendent of Carlisle High School who smelled of cigars and cinnamon balls. Pfanstiel was a veteran of World War I, the "war to end all wars."(Below, left) Jake Earlywine, the author's buddy and neighbor, in his 1944 high school graduation picture. Jake's family participated in rendering a hog each autumn in the Mathias family's backyard.(Below, right) Author's playmate and pal Horace "Spud" Marshall, occasional fly money champion and hammerer of catfish. (Courtesy of Nicholas County Library)

Charles and Frank pose outside their home in
September 1931 on Frank's first day of school.

Charles Mathias, age
eight, in 1936.

Frank Mathias, Andrew Metcalfe, and
his mother, Elsie Metcalfe, during a
1932 jaunt to the Carlisle reservoir.

Andrew Metcalfe, the author's
neighbor and brotherly friend,
was killed in action in Italy
during World War II and
earned the Silver Star.

Carlisle High School band, May Day, c. 1938. Author (behind bass drummer) has the only smiling face in the band. Friends include (front row, left to right) drum major Andrew Metcalfe; trumpeters Charles Sexton, Ben "Pokey" Pumphrey, and Bobby Cunningham (fifth from left); Marion "Steamboat" Evans (second row, third from right); baritone player Tom Carter (back row, center); bass horn player Billy Harper (back row, right); and Frances Henry (standing in front of Harper). Courtesy of Viola Pumphrey.

Floodwaters of January 27, 1937, just to the rear of the boys posing on Market Street in Maysville, Kentucky. (Left to right) James and Robert Clarkson, Walter Hines, Charles and Frank Mathias. The Clarkson boys later served in the army, Hines in the navy.

(Left) The author in 1937, age twelve, displays his "tenderfoot" Boy Scout badge.

(Below) Author's sketch of Black Hawk Camp.

(Top) Charles Mathias, six years old in 1934, wets his line at a favorite fishing spot, the Carlisle reservoir. (Right) The author at age eleven in 1936, in a photo taken in a carnival booth.

(Left) Bryan-Hunt Wholesale Grocery Company salesman Charles "Lucky" Mathias, shiny shoes and all in 1922.

An amazingly exact likeness of the author's grandfather, Kentucky State Representative John B. Furlong, that appeared in a magazine advertisement a few months after his death.

(Right) Frank and Charles "Speck" Mathias in 1937, ages twelve and nine.

Charles and Frank Mathias on May Day, 1936, dressed in typical summer attire of white shirt and white duck pants.

Lucky Mathias's practical-joking friend Ambrose Rogers "Tickie" Fisher holds his wife, Achie, while displaying a typical Jazz Age look with his flared pants and late 1920s auto. (Courtesy of Kay Fisher Hall)

(Left) The author's lifelong buddy Joe Beatty. Both of them survived drinking from Brushy Fork Creek, Carlisle's open sewer. When he failed the army's physical exam, Joe was heartbroken, a typical reaction for the GI generation. (Class photographs courtesy of Nicholas County Library)

(Right) The author shared many adventures with Marion "Steamboat" Evans, from swimming in the city lake tank to climbing the high railroad trestle at Black Hawk. Evans was a marine rifleman on Iwo Jima.

(Left) The author's lifelong buddy David Harper, age seventeen, who joined Mathias in many grade and high school episodes as well as Sunday mass with the town's tiny Catholic congregation.

(Right) There is probably no better example of the GI Generation than cousin Bob Mathias, a paratrooper discussed by Stephen E. Ambrose in *D-Day* as an example of what Hitler was up against in his overconfident belief that democracies produced weaklings. Bob was the first American officer killed by German fire on D-Day.

(Left) The author's buddy Bill Hopkins, who became a private with the Ninety-first Infantry Division. He was killed in action in France in 1944.

(Right) Nate Young, a buddy of the author, in his 1944 high school graduation picture. Nate was destined to serve with the First Infantry Division—"The Big Red One"—in Europe.

Nicholas County Courthouse, Carlisle, Kentucky. As a child, the author shook hands with many of Kentucky's prominent politicians on the courthouse steps, enjoyed "hillbilly" music in courtroom concerts, and flew model airplanes from the clock tower.

The author's bandmates: Emory Griffith "Griff" Asbury (left), who became one of the U.S. Army's champion rifle marksmen, and Bob Cunningham, destined for the United States Air Force in World War II.

Pen and ink sketch by the author of the high railroad bridge over the confluence of Fleming Creek with Licking River. The "trestle" was a favorite target of climbers and thrill seekers from Camp Black Hawk.

Lovely Lillian Marie Furlong, described as the author's "Auntie Mame," is seen here as the presiding beauty of Maysville's centennial celebration of 1933.

The Maysville hillside home of the author's grandparents, John and Elizabeth Furlong, at 122 East Fifth Street.

Downtown Maysville, originally Limestone, Virginia, and a pioneer gateway to Kentucky. The Simon Kenton Bridge connects the town to Aberdeen, Ohio. The author and his pals often swam from the three piers near the bridge.

(Right) Walter Hines Jr. in 1943.

Frank Mathias (far left), age six, with his favorite cousin and partner in Maysville shenanigans, Walter "Doc" Hines Jr., age five, in 1931.

(Right) The author's "Uncle Doc," Oliver Morris Goodloe, Maysville Public Health Director, at age thirty-nine. Described as a "fast flying physician," Goodloe later served as Commissioner of Health for Columbus, Ohio. Courtesy of Betty Goodloe Arsuaga.

Maysville buddy Glenn
Mattingly at seventeen. A
fellow river-surfer and
musician with the Kentucky
Kavaliers, Mattingly became a
lieutenant in the World War II
air force.

The author's buddy John
E. Soper in his 1943 high
school graduation picture.
Soper and Mathias wound
up World War II on Luzon.

The Kentucky Kavaliers Dance Band performing at the Maysville Armory. Left to right: (front row) bandleader Clarence Moore and vocalist Charlotte Newell; (second row) saxophonists Frank Mathias, Gail Clark, Verna Ellis, Don Wood and vocalist Wenonah Jones (seated); (back row) trombonists Leo Caproni and Shelby Cox, trumpeters Gene White and Glenn Mattingly, drummer Wayne Cablish, and pianist Virgie Whitaker.

(Right) A front yard get-together in 1939. (Front row, left to right) Frank and Charles Mathias and cousin Mary M. King. (Second row, left to right) Lucky, Nannie, Aunt Katie King, Lucky's cousin Agatha Funken, and Uncle Joe.

(Left) The author's mother, Nannie Furlong Mathias, on her bungalow steps about the time the author left for the army, and at a time when she and Carlisle began to "wear well" together.

(Right)
Frank Furlong Mathias,
age seventeen, 1942.

The courthouse yard's list of veterans forms a backdrop for the author and classmate George Judge, both just returned from World War II in 1946. More than forty of Nicholas County's GI Generation never made it home, having been killed in action: ten of them were the author's playmates or pals.

from Katie King, his farming sister, he felt he could also learn to make butter and cheese.

Dad was as good as his word. Verna Stone helped him pick out a nice cow at the stockyards. He found he could pasture it near a barn on the East Union road. The place housed a walnut-picking industry, but an attached shed would be perfect to shelter and milk the cow. It was just about two blocks from home and about two hundred yards from the Catholic Church. Perhaps he could combine going to church and milking the cow when the opportunity offered. Lucky thought he had it all figured out.

Dad's venture into dairying brought sly comments from his friends. "Lucky," Ed Metcalfe advised, "I'm an old cowpuncher and I can tell you you're going to have to buy a hand warmer once the weather gets cold."

"What are you talking about?" Lucky asked, a puzzled expression on his face.

"Why, Lucky, I though surely you were more sensitive than to ask such a question. Just place yourself in your cow's position; how would you like someone with icy hands messing around with your teats on a winter morning?"

A few days later Dad ran into Everett Pfanstiel uptown. "Lucky," Fanny said in a serious tone, "I can offer you a real bargain if you're in a buying mood. I've got a genuine Colt six-shooter you can have dirt cheap."

"What in the world are you talking about; the last thing I need is a pistol."

"Why, Lucky," Fanny replied with a smile, "I was only trying to help. They tell me you're running a head of cattle out there on the East Union road. Don't you know that area is literally alive with rustlers?"

Another friend, A.R. "Tickie" Fisher, was eagerly lying in wait for Dad at his lumberyard. The yard was only a block from our house, and Dad often hung out there with Tickie, the hired hands, and some old-timers. It was a congenial large office, with a big stove and comfortable benches and chairs. Practical jokes were likely to be sprung at any time.

Lucky had no sooner entered the office than Tickie told him

he had heard tell of his cow. All of the loafers perked up at this unusual information. Dad assured Tickie he had heard right and hinted that he was going to save a lot of money on milk. Tickie interrupted with a question presented in a very serious tone and manner: "Lucky, has that cow of your had its shots?"

"Shots? Shots? What do you mean, Tickie?"

"Why, Lucky, I was sure you knew; a new government regulation says that all milk cows must have a series of expensive shots administered by a vet. It's only right, I think you'll agree, to protect our children and womenfolk and any others who drink it. Let's see, if I remember, the shots include rabies, typhoid, malaria, tularemia. . . ."

Lucky interrupted: "That's an expensive list for sure, and there isn't a vet anywhere near here—just like the damned New Dealers to get this stuff going!"

"Now, now, Lucky," Tickie cooed, "you always tell us how much you like FDR and his New Dealers, and here we find you've turned against them." The loafers nodded in mock agreement. "And Lucky," Tickie continued, "you never let me finish listing all the shots required. Cows also have to have shots for mumps, measles, impetigo, pinkeye, hives, warts, seven-years' itch. . . ."

By the time Tickie got to pinkeye, Lucky knew they had him, and he joined in the fun. "You birds are going to be sorry when my cow has quintuplets like the Dionnes. I'm going to name every ugly calf after each one of you, starting with Tickie!"

After the fun of getting started was over, Dad faced the routine of milking the cow every morning and night. Costly feed had to be supplied when winter shriveled the grass. This ate up the profit, while the constant call to milking shoved an irksome time clock into Lucky's easygoing way of life. What happened next bore out earlier predictions: Lucky sold the cow in early February and regained his happiness. Unfortunately, Ed Metcalfe lost his just at the same time. The Metcalfes had continued buying the farmer's milk in spite of Mom's warning. Ed began feeling "poorly," with fevers and fatigue. His illness was finally pinned down as undulant fever (brucellosis), a severe disease contracted by drinking milk from infected cows. It took him several months to recover.

Lucky did well on the animal front in spite of the cow, and he was destined to do as well on the vegetable and mineral fronts in waging war against the Depression. Dad took great pains to have the earliest homegrown tomatoes on the market. If he had them, which he always did, he could sell them in quantity to every grocer in his territory. Even Kroger and the A&P bought them, for nothing beats homegrown tomatoes after a winter of eating the hothouse kind.

Dad grew his tomatoes in our backyard and Uncle Joe's, a combined area of one-third of an acre of very fertile soil. He grew his own plants and had them in the ground for the first of spring weather. Each plant was fastened to its stick with a V-shaped metal strip crimped on the ends to hold it in place. Lucky invented the device to save tying the plants with string. Before long a similar device appeared for sale over a wide market. He never knew whether his idea had been pirated or whether the simple idea had also occurred to someone else. In any event, his early tomatoes brought victory on the vegetable front, adding cash to our coffers.

Dad scored a lasting victory on the mineral front by buying coal from private miners. Our bungalow was mostly heated by a floor register above our $43.50 Sears, Roebuck basement furnace. It burned an average of some twelve tons each winter. Lucky paid over $100 a year to Tickie for coal and saw no way to avoid doing so. The solution to this problem knocked on our door one late summer afternoon. Dad answered the door to find a horny-handed man standing there in overalls and heavy work shoes. After a brief introduction, the conversation went about like this:

"Mister Mathias, I was told you got a coal burnin' furnace; is that right?"

"That's right, burns as much as fifteen tons some years. What's on your mind?"

"Well, sir, I'm one that can cut your coal bill; I've got my own mine up in th' mountains and I've drove down a load I'm sellin' for six dollar a ton. How does that sound to yuh?"

"Right off I'd hafta say you've got the best price around if it's good coal—no clay, slate, and stuff like that." Lucky was impressed.

"It's good coal, sir, jist come see for yoreself. I'm parked over yonder."

Dad checked the coal, and as far as he could tell, it looked as good as the bituminous coal he bought each year from Tickie. The miner, as Dad knew, ran a "jack-leg" drift mine, one with a horizontal walk-in shaft following a coal seam into the mountainside. Such coal was cut, wheelbarrowed, and loaded by hand. Hundreds of these mines operated throughout the commonwealth's vast coalfields to fill the heating needs of the owners. The Depression and automation, however, forced thousands of miners out of work. Eventually, some three million people fled Appalachian coal country seeking work and a new life in distant cities. Burgeoning defense industries after 1939 soaked up this horde of jobless migrants. But many refused to leave their familiar homeland, turning to mining and selling coal to luckier people elsewhere, in this case, "down in the Bluegrass." The man at our door was one of these.

Dad bought the coal and ordered another load as soon as it could be trucked down from the mountains. The miner and his son shoveled the coal from their truck down our basement coal chute. Each year Dad's standing order with this miner saved him two to four dollars a ton. Within two years this was enough to have more than paid for our Sears furnace!

Tickie Fisher could look from his office window and see that a jack-leg miner was unloading cheap coal up at Lucky's house. He could not really blame his friend, for the Depression bred an economic tolerance into people either unknown or misunderstood by the consumer society to come. But when Lucky came down to loaf and chat, he told him he would have a cold home the coming winter. Tickie and the others worked up such a case against jack-leg coal that they talked themselves into concluding that the stuff probably would not burn at all. "Poor Lucky," they sighed.

Lucky put up a good front, but he secretly thought they might be right. After all, he knew next to nothing about coal and had bought it with price instead of quality in mind. When he got home he stirred up a fire in the furnace, much to Mom's amazement; it was a steamy September day. The coal was top-grade bituminous and burned beautifully. "I'll get that bunch down at Tickie's," he thought as he put the fire out.

Dad took me with him, and we arrived down at the lumberyard office early the next day. Tickie had not arrived, so Dad beck-oned to Billy Vaughn, a friend and foreman. "Billy," he said, "I'm going to play a trick on Tickie and the crowd if you'll help me." He told Billy what he had in mind; Vaughn chuckled and agreed to help. As requested, he brought Lucky a fine, blocky piece of coal from Fisher's "Number One" pile. Dad wrapped it in a newspaper and waited for the boss to show up. Loafers filtered in as well as customers. Soon Tickie arrived and almost immediately asked Lucky what he had wrapped up in the newspaper.

"Tickie, you and the boys told me yesterday that I'd made a big mistake in buying that jack-leg coal. I don't think I did, so I brought a big chunk of it down to try out in your stove. Get a fire started and we'll see who's right."

Tickie of course accepted the challenge and soon had a fire going. A crowd gathered to see what would happen. Dad stepped up and laid his coal on the fire. It caught and burned brightly, send-ing flickers of light into the dark corners of the big room. Interested faces looked in at the open stove door as Tickie began talking down the coal.

"Lordy, Lucky," he chortled in his twangy baritone voice, "look at the water oozing out of that junk. It would likely rust out a stove in a few weeks." He broke it up a bit with his poker. "I just wish you all would look at the slate and clay falling out of that slab. It's a wonder the stuff holds any fire at all." Everyone shook their heads in agreement, even though the coal was burning furiously. Dad then called Vaughn over and asked him where the coal came from.

"I picked it up this morning for Lucky off the Number One pile just outside this window," Billy said, pointing so that everyone could see.

A roar of laughter greeted Billy's words, not the least coming from Tickie. Lucky was now one up on him, not that Tickie minded; he could get even. A month or so later, when the coal truik was old hat, Tickie asked Lucky if he had heard the good news. Lucky bit.

"What news is that, Tickie?"

"Why, Lucky, a hide plant is coming to town. I hear they'll be curing all sorts of animal hides to make leather."

"That *is* good news; where are they going to build it?"

"From what I gather, they intend to put it on the old Growers' Tobacco Warehouse lot, right across the street from your house."

"The hell they are," Lucky exploded. "Those things stink like the devil! There'll be burning hair and bristle; rotten meat will peel off the hides."

"Now, now, Lucky," Tickie chided, "these are hard times. Just think, they tell me twelve men will be hired right here in town."

"Has anyone else heard of this thing?" Lucky asked with a suspicion-tinged voice. The loafers sitting around the office all agreed with Tickie's story but added that such a nuisance should be located out in the country. Fisher said he believed they were right; but the town had no zoning laws, and jobs are jobs; yet if the thing were built it would cut the value of any homes within smelling distance.

Lucky was sucked in. Without checking further, he drew up a petition against the "hide plant," asking Tickie and the gang to sign it. They signed it, of course, and he took it around the neighborhood that afternoon getting other signatures and creating concern about defending against such an outrage. Ed Metcalfe was so mad he drew up his own petition and took it around town getting signers. Uncle Joe joined him in the effort. Somewhere, probably at the courthouse, one of the petitioners found out that none of Carlisle's administrators had heard of a hide plant, much less given permission to build one. Informed of this, Lucky charged back to the lumberyard office. He asked Tickie point-blank: "Where in God's green earth did you get that information about a hide plant?"

Ambrose Rogers "Tickie" Fisher looked up from his desk with an expression of puzzled innocence: "What hide plant, Lucky?"

14

Cops, Robbers, and Characters

Nicholas County has always been a safe place to live, but this is not to say that crime, such as it was, took a holiday between the wars. We kids sometimes penetrated the trappings of shady activities better than adults. Take "Hinky," for example. He was a kindly appearing soul who puttered around Courthouse Square most Saturday afternoons. Hinky always wore a long black overcoat that hung down to the calves of his legs. He invariably tipped his floppy felt hat to the ladies, revealing salt-and-pepper gray hair, and he had an encouraging word or two for one and all. On Poppy Day Hinky sported a large cluster of red paper poppies pinned prominently to his overcoat lapel. Aunt Elsie Metcalfe and the Legion Auxiliary ladies who sold them praised the lanky old widower for his patriotism. It was said with pride that Hinky had been "over there" during the Great War "making the world safe for democracy." Some said sadly that he had been "shell-shocked" and that was why he just fooled around, living alone in his little farmhouse. And we kids added to this wartime legend, assuming that "Hinky Dinky Parlez-vous" was a song dedicated to Hinky.

Whatever Hinky had or had not been in the past, one thing was certain about him in the present—he was a bootlegger. Inside that long black coat were sewn numerous small pockets, each one sized to hold a flat little half-pint bottle of booze. Pat Conley, Davey Harper, and I caught him in action one afternoon in the courthouse men's room. We burst into the room as he took out several bottles for customers. They grinned at us, paying no more attention as we went on to use the facilities. Hinky collected fifty cents for his half-pints, and it was probably homemade moonshine. When I told Andrew about it, he paused in surprise, then saw his chance: "I guess we'll have to look at Hinky from now on through rose-colored bottles!" And so we did.

Liquor was hard to control in Carlisle during the Depression, whether the town was wet or dry. The *Mercury* often carried news of liquor raids, such as the issue of January 10, 1935, which revealed that a raid on a Dorseyville home gleaned twenty pints of moonshine. Licensed dealers complained to the editor that moonshiners were ruining their business. "Moonshine can be bought at fifty cents per pint in Carlisle," they grumbled. If Hinky was selling "shine" in his half-pint bottles, he was making 100 percent profit. No wonder he could afford a big bouquet of poppies instead of the usual one.

Courage growling out of a whiskey bottle—or maybe it was just hormones—brought about the summer Saturday afternoon knife fights uptown. They were frightening to watch. The fighters were nearly always farm boys who had come into town after a hard week's work in the corn or tobacco patch. They were mostly dressed in the stylish hot weather fashion of the era: white duck pants, white shirt with rolled-up sleeves, and either black or two-toned shoes.

They were looking for trouble, so it did not take much to start a fight. A dirty look or an insult brought a march of the two lads and their confederates, with other hangers-on, such as us kids, into the graveled alley behind the Ford garage. Sumac, ivy, and other bushy growth hid the alley from view.

Rules of some sort were followed, for I never heard of anyone being killed in these affairs. The fighters dealt only in slashing instead of stabbing, the object being to split the opponent's skin and shirt, leaving long bloody streaks across backs, shoulders, and arms. And flying hair was always a part of the scene. These older boys wore their hair in a pompadour, a style in which long hair was brushed straight back from the forehead. Brilliantine was used to hold it in place, but the sweat and action of a fight soon had it flying, finally plastering it in long, greasy strands across the fighters' faces. Within five minutes or so, the police showed up with no-nonsense billy clubs and the fight was over. The proud fighters, strutting like game-cocks, laughed and joked with bystanders all the way to their night in jail. They had a lot to talk about the next week as they chopped weeds and milked cows. Few could dare tell them that manhood was more than this. But a few years later they turned into men after all, at such places as New Georgia, Midway, Ploesti, and Omaha Beach!

Judging by what I have seen in the weekly *Mercury*, only in the last week of January 1935 was Nicholas County in the throes of a "crime wave." The January 31 issue reported that "three youths" stole $120 from the Carlisle Mill and Supply Company. They admitted also to having stolen two or three bags of flour a week from the mill for over a year. And adding insult to injury, they confessed to stealing about ten dollars from the *Mercury* office earlier in the week.

What might well have resulted in a lynching also occurred that week. A local white woman "was struck by a Negro." The culprit was caught and taken to the Lexington jail for his own safety, for "feeling is said to have run high." I have no memory of this incident. Subsequent issues of the *Mercury* and personal inquiries in Carlisle failed to reveal the outcome of this affair.

Crime and criminals received so much newspaper attention that kids identified with them and the G-men who pursued them. Any pretty afternoon after school was excuse enough for our gang to gather in a backyard for a fast game of cops and robbers. Whoever hosted the game had the right to call himself after one of our favorite gangsters of the era, whether John Dillinger, Machine Gun Kelly, or Pretty Boy Floyd (Bonnie and Clyde Barrow and Ma Barker, being "sissies," were never considered). A similar right of choice came with cops, and J. Edgar Hoover led the pack. Hoover's lieutenant Melvin Purvis came next, for he had killed Dillinger at a Chicago movie house. But everyone had his identity as a G-man or gangster as we laid ambushes and ran about shouting and shooting cap pistols. We were unaware that Nicholas County would soon host the "real thing," achieving notoriety not only for a bank robbery but even more for what happened when lawmen closed in on the robbers.

Moorefield is a village set in a fertile and prosperous farming area. Several churches, a grade school, a general store, and a small bank were strung along the main thoroughfare, state Route 36. The bank, seven miles from the closest police station, was seen as an ideal target by two gunmen. Harve Wilson, the banker, did not look like the type to cause them any trouble. A hit-and-run robbery was planned and carried out on a summer day in 1938.

The banker was held at gunpoint as the money was taken; the gunmen then ran for their car. By this time Wilson had unlimbered his pistol and blazed away at the swiftly retreating getaway car. Rumor had it that "Harve put four bullet holes in the back window you could cover with your hat." Lucky and Wilson were fast friends, and Dad repeated this rumor often.

Wilson shot well, but failed to wound either robber and they drove into hiding along an overgrown riverbank. Lawmen of course had been on their trail since Wilson had telephoned them of the robbery. Several days later the Nicholas County sheriff and his men closed in on the pair, sneaking silently through a thicket of sand willows and underbrush. The robbers' first indication of trouble was also their last one: the sheriff's stern voice commanding them to put their hands up. They stood up slowly, hands in the air, and faced the lawman. To his horror and heartbreak, one of them was his own son. He did his duty and arrested them. The money was recovered and the robbers did time in the state penitentiary.

Carlisle had its share of citizens known as "characters," either affectionately or otherwise. Most "normal" citizens, perhaps in the splendid tradition of their English forefathers, generally relished the presence of eccentricity in their midst. Whenever a class system is in force—and a mild one existed in Carlisle—acceptance of personal "differences" is easier, for each citizen is secure in his own social class or category.

Carlisle's mild class ranking was based mostly on money and membership. There were no people of real wealth in the county, but in hard times wealth is relative. A professional man making five thousand dollars a year was seen as an economic aristocrat by clerks, teachers, and craftsmen earning one-fifth as much or by laborers and people on relief rolls with much less income than that. Money added to one's rank.

Church membership was the other major indicator of class in Carlisle. There was no Episcopal church, but other mainline Protestant denominations enjoyed high status: Christian, Baptist, Methodist, and Presbyterian. Masons ranked with these groups. Those belonging to Holiness churches—"holy rollers" they were called— or to no church were usually thought of as a lower social class. We Catholics numbered but eighty in a county population of eight thousand and were often viewed as proof of the persistence of error in an age of truth. We were too few to be seriously reckoned with, yet we stood as Reformation "holdouts" as well as members of an interesting but "puzzling" worldwide Christian communion. For these uncertain reasons we bobbed up and down in status, especially during the heyday of the Ku Klux Klan.

African American citizens were only vaguely thought of as partners in the above system, for theirs was a segregated bottom-class existence mostly ignored by whites unless they failed to "know their place." They were probably the only people in the county who could have not the slightest doubt as to their position in the scheme of things. Their white neighbors may have sinned more against them by omission than by commission. All in all, the town's mildly structured society offered fairly free rein to the somewhat "different" folks who lived, loved, schemed, cheated, joked, worked with, and greatly interested the rest of us.

There were "lovable" as opposed to "distasteful" characters, only Hinky being both, depending on who he was talking to at the time. My uncle Joe, however, fell under the first category. He tilted from side to side like a roly-poly as he walked about, and he was always in a fussy sort of good humor. One of his favorites was Eugene Neal, and whenever the two met outside Neal's grocery, Uncle Joe often paused to give him a compliment, once saying, "Gene, I think you're a promising young man."

"Thank you for your compliment, Uncle Joe," Gene said, wondering what his unpredictable old friend would say next.

"Think nothing of it, Gene," Uncle Joe snapped. "They say you'll promise just about anything!"

Like most bachelors, Uncle Joe was occasionally beset by jokers and even a few well-meaning folks who asked when he was getting married: "Just as soon as I can find somebody with more sense than you have" was his much admired reply. He lumped his hard-won knowledge of the world's pitfalls, gleaned from years as a horse-back letter carrier, fire chief, tailor, and insurance salesman, into one often cited formula: "You can't do nuthin if you ain't got nuthin to do nuthin with." He applied this maxim to just about everything: labor, education, intelligence, business, religion, government, farm-ing, and even to his failure as a fisherman as compared to Lucky. Bill Conley, a local lawyer and friend, received a bit of counseling from Uncle Joe one day: "You lawyers get us outa the kinda trouble we'd never be in in the first place if there wasn't no lawyers." And he once told Mom that one of her sisters was "shy about tellin' her age—about ten years shy." He was right, and Aunt Pauline treated him with greater respect from then on.

Perhaps the best loved of Carlisle's characters was a barber, a smallish, gray-haired man in his fifties. J.H. "Cap" Fulton enter-tained the customers in his small shop with outlandish lies and out-rageous exaggerations. He also ostentatiously bragged and cheated, W.C. Fields style, while shooting pool at the uptown billiard parlor. Cap's numerous followers were ever trying to "put one over on him just to see what he'll say." A notable effort to this end had to do with a turnip. An admirer carved one to look remarkably like shav-ing soap and slipped it into Cap's counter mug. To everyone's de-light, the next customer was one of those men with a tough, bluish beard. Fulton thrashed his brush mightily, trying to foam up a suit-able lather. He managed a thin lather from residue in the cup and brushed it on while complaining about "this gol-darned wartime soap." He stropped his straight razor, sized up the man's jaw, and applied the blade with a long-practiced downward stroke. ZIP! The customer fought free and leaped from the chair, nursing a bright red streak down his cheek. While Cap was apologizing, he discovered the "soap." He knew he had been had, and he chased the laughing onlookers out of his shop to spread yet another tale about the town's favorite barber.

Fulton's tales often attracted Warren Fisher, the prize-winning editor of the *Carlisle Mercury* and ready defender of local talent. Whenever he wrote about Fulton, he referred to him as "the Baron

Munchausen of the shears," in reference to an eighteenth-century adventurer widely known for the exaggerated telling of his exploits. In the *Mercury* of January 24, 1935, the editor noted sadly that he had a death to report: "Cap Fulton's dog 'Dee' has died." The shaggy old dog had snoozed fitfully for years at Cap's feet, and some said that it changed color weekly from hair clippings falling on it. The editor sympathized with Cap's vigorously held claim that Dee was a thoroughbred and eligible for registration with the American Kennel Association. Fulton had always intended to register the dog, Fisher wrote, but said he could never truthfully and honestly decide whether Dee was a greyhound, fox terrier, border collie, or English bulldog.

A rugged looking man of delicate Victorian sensitivities was old "Chesty," a bachelor who spent many of his later days sitting in the courthouse or outside, as the weather dictated. His noblest work came in preventing toddlers from dipping into the contents of the big brass spittoons strategically placed in courthouse hallways and offices. Whenever he failed, he excused himself by rolling his eyes and crying, "I can't be no mama to everbody everplace at onc't!" This caused a few who did not know Chesty's background to nickname him "Mama," but long before this he had practically tattooed himself as "Chesty," and with good reason.

Chesty never referred to parts of the female body for what they were but coined delicate names for each. This extended beyond calling a navel a belly button and indeed beyond the human body itself. Piano "legs" were off limits to him; he called them "limbs." His nickname attached itself to him at a church picnic when he spied a particularly appetizing chicken breast at the end of a lengthy table. A sudden lull in the conversation came just as he pointed and shouted: "Would somebody down there kindly pass me that big lady chicken's chest!" With these words, Chesty invented himself.

"That G.B. sure is a character!" most of us said when we talked about Granville B. Leonard, Carlisle High School's "Smith Hughes" man. None meant that this likable bachelor, who earned extra pay teaching agriculture under the federal Smith-Hughes Act, was a character nearly so much as a "son of a gun," a term of indulgence and affection often said in the same breath as "he-man."

Leonard was bulky of body and walked as if he was on his way through a cornfield or cactus patch that only he could see. His sway-ing gait might well have earned him a role as a sod buster or cavalry-man in a John Wayne movie. But unlike such actors, he was the real thing. And he was also a master teacher.

Leonard of course taught farm boys and directed the 4–H Club, but he was noted in the student body for his General Science course. He strode heavily into the classroom one day complaining about the winter weather as he brushed snow from his shoes. He casually dropped three sticks on a front table as he went to the blackboard and lectured on lizards. No one noticed when the three sticks moved, slowly at first, then thrashed, curled, and began crawling on the table. Suddenly the class came to life as the "sticks" turned into live snakes—this amid a turmoil of shouting, squealing, and overturned chairs. Leonard's frozen harmless snakes and their revival as they thawed out in the warm room made an unforgettable biological point.

On another day he brought two jars to class, one filled with Coca Cola, the other with alcohol. He placed an ounce of liver, tied to a string, into each jar, saying we would check the experiment tomorrow. The next day we found that the Coca Cola had dissolved the liver, but the alcohol had seemingly preserved the meat.

"Mr. Leonard," a student asked, "doesn't it look like we'd all be better off drinking booze than coke?" The class chortled and laughed in approval.

Leonard probably expected this, and he replied: "Nate Young's got a point there, but as for me, I've found that Coke tastes a right smart better than embalming fluid!"

A man lacking even a little of the patience of G.B. Leonard was Seamus O'Toole, an Irish farmer of great height and girth. My first close contact with O'Toole was on a Saturday afternoon as I at-tempted to deliver *Grit*, a national newspaper for rural readers, to a second-story saloon. As I started up the long enclosed stairway, a commotion at the top caught my attention. O'Toole stood there with massive legs spread, one huge arm holding a smaller man while he sent another hurtling down the stairwell. I leaped back as the first one crashed at the bottom, then watched in awe as the big Irishman flung two more lads down to the bruised and battered pileup on the landing. My dad owned the building, which had a dry cleaner on the first floor, so I felt reasonably safe in making my way up to the saloon to deliver the paper. The bartender said that the boys had tried to throw O'Toole out, just to see if they could. They learned better the hard way. But by the time I left the defeated lads were back upstairs drinking and laughing with O'Toole as if nothing had happened.

Seamus was unable to whip machinery as decisively as he did men. Moreover, he was an "animal man," it was said, whose main talent lay in having his way with the horses and mules and other animals on his farm. There was some truth to this. One Saturday afternoon he drove into town to shop, his Terraplane sedan's isinglass windows flapping in the breeze as he skidded into a graveled parking space in front of the courthouse. Horses and buggies shared these spaces. After shopping, O'Toole applied the crank to start the motor, but it snapped savagely back at him, injuring his arm. Just as quickly he pulled out the crank and smashed a headlight, sending it clattering into the street. Seamus backed his ears, gritted his teeth, and shouted in triumph for all to hear: "That'll be teachin' you to kick me, you di-r-r-ty damned beast!"

Although Carlisle had no authentic house of ill repute, this is not to imply that it had no amateurs or characters fishing the shallow backwaters of the world's oldest profession. Most eventually "got religion" and became solid citizens but at the same time attracted gossipy attention either as "Jezebels," "weekend warriors," or "unsavory characters." In spite of them and their customers, Carlisle was, by modern standards, comparatively free of illicit sex, and what there was was usually seen as a wrong demanding repentance rather than the permissive pursuit of an "alternate lifestyle" or an animal drive free of consequences. And fearful consequences lurked, for neither contraceptive pills nor penicillin were available. Most of my classmates and I entered service as virgins but hardly repressed ones. We had grown up talking sex, observed farm animals in action, petted and smooched with dates, knew the latest jokes and gossip, yet were still able to believe that the safest and sanest sex came only through love and the marriage bed.

It is no longer spoken of in passionate whispers, even by the few left to remember that disturbing between-the-wars love affair. The issue was simple: the man loved the woman and the woman loved the man. Simple or not, they were unable to marry in Carlisle, or even in Kentucky. They probably could have done so in nearby Aberdeen, Ohio, some said, because Aberdeen was known at that time as a "Gretna Green." In any event, they left their Nicholas County homeland, then married and settled north of the Ohio River. The man was white, the woman black.

There was a character I never heard called anything but "Germy." Germy told most everybody that he was a lot like Will Rogers: "I never meet nary a soul I don't like unless they git up too close." We understood what Germy was driving at, knowing his terrible fear of germs.

He was in his fifties, lean and lanky, usually unshaven, and often wearing a brown patchy all-season sweater and baggy pants. His attire was not unusual in a hardworking rural community, but his gloves were. Germy wore brown cotton gloves the year round, holding his hands out from his body like a praying mantis. He did a coy, sideways dance whenever he met someone on a narrow sidewalk to avoid their germs. Nor was he ever to be seen in movies, school, or church assemblies, places where germs congregated. I have forgotten any details of his life, if I ever knew them; Germy was simply a part of the Carlisle street scene and accepted as such.

The citizenry never molested Germy, but the same cannot be said for "Goosey Ben" Bragg. Like several others, Bragg roamed the streets pushing a cart in which he collected household garbage for hog slop. But Ben had an unusual affliction; whenever anyone goosed him he went into near acrobatics, whooping, leaping, running in circles, and laughing! His garbage often cascaded from his cart into the street at such dramatic moments. He was of course a target for high-school boys. One leaned out and goosed him as he walked the aisle of a crowded court-day courtroom. Ben flew fully into his act, leaping the rail between court and audience and sending lawyers and secretaries running for cover. The audience erupted with loud laughter as the sheepish out-of-town lawyers returned to their seats.

By this time Bragg was happily and safely seated amid an appreciative audience.

Two frequent house visitors, wrongly considered characters by many, were "the drippins woman" and Uncle Henny, the "coffee eater." The former came to collect bacon drippings, the latter to collect garbage.

"The drippins woman" always knocked loudly on the front door before walking in: "Here again, Miz Mathias—comin' fur my bacon drippins!" She, her gawky nephew, and mom always went into the kitchen "to sit a spell," drink a cup of tea, and lightly gossip about the state of drippings in the neighborhood. She wore a bonnet and faded dress that hung just above ankle-high white tennis shoes. Her nephew wore outgrown, faded bib overalls over a patched shirt and tennis shoes. Such attire came to college campuses in the 1960s, but in the 1930s our visitors were neither "making a statement" nor trying to "identify" with poverty, they were honest-to-god poor. Her drippings (grease) were mixed with lye leached from wood ashes to make soap.

A gentle back-door knock announced Uncle Henny, an aged black man. He too "sat a spell" with us before collecting our garbage for hog swill. His "fee" was a cup of coffee, which he spooned full of sugar, then ate out of the cup—thus his characterization as the "coffee eater." And he was not one to offer unearned praise: "Next to Mrs. Metcalfe's," he often told Mom, "your coffee eats better than any in town."

All drug addicts between the wars were lumped together as "dope fiends." Carlisle had one whom I shall cal "Val." Val sometimes tried to talk a doctor's son into filching morphine from his dad's supplies. The boy refused him, warning his dad and telling his buddies about it. One afternoon we learned that Val's hideout to inject his arm with morphine was the thick horseweed patch alongside the high playground fence. He never suspected kids were watching him through knotholes from the other side of the fence. What he did scared us, so we were breathlessly quiet until he left. We heard sinister tales of "reefer madness," and these, combined with lurid accounts of sinful dreams in "Chinese opium dens," made us marvel that Val was able to keep up pretenses, for he was always spoken of as "one of the nicest men in town."

Several years later I was injected with a heavy dose of morphine in an infantry field hospital in Luzon. I thought back to Val and the horseweed patch as the medic shoved the needle into my arm. "Sinister opium dreams are coming my way," I told my fevered self. Instead, it brought blessed relief from the craziness and fever of the first of a series of malarial attacks. Heavy doses of atrabrine quickly reduced the deadly severity of that first attack. Val had his own private battle with drug addiction, but I now know there was no pretense involved in his being "one of the nicest men in town."

Between the wars, "homosexuality" was a borderline word few used and fewer felt free to discuss. But most communities did acknowledge one or more "queers," and citizens old enough to drive knew who they were, if not exactly what the label meant. Several Nicholas County men—and they were helpless to gain redress— were branded with this odious title. Few supposed, however, that women could be homosexual (as distinguished from "queer"), or much of anything else besides wives, teachers, nurses, and telephone operators, so they were generally exempt from suspicion. Indeed, the use of the word "lesbian" would have puzzled all but a well-read few, like the one I heard "identify" it as "a country in the Holy Land with Beirut as its capital."

Whatever the adult sexual orientation of the man who approached me one sunny Saturday morning may have been, one thing is certain: he was a scheming child molester. Two twelve-year-old pals and I were sitting and chatting on steps alongside a Main Street business building when he walked up. We had seen him around town but were unacquainted. He cracked several good jokes, then handed us some magazines: "See what you fellows think of these rascals!" he chortled. We gasped at the contents. They were nudist magazines, far racier than the *Spicy Westerns* on the drugstore racks. We whistled loudly as photo pages of naked men and women spun before our eyes. He was calling himself "Hotsy" when we attracted attention. A shadow darkened our sunny scene. A pal's father grabbed a magazine, glanced at it, then grabbed little "Hotsy's" shirt up around his neck and knocked his head hard against the building wall. He immediately dragged my whining pal up a nearby alley for a whipping. Bruised "Hotsy" scurried away, and I ran all the way home, keeping my mouth shut for the rest of the day.

On almost any Saturday afternoon Uncle Moss Mohrs staggered around Courthouse Square until the constable gently collared him and took him to jail. Uncle Moss was the "town drunk," but by no means the only one in town. All of the others were summed up in Uncle Moss when one was talking about the perils of "Old Dog Liquor," as the preachers called it. Some said Moss spent more time in jail than the jailer, which was not true but still made a point. He was sobering up one morning when he witnessed several "jailbirds" digging an escape hole through the rotten concrete floor with ordinary kitchen spoons. He knew better than to interrupt, but when the last one slid through to freedom, he called the jailer. "Willy," he said as the jailer arrived, "them three fellers you brung in here last night has done spooned their way out of your jail!"

Mohrs's alcoholism endured until the Vietnam War, but one Saturday at noon he unaccountably went to his room to sleep off the booze. He lit a cigarette and went to sleep. It was to be eternal sleep, for the mattress ignited and Uncle Moss and his feisty little bulldog died from smoke inhalation.

Franklin A. Hornbuckle was said to be one of Carlisle's "big bean and cabbage men," and he looked it. He carried a gold-knobbed cane, wore ivory spats over shiny shoes, and draped his portly body in finely striped dark suits. There were no men of real wealth in town, but in any lineup of Carlisle's businessmen, a visiting New Yorker would have believed Franklin to have been one. As if in secret contempt of this hard-earned image, Hornbuckle came out with the lightning bugs on many summer nights and peed at length into the huge spirea bushes surrounding his spacious front porch. Undoubtedly his wife knew he drank a lot of beer, but she probably never knew how he was getting rid of it. In fact, no one except us kids found this out.

We often chased and bottled lightning bugs through the big yards around Hornbuckle's and played hide 'n seek when the spirit hit us. One night Davey Harper and I were hiding in the spireas when we heard his heavy tread on the porch above us. We lay there in puzzled silence as we began to get wet. Was it raining? A glance up through the tangled spirea revealed that it was not rain that was wetting us. We scooted on hands and knees around the porch to a hose faucet and cleaned up. Although Hornbuckle never caught on, the kids did. Anytime a hide 'n seek game was in progress in his yard, the kid who was "It" knew there would never again be any hiders under those spirea bushes.

I never played hide 'n seek with Espy and Ospy Mulligan because we met only in the daytime. They were identical twins who wore long hair "like Jesus" and who lived in a rusty tin-roofed, clapboard shanty within walking distance of a country grocery on Dad's route. They hung out at the grocery, and Speck and I played with them whenever Dad took us on his route. We became pals. One day Dad pulled in beside the grocery and Speck and I were puzzled to find the twins missing from the scene. Just as we walked up the porch steps, Mrs. Mulligan came out the door.

"Howdy, Mrs. Mulligan," I said. "Where are the twins today?"

"Why, Frank, they're workin' and won't be here today. And sumthin' else is, they ain't twins no more; Espy's done got hisself a haircut."

John Lawrence ran the last blacksmith shop I ever saw in action. When he felt like it, he beckoned us kids to come and stand just inside the wide sliding doors and watch him work. He wore a heavy leather apron over his overalls and sturdy shoes. Both were pitted by hot metal. We gasped in admiration as he heated metal in a rasping blast of blue flame, then hammered it into horseshoes or farm implements amid lofty showers of bright and dying sparks. He shaped everything on his big anvil, his hammer pounding out sounds like a carillon stuck on one note. Sound and smell combined unforgettably when the smith dunked the white-hot metal in his wooden water tub, the sizzling steel provoking a cloud of steam to blend with the shop odors. This smell of hand-worked iron is a good smell.

The blacksmith shop was a rendezvous for a group of middle-aged friends. They sat there several hours a day playing euchre, a card game played with thirty-two cards, all the cards below seven except the ace being removed. They were to the blacksmith shop as Lucky's friends were to Tickie Fisher's lumberyard. And they played good-natured practical jokes on each other with the same gusto. One of the regulars was Charlie Ross, a jovial and well-liked letter carrier. Ross, like Lucky, was a bit short of patience, thus an ideal target for jokers.

Charlie dropped by one hot day for a few hands of euchre, hanging his big leather mailbag on a wall spike. After a few games, he hoisted the bulging bag to his shoulder and continued walking his hilly route. By noon, Ross was certain Father Time had caught up with him; he was sweating and wishing the day would end. Around two o'clock—by this time his usual springy steps had turned leaden—he became suspicious of his mailbag. No matter how much mail he delivered, the bag seemed heavy as ever. With a sudden sinking feeling, yet one tinged with discovery, he turned his bag upside down. Seven or eight pounds of horseshoes clanged down on the sidewalk!

Two citizens of Carlisle held a special place in the minds of us kids. One was a girl we seldom saw but always looked for. She sometimes peeked from behind the curtains of her second-story window but just as quickly vanished from view. She looked to be our age. Older folks shushed us up whenever we inquired about her. I never found out her name or who her folks were, but rumors abounded as to why she was never let out of the house.

I felt both sorrow and pride for a man I never saw but heard much about. We were strongly warned never to shout or make noise when passing his home or to disturb the peace of his dwelling in any way. The warnings were issued with considerable force, and I never knew any kid to disobey them. Peace prevailed in his neighborhood. He was an honored and decorated veteran of the Great War and was slowly and painfully dying from lungs burned by mustard gas on the Western Front.

15

Summertime

Each year I faced summer like a miser counting his gold. The hoard of days from May Day to Labor Day were my treasure and were approached with the greedy hope I could somehow spend them yet keep them. May Day annually gave tangible form to my naïve hopes.

May Day is a traditional spring festival in many northern countries. The old Soviet Union, for example, celebrated it as an international labor holiday. Although not as widespread as it once was, May Day festivals in the United States usually follow English tradition in the crowning of a May Queen and winding of a Maypole. Carlisle between the wars followed form, with the citizenry joining the schools in making much ado over May Day. The gymnasium was spangled with flowers and colored streamers. A costumed herald, accompanied by a trumpeter, announced the arrival of the radiant and richly gowned May Queen and her attendants. She was always a high school senior, duly elected for her beauty and personality. After the queen was enthroned, a festival theme—good health, patriotism, rural versus city life—was enacted by costumed students.

I spent my first five May Days costumed as a brownie. Brownies are helpful elves or goblins in English folktales. Whenever teachers staging the event had more children than they had parts, they costumed us as brownies and stood us here and there as background to the action. My half-pint size doomed me to brownie status until I rebelled in sixth grade, winding up as one of twenty blackbirds in a huge paper pie.

Once the lovely Maypole was wound and blue ribbons were ceremoniously awarded to the certified healthy students, the make-believe ended and everyone stepped back into the less than healthy and financially strapped real world lurking outside. But we never thought of it that way, remembering it as just one more happy May Day as we joyfully surrendered to summer.

Summer's boyhood action often centered around a privy in Uncle Joe's backyard. It was abandoned when flush toilets came to Main Street, but it remained a well-built and roofed clapboard "three-holer." Now odorless, it gradually was adopted as a clubhouse, the horizontal inside braces serving nicely as shelves. Adults ignored it; they had had enough of privies, remembering icy winter nights and summer wasp nests and spiderwebs. But this greatly enhanced its value in our eyes.

The privy entered my life in an unexpected way when I was about nine. An "only child" girl was visiting a pal's home and began playing with us boys. She deftly trapped bumblebees in a jar held against hollyhock blossoms, and I liked her. One afternoon as we sat listening to the buzzing of her embottled bees, she asked me a personal question, the first I had ever received from a girl. It was posed in a very matter-of-fact manner: "Do you have a dingus?"

"Sure," I replied, "I guess everybody has a dingus, don't they?"

"I'll show you mine if you'll show me yours," she said, setting her bee jar down.

With no further discussion, we walked over to the privy and dropped our pants. She seemed satisfied with the view, but I was flabbergasted—there was nothing to see! I knew boys and girls were supposed to be different and guessed that this must be it. An hour or so later Peanuts Bailey dropped by. He had several sisters and knew a lot about girls. I told him what happened and described what I had seen. "They're all that way," Peanuts said, with a disinterested shrug.

I felt smugly superior after that whenever I wrote my name in the snow, wet down campfires, or forced a head-high stream up the back of a barn door. By the time I started high school, however, I began to understand that I had been living in a fool's paradise.

Several years later the privy served as a stage for a family drama of some consequence. It began with Speck's discovery of a hidden box containing twenty-four 12–gauge-shotgun shells. They were old and they were dangerous, being enclosed in yellow instead of modern red casings. Dad's brother John had left him a shotgun and these shells when he moved to Texas. Lucky seldom hunted, so the gun and shells had gathered dust since the mid-1920s.

When Speck showed me the shells—he was about nine and I was twelve—I knew opportunity knocked. "We'll have fireworks!" I said excitedly. "I'll take them out back and you get the butcher knife. We'll cut them open and take out the powder and light it with a big WHOOSH! It'll be just like what Tom Mix did last week when he poured the trail of gunpowder into the rustlers' cave." Speck came back with the butcher knife and I hacked some shells open. A small pile of gunpowder had accumulated when Dad walked up. "What in the world! Where did you two find those old shells? Good Lord, gimmie those things before you blow yourselves up." He scooped them all up and threw them down the privy. "Don't go near them," he commanded, and went back to chatting with Cousin Otto Bedinghaus on the front porch.

Cousins Otto and Emma Bedinghaus had driven to Carlisle from Chillicothe to spend the weekend with us and Uncle Joe. They were well off, spoke German, and often left Speck and me a half dollar each. In spite of my warnings, they always slept in Uncle Joe's bedroom with the death clock in the wall.

The temptation was too great for Speck and me to heed Dad's warning. "You've got to climb down and get those shells," I told him. "We'll take them to Spud's or Popeye's, or somebody's where Dad can't catch us." Speck was agreeable. He had often climbed in and out of the privy pit to hide while playing cops and robbers. The long-abandoned privy offered easily climbed stone walls ten feet down to a dry bottom. Speck squinched his small, agile body through one of the holes. I watched his red hair disappear as he dropped into the dimly lit pit to search for the shells. "I can always count on Speck," I thought, but added, "Besides, he's too dumb to know better."

Neither Speck nor I had anticipated Cousin Emma Bedinghaus's condition. Cousin Emma was not a woman physically to attract favorable attention. Uncle Joe described her as "a hefty frau," while Nannie believed her to be "a bit stout." Speck and I called it as we saw it: "Cousin Emma is a fat lady," we said. In any event, Emma was chatting with Uncle Joe in his living room when diarrhea hit her with an urge for quick action. As she headed for the bathroom, Joe shouted after her: "The plumber hasn't come yet to fix the commode—you'll have to use the backyard privy, Emma!"

Emma now rallied her portly self for a dash to the privy. I heard the backdoor slam, and here she came, rounding the hoot owl house with a grimly determined set to her jaw. I sensed disaster for Speck. By this time I had scooted into hiding behind our garage with no way to warn him. He thought I was still in the privy. Emma rushed in huffing and gasping and immediately let fly a withering blast.

Speck was astounded, then enraged. He began fighting back, shouting my name as he hurled rocks and shotgun shells up at the hole from whence came his misery. Cousin Emma was completely distraught, tripping over her undergarments as she surged out of the privy screaming, "Lucky! Lucky! Come quick! One of your boys has fallen into the outhouse! *Hilfe! Hilfe!*" I knew that was German for *Help! Help!* And I also knew I was going to be in big trouble for help was on the way.

Dad and Cousin Otto came running around the house from the front porch, with Otto in the lead. Dad sized up the trouble and yanked Speck up through the hole so hard he skinned his legs. I hated to hear him ask where I was, but I walked over from the garage, mustering a look of complete and puzzled innocence. It may have been one of my best acting efforts, but it did not work. He bent me over, using his belt to thrash me while Mom took Speck to the bathroom for a scrubbing. The plumber showed up an hour later, never to know that his belated arrival created a conversation piece for years to come and probably prevented the Mathias boys from blowing themselves up!

Tobacco's influence on Nicholas County was total, extending to an annual event that took place in our privy. It was almost a civic duty for Kentucky men to chew and smoke. We boys imitated our elders by smoking free substitutes such as corn silk, street butts, or sweepings from tobacco barns. This was usually done only for fun and seldom to my knowledge from addiction. Our favorite substitute was the easily come by "Indian cigar." These foot-long, slender, beanlike pods droop by the hundreds in late summer from catalpa trees. We picked them green and hid them in protected places to cure, blacken, dry, and become smokable. This is where the privy came in.

Each year someone started our annual smokers' parade by dropping by to say that the Indian cigars had ripened and he had brought some to hide in the privy. This ignited an unplanned yet inevitable movement toward a "big smoke" each year. The catalpa beans were laid around the inner eaves of the privy, out of sight yet protected from moisture. Soon, James "Shotgun" Cannon might bring in another batch. (Shotgun bore that nickname because he was judged too small to be a cannon.) The parade picked up tempo with Spud Marshall, Gerald "Butsy" Barlow, James Hughes, and others adding their cigar stocks to the outhouse. We had not the slightest intention of smoking them all; just knowing they were there satisfied our craving to feel that once again we had put one over on adult rules and authority.

By early autumn all was ready. The gang brought wooden kitchen matches (book matches were seldom seen), and each chose a ripened cigar. Their dry, fluffy interior holds fire and burns easily. The hard ends were bitten off, matches applied, and the privy puffed full of blue smoke. The taste is chemically acrid but not unpleasant. Smoke drifted out of eaves and cracks, yet we were never noticed. We resembled a bunch of ragged little businessmen at a convention. Finally satisfied, each threw his cigar down a hole, as if to say we had made our point for yet another year. The meeting adjourned until next fall's "big smoke," but before then a smaller meeting took place that deserved to be called the "big dirty drink." It had to do with apples.

Few Carlisle kids ever got infantile paralysis (polio) because we "inoculated" ourselves by the things we ate and drank. I offer proof of this issuing from a 1936 drinking spree I engaged in alongside reekingly filthy Brushy Fork creek. Its beginnings were innocent enough. Candy was scarce so fruits filled in. Since my backyard apple tree was loaded with bland cooking apples, Joe Beatty and I decided to roast some on an open fire, then sprinkle brown sugar on them while hot. It was our own recipe.

Brushy Fork was just a block away, so Joe and I quickly had a driftwood fire centered in a hollow stack of rocks. Our apples lined the top edges, where overlapping flames could singe and roast them. We had barely gotten under way when Joe's older brother Kelley walked up. We invited him to the feast, not because he was a likable fourteen-year-old but because we had a great surplus of apples. Kelley noticed we had nothing to drink. "I know where a hose and screen is," he said, jumping up. "I'll run over to the house and get them." We wondered what he had in mind even as we dodged a few clods thrown at us by Donnell Baugus, "the bully of Dorsey Avenue." Fate later gave paratrooper Donnie a hero's death during the 1944 Normandy invasion.

The apples were sizzling nicely when Kelley returned. He laid a ten-foot length of hose under rocks on the shallow creek bottom, then propped up the downstream end so that it spurted water steadily. As he crimped a piece of window screen over the upstream end, he smiled triumphantly into our puzzled faces. "We've got good drinking water now," Kelley said, with all the authority of a skinny Oliver Hardy. "When any water runs five feet in the dark it get purified, and it's plenty dark inside that hose. The screen will do a good job, too. Let's have a drink," he said, producing a tin cup.

Joe and I were a bit leery but not for any valid reason. A valid reason would have been that Carlisle had no sewage system other than Brushy Fork. Sewage and fetid debris entered and drifted down it twenty-four hours a day. Kelley defended his project: "Look, there's nothin' to worry about; I even doubled the length of the hose. Besides, the screen catches all the big stuff." He passed the cup around. I took it, thinking that "if Kelley Beatty isn't old enough and smart enough to know, who is?" Joe reached the same conclusion, and the three of us feasted on sugared apples every day or so, chased by some of the tastiest water ever to come out of a hose.

A few summers later a patriotic venture brought a run-in with even better tasting water. It began when Steamboat Evans spotted me one day eating a hot dog at a window table of the Little House with the Big Eats. He came in. "How come you're lucky enough to eat out?" he asked, his voice tinged with envy.

"Aw, Mom, Dad, and Speck went to a grocer's funeral in Flemingsburg; I played sick and they gave me a quarter to eat out."

"Lucky you! D'ya know what Cunningham and I are getting ready to do?"

"No tellin,'" I said, but I was interested.

"We're goin' out to climb one of the lake tanks and plant the American flag on top. Wanna go?"

"Do I," I gurgled, choking the words out as I stuffed the rest of the hot dog in my mouth. "Let's go!"

Our pal Bobby joined us at Radio Hospital, the Evans's business, where Steamboat picked up a yard-long American flag. He paused long enough to show us his new, handmade forty-five-power telescope, "too powerful," he complained, "to see anything good in the apartment across the street." Bobby and I looked, judging the three girls who lived there to be perfectly safe from Steamboat's imperfect telescope. We hiked a mile to twin hundred-foot-high hilltop water tanks near Carlisle's two reservoirs and pumphouse. We easily ignored a KEEP OFF sign, seeing ourselves as modern Pearys and Amundsens, explorers who had planted flags at the poles. Besides, the odds were in our favor, for no fishermen were in view on either lake this summer day.

The ladder on the older tank looked better, so we decided to climb it. Staring up the dizzyingly tall supports gave me second thoughts. But what would Steamy and Bobby think if I was so unpatriotic and cowardly as to back out from planting the Stars and Stripes atop the highest point in the county? The small steel ladder, solidly welded to one of the four support columns, led to the top. Steamboat led the way, climbing slowly but surely up past the horizontal girders. I followed him, gripping tightly and worriedly as I went. Small birds, astonished to see us, flew from nests in the girders and chirped insults as they circled us. Much worse were nesting wasps Steamboat unavoidably stirred up. Bobby and I waited for them to settle down before inching by. Cunningham was ten feet below me. When I looked down I scared myself with the view of the distant ground. My palms were sweaty. I mumbled hopefully, "If I can just make it to the deck around the tank's bottom I'll be okay." And so I was.

Steamboat hauled me over the railing and onto the deck. Bobby joined us and we enjoyed a magnificent view of the surrounding hills, fields, and town, an unexpected bonus to our patriotic venture. Both lakes glistened in the sun; the distant courthouse clock bell struck three. Mathers' Woods loomed to the northwest. A train trailed smoke as it puffed toward town from the southwest. Uncle Joe undoubtedly awaited it. We circled the tank to take in views from all directions. "This must be what it's like to be up in an airplane," Bobby cried, the wind creating muffled echoes of his voice against the tank's metallic sides.

"It's time we plant the flag!" Steamboat shouted as he climbed up the tank ladder. Bobby and I followed our older pal, now full of confidence, the terrors of the climb forgotten. By the time we joined him at the top, Steamy had his three-foot flag fluttering in the breeze. It was tied to a steel stem of some sort, probably a lightning rod. Our pride soared as the wind stiffened the fabric, displaying our national banner against the blue sky above and the earth colors so far below. Five years later Pvt. Marion Prather "Steamboat" Evans was a marine rifleman on Iwo Jima when a much more dramatic flag-raising took place on Mount Suribachi. After the war he maintained with tongue-in-cheek that he, Cunningham, and I should again plant the flag on the lake tank but this time take a cameraman along.

We were about to head back down the ladder when we saw the trap door. It opened into the tank, illuminating the interior as well as a ladder leading down into the stored water. "Let's take a swim!" Steamboat cried. "They won't let us swim in the lakes so we'll swim in their water tank instead." This was an appealing thought. Every kid in town had long yearned to swim in the attractive, clear reservoirs, but "rules are rules," the old folks always said. We stripped off, hung our duds on the inside ladder, and had a pleasant swim in and around the hundred-foot level of Carlisle's drinking water.

The trip down and back to town was uneventful. For some weeks thereafter I thought of every drink of tap water as something special, even better than that earlier provided by Kelley Beatty's hose down on Brushy Fork. But Steamy, Bobby, and I thought it best to keep this part of our flag-planting venture to ourselves, which we did.

The lake tank was not the only high spot of summer adventure. The courthouse clock tower rose one hundred feet above ground level, though it lacked the additional hilltop elevation of the lake tanks. We model-plane builders viewed the clock tower as a magnificent launching platform for our feather-light planes of balsa wood, tissue paper, and hand-wound, rubber-band-powered propellers.

Balsa wood models had lives of their own. Intricate plans and templates were scrupulously followed as straight pins, razor blade, cement, and patience gradually brought the wood and tissue to its destiny as a creation capable of flight. Few could cut and glue a model together without gaining insight into the skeletal form and function of all structures, whether of buildings, ships, planes, or even the human body. They were a joy, not merely fun, to build and to fly. A good Comet brand model kit cost as little as fifteen cents, an investment in pride, joy, and insight probably unequaled during the Depression years.

Classmates flying models from atop the courthouse caught me unawares until I saw them in action one afternoon. Someone, perhaps Walter Robbins, our supreme modeler, discovered a hidden stairway leading from the ground floor to the attic and opening also into an alcove behind the judge's bench. (This may have been an "escape hatch," for the courthouse had been built during a time of feuding and harassment of Kentucky judiciary.) Once one reached the pigeon-infested attic, further stairs opened onto a small, fenced deck atop the tower.

Each of us brought planes designed cheaply from leftover scraps and pieces of balsa and tissue. We flew them when winds were light and proudly watched as tiny propellers pulled them free of courthouse updrafts, setting them into glide paths that often reached the roofs of business buildings or drifted them down amid Main Street traffic. We were tolerated because the light planes were of interest to adults and damaged nothing. After all, this was an era when citizens rushed outside to view the mystery of flight anytime they heard an aircraft motor.

We were unable to let well enough alone. Someone tied a kerosene-soaked string to the tail of a model and lit it as he launched it. When the fire reached the plane, it went "down in flames," like Spitfires and Messerschmidts then "flaming out" in the ongoing Battle of Britain. We felt patriotic as we watched flaming Nazi-marked planes crashing down on the roofs of nearby businesses. And that is what wrecked us. The owners of businesses and parked cars did not share our view of fireballs landing on their property. One day we found the attic doors padlocked, each with a sign: "Keep Out: This Means You."

I supported my model building, among other things, by collecting and selling scrap iron desperately needed by Japan's brutal war machine. My pals and I knew little of this and avidly searched the metal out, for the pay was good. Nothing escaped us, whether rusty spikes and bolts along railroad tracks or odds and ends in the debris of old warehouses. John Lawrence's abandoned blacksmith shop was bought by Lucky for other purposes, but I sifted out hundreds of horseshoes and metal pieces for sale. While we were collecting scrap iron, adults often predicted that "that stuff is going to Japan, and they'll be shooting it back at us before you know it." I could not have cared less, for my naïve mind centered only on the coins paid for it. Then came war, and I wound up fighting the Japanese war machine. If a genie had appeared and marked some of the myriad shell fragments that came my way, at least one sliver might have read: "Collected by Corporal Mathias at John Lawrence's old blacksmith shop, Carlisle, Kentucky, June 23, 1940."

Model building and scrap collecting gave way to worry about Nannie during the summer and autumn of 1940. She said she had heart trouble. There were many symptoms. She tired easily and was unable to sew, sweep, and cook as vigorously as she had in the past. Whenever we had visitors she perked up, serving and entertaining admirably, but she claimed exhaustion as soon as they left. She reminisced often of her teaching days in Colorado and Iowa, allowing no excuses for Dad's not having lived up to his premarriage promise to move out west. She went to Carlisle's three doctors, each of whom failed to find any heart trouble. She tried her luck in Maysville, "where the doctors have some sense," but they offered the same diagnosis. Doc Goodloe, her brother-in-law, delicately suggested that perhaps her fifty-two years were catching up with her. She doubted this but accepted his offer to schedule an examination by a renowned but high-priced Cincinnati heart specialist.

Dad and I drove Mom to her appointment, catering to her palpitations and a broken elevator by nearly carrying her up a long flight of steps to the specialist's office. We read out-of-date magazines for an hour, hoping for the best, and that is what we got. The door opened and Nannie and the doctor entered the waiting room grinning and laughing. Her health was excellent, she had no heart trouble, but she needed to cut back on her excessive coffee drinking. This had caused her palpitations. A happy Mom led the way as the three of us frolicked down the steps we had so carefully climbed sixty minutes before. It seemed at first glance that all it took to gain Nannie's belief in a medical diagnosis was a fifty-dollar-an-hour fee. But Lucky knew better, advising that "all of us are going to love Mom a lot more and tell her so every day." It worked. She lived happily until 1970, more than long enough to abandon Maysville for a long overdue love affair with Carlisle!

Each summer Mathias relatives from afar visited us, for Lucky and Joe were the only Mathiases left in the old hometown. I relished the visits of my many lovely female cousins, loving the smell of perfume around the house. And older boys in town flattered my ego by asking introductions to cousin Marjory, Marita, Rosemary, or whomever. Andrew Metcalfe of course had an inside track and courted many of them, but his life's destiny was linked to that of cousin Bob Mathias, of Washington, D.C. Bob often came to Carlisle with Uncle Harry and Aunt Catherine's family. Harry, the oldest of the six Mathias boys, had started work as a printer for the old *Carlisle Democrat* but in 1915 had taken a job in the Government Printing Office. Robert Mason Mathias was born to Harry and his wife, Catherine Marshall of Frankfort, that year.

Bob Mathias was a talented young man whose life, like Andrew's, was cut short by World War II. He was an artist for the *Washington Post* but an unusually tough one, for he boxed his way to the 1937 national amateur welterweight title. With the coming of war, Bob joined the paratroopers of the Eighty-second Airborne Division and, as discussed in the introduction of this book, became the first American officer killed by German fire on D-Day.

Bob, his parents, and five brothers and sisters spent time with us most summers. There were few of the attractions held essential to modern life, such as television and plenty of money available for all sorts of entertainment, so we made do with conversations, books, games, races, and singing together and in general entertained each other. It was probably entertainment enough for Bob and his brothers and sisters—big city kids—to wander around little Carlisle and its rural environs, listen to the serenade of bullfrogs, screech owls, and roosters every night, and ponder just a bit better the life their father must have led in this tiny village before moving to Washington.

After some days in Carlisle, Uncle Harry always took Bob and the rest to Frankfort for a visit with his wife's family, the Marshalls. Aunt Catherine was one of the thirteen children of Ben and Emma Marshall. Ben (for Benona) Marshall weighed 258 pounds and stood six feet, two inches, in contrast to Emma's four feet, ten inches! Ben, well known throughout Kentucky, served in public life in Frankfort and in the commonwealth for half a century. His most important office was collector of internal revenue for the Seventh Kentucky District, to which he was appointed by President Woodrow Wilson. But Marshall took the most pride in having been captain of Company A, Kentucky State Guard, during the turbulent months that followed the assassination of Governor William Goebel in 1900. When all is said and done, Lt. Robert Mason Mathias, with a German cobbler for a granddad on one side and an Anglo-Saxon politician on the other, drew strongly from both sides to become a truly American patriot.

16

Hanging around Town

Carnivals were welcomed to town each summer. They set up rides, the midway, and living quarters on Jackson Field, the pasture where autumn football games were played. Unlike the movies, they were live, gaudy, and challenging, appealing to all five senses. One could risk a few cents gambling, or be the big man by ringing a gong with a sledgehammer, or eat cotton candy and caramel apples, or best of all, walk back and forth on the midway exchanging glances and quips with girls who were there for exactly the same purpose. And anyone jaded with the usual offering had only to visit the "Freak Show." Over the years I saw a man who looked like Popeye, one who ate small but live chickens, another who was tattooed from neck to toes, a "giant" no taller than many modern basketball players, a "fat lady" who might easily play second fiddle to numerous fatter ladies and men hogging modern supermarket aisles, the usual midgets, but also a heartrending man without arms or legs. "An awful way to make a living," was the usual comment directed at the "freaks."

Brazenly advertised "Stella by Starlight" occupied an off-the-midway tent one year. Those daring to enter were promised a view of "the human form in all its glory!" The heroine cavorted naked between a bright light and a smoothly stretched sheet, posing in suggestive silhouettes for the whistling and snorting male audience out front. Speck, James Hughes, and Joe Roundtree managed to squirm their heads under the tent, seeing her in the flesh before a "carny" grabbed their feet and pulled them out. Their descriptions of Stella grew in vividness and detail over the following weeks.

I had nothing like that to brag about, but I did wrestle a Gypsy at the 1940 carnival. I arrived with a quarter in my pocket, but before I could spend it I noticed several acquaintances wrestling off to one side. When I walked over, I was challenged to a bout by a smirking stranger. He was my size and age so I lined up opposite him. We wrestled for a few minutes, then he gave up. "You whipped the Gypsy," the other boys said, and I strutted away feeling I had done something worth bragging about. I had heard of Gypsies somewhere, probably in the movies, and now I had licked one. This called for a treat, perhaps a caramel apple. I reached into my pocket for the quarter. It was gone. With a sinking and helpless feeling I realized I had not licked a Gypsy after all.

Gypsies and carnivals were once-a-summer challenges, but bees and wasps offered chances for risky daily duels. Their numbers were truly great in this era before powerful lawn and field insecticides. They and their butterfly allies were summer cousins, brushing wings with kids' elbows at every seep or puddle. We competed under grape arbors and uneasily shared flower-dimpled lots and pastures. It took courage to pinch a sitting wasp's tiny waist between thumb and forefinger to show off to an amazed girl as its stinger darted harmlessly in and out of its sleek abdomen. Bumblebees were not built for this, but they foolishly let kids transfer them from blossoms to bottles; we relished the peril before flipping off the lids and rolling the bottles to let the black and yellow bees tumble out and take wing.

"Let me put a bee in your ear" meant one had gossip to pass on, but this saying turned into painful reality for a classmate one afternoon. The *Mercury* of August 1, 1935, noted that "June Stewart . . . was brought to Carlisle . . . and given an anesthetic while a local physician removed a honey bee from her ear. The bee had lodged there the day before."

"To have a bee in one's bonnet" is to be obsessed with one idea, a perfect description of Bummie one afternoon when a bumblebee became entangled in her hair. It buzzed in puzzled fright as Andrew and his distraught grandmother ran in small circles on the lawn trying to give the bee an escape route. Spud Marshall and I joined the quarrel. Andy lit his dad's pipe and puffed smoke into Bummie's hair as she bent over. The bee flew out and we sighed in relief, but after circling her head the nicotine-dazed creature flew back into her hair. Andrew stood there, fuming helplessly as he held an empty pipe, but the bee quickly recovered and flew away for good. While we laughed, Andy came up with a saying to fit the occasion: "The bee 'put the bee' on Bummie, but we 'put the bee' on the bee!"

No one, however, had ever "put the bee" on wine hidden and forgotten in Uncle Joe's closet. He was the type who never opened Christmas presents until summer, so it can be doubted that he remembered it was there. In addition, family skeletons as well as wine came out of that closet one summer afternoon. Speck and I were rummaging through stacks of woodcarvings in the closet, mostly of cuckoo clocks and picture frames. They had been carved by relatives, past and present, in Germany's Black Forest. We admired the craftsmanship, wondering how or why they wound up in the closet. More to the point, they covered a flat leather case in one corner. Intrigued, we popped the metal spring latches, opened the lid, and stared with mounting excitement at six sample pint bottles of fine wine! "Maybe we oughtn't drink this stuff," I said, but we did.

The wine tasted snappier than Kool-Aid, but the more we drank the better we liked it. Uncle Joe walked in, having returned from his usual date with a train. He stared at us, mumbled something, then turned and trotted next door, shouting, "Nannie! Oh Nannie! The boys have gotten into the wine! The boys are into the wine!" Mom was soon assessing the evidence: guilty looks and several empty or half-empty wine bottles. We had sampled several bottles before finding the sweeter ones. She listened angrily to our slurred speech, then hustled us home after we made rather sloppy apologies to "good ole Uncle Josie." "Wait 'til your father hears about this," she said grimly. "Just you wait."

Lucky was no prohibitionist, for he had helped Joe run off batches of home brew before repeal, but he was wary of anything stronger than beer. His father had been an embarrassingly heavy weekend drinker, and his brother Edward had died of alcoholism. Ed had contracted the dam impounding the Carlisle reservoir and had done well for years. He began drinking in his forties, lost contracts, and finally took the one job he should have avoided—that of a specialty man for a wine company. The closet bottles had been ones he used in his promotion work. Speck and I knew nothing of this as we anxiously awaited Dad's return from work.

Lucky heard the news while unloading his satchel and sample case. He must have had a good day, for his mood was one of amusement mixed with concern. "Poor old Ed," he sighed. "Joe should have thrown that stuff out years ago." He sat Speck and me down on the back porch steps for a lecture.

"Did you two have so little sense as to go into Uncle Joe's house and take things? I thought you loved Uncle Joe," he said, slanting his head and voice as if having to question an obvious truth. Before I could answer that we did, he revealed his brother's disastrous encounter with alcohol. "Your Uncle Ed died from drinking too much of the same stuff you two got into this afternoon. Remember him?" he asked, nodding at me. I nodded back, but my memories were those of a four-year-old, of a tall man pitching me on high, laughing and catching me as I fell. Speck listened with wide eyes and trembling chin. "And your Grandpa Mathias," Lucky continued, "embarrassed all of us more than enough. Sometimes he passed out drunk, and his card-playing pals loaded him into the back of his wagon. They slapped old Brack's rump and the little horse pulled him through town to the shoeshop where we lived, then whinnied for help. We boys carried him inside where Mom put him to bed. How would you like it if I came home that way every month or so?"

By this time we were crying and mumbling that we would not like it at all. Uncle Joe walked up as Dad hammered home a final point with great conviction: "Just remember this—there never was a Mathias who could handle whiskey. I learned that from watching my father and I've not drunk over a quart of whiskey in my life." Turning to his brother, he asked, "Isn't that right, Joe?"

Uncle Joe nodded in agreement but took up for his nephews

as usual. "Lucky," he frowned, "you oughta quit pickin' on 'em; I've dumped that wine down the sink, and I don't think they knew any better anyway, did they Nan?"

Mom agreed, having switched sides once Dad started us crying. This irked him, but he shifted emotional gears and turned to the humorous side of the episode. We all laughed as Speck and I told how the wine affected us. In the long run, however, the laugh was on my brother. Speck died of alcoholism at age fifty-seven, having outlasted Uncle Ed by seven years. Lucky pegged it perfectly on our day of wine and roses: "There never was a Mathias who could handle whiskey."

Hanging around town offered much more than a wine party at Uncle Joe's, for Carlisle boomed with new construction in the late 1930s, but its need for a new jail went begging. By 1938, New Deal projects underway or completed in Nicholas County included a second reservoir, a seventy-five-thousand-gallon auxiliary lake tank, several new streets, and a National Guard armory. This was good, but by far the most immediate need was for a decent jail. My buddies and I seldom passed the ramshackle old structure without ogling its tiny dungeon windows or pausing to shout up at the grinning prisoners. They shouted back from tall, high windows, their fists clenched around thick, rust-discolored bars. Boys or girls were sometimes there, running errands for a father, uncle, or brother, bringing snacks or tobacco from Neal's Square Deal, and tying the stuff to strings let down for the purpose. This was illegal but went on with little interference. Escape tools were probably smuggled in this way. On June 19, 1940, the local paper reported that "six jailbirds dug through the rotten concrete floor, dropped to the basement and escaped." Nine had escaped the same way a year before and several others before that. The editor might have deduced, with more truth than humor, that these men possibly left to find a bathroom, for he later reported that the entire jail was served by "only one commode!" Each time the escapees were soon caught and returned to their respective window spots, chatting as usual with passersby and probably planning their next escape. Fortunately, the town's volunteer firemen were never called to the jail; a terrible tragedy might have entered Carlisle's records if the building had caught fire.

Danger or trouble in today's world is often announced by sirens: fire, police, ambulance, or tornado. By contrast, the brazenly insistent ringing of Carlisle's fire bell stirred its citizens to action even quicker than the alluring hum of an airplane overhead. Both involved conflicting human urges, the first for destruction, the second for progress. Destruction had the upper hand on a summer night in 1940. Speck and the fire bell sounded off together: "The stockyards are on fire!" he shouted through an open window, while the compelling rhythm of the bell brought townspeople running either to combat the conflagration or to see the frightful drama.

The neighborhood emptied as we rushed toward the rapidly expanding fire. I stumbled, bit my tongue badly, quickly returned home for a washrag, then stood gawking with it stuffed in my mouth. Great gouts of flame swirled into the black sky, the fire's steady roar a background for the frantic cries of trapped animals and the crackle of collapsing stalls, roofs, and offices. The volunteer firemen and their small engine were hopelessly outclassed. Arson was blamed for the forty-thousand-dollar loss, only one-fourth of it covered by insurance. A heavy blow was dealt the county's farm economy. I was sure I would never see the likes of this fire again, but five years later I watched wartime Manila burn, my all-time contact with the human urge for destruction.

Moving the subject from fire and destruction to Kentucky politics is a worthy move, yet some might argue that fire and destruction often marred commonwealth politics, citing Civil War times and the assassination of Governor William Goebel as examples. Others, such as James Hilary Mulligan attacked the issue in perhaps the most widely quoted lines of poetry from the commonwealth: "And politics—the damndest / in Kentucky," from his seven-stanza poem *In Kentucky* (1902). I can agree with his poetically made point, yet boyhood experience dictates that Kentucky politics walked a tightrope between grandest and damnedest. On any one day I might accept free textbooks from the state's largesse, but on the next witness votes being bought for half-pints of booze at "Mathias No. 1." Mathias No. 1?

It does a kid good to see his name bantered about town. Whenever there were elections I took pride in the many references to Mathias

No. 1 and Mathias No. 2. These were two of eighteen county voting precincts originally located in shops or businesses owned by Grandpa or Uncle Joe Mathias. Speck and I were unsure what precincts were, but we liked seeing the family name pop up at election time.

Politics came easily to children growing up in Kentucky's county-seat towns between the wars. The historian Robert M. Ireland tellingly labels the state's 120 counties as "little kingdoms." Before the passage of a judicial amendment to the state constitution in 1975, each of Kentucky's overabundant counties was headed by an elected county judge who wielded legislative, judicial, and executive powers—kingly authority indeed! In many ways, the commonwealth's governor was only first among equals in relation to these 120 judges. Moreover, nearly every governmental post was elective, thus any kid growing up in a county seat was forced either to fight, take sides, or lie as classmates' fathers vied for such posts as jailer, coroner, county surveyor, constable, justice of the peace, county clerk, county attorney, assessor (property evaluation administrator), and sheriff. By the time I was ten I had devised a shifty answer to this question: "Is your dad and mom gonna vote for my dad?" Stating a truthful "I don't know" never ended the matter. Instead, I learned to look my questioner in the eye and say, "They like you and your dad." That usually worked.

It was easier to evade commitment on local elections than on state or national ones. Local politicians could not afford to offend people they saw every day. But state and national elections brought the two parties into angry conflict over Depression realities, generating heated debate. More often, however, in strongly Democratic Nicholas County, it was that party's gubernatorial primary, or sometimes the conflict over a vacant senate seat, that embroiled the citizenry. And Albert Benjamin Chandler's name was usually involved in some distasteful way.

"Happy" Chandler became lieutenant governor under the colorfully named Ruby Laffoon in 1931. For years thereafter he was either governor or trying for a United States Senate seat. Happy was not liked in our house, Dad invariably referring to him as "Crappy Handler" or "Kentucky's little blabbermouth." Since he shared this opinion rather openly, he lost some customers along his route but replaced them with an equal number of Chandler haters. I imitated Dad, of course, thinking it was cute to call Happy "Crappy," never having learned that politics is the art of compromise. A lesson was on the way.

By 1938 my pal David Harper and I could remember standing on the courthouse steps and being patted on the head or shaking hands with such state politicians as Chandler, King Swope, Tom Rhea, Keen Johnson, John Young Brown Sr., and Alben Barkley. It was Chandler's 1938 attempt to oust Barkley from his Senate seat that led to the only fistfight I ever had with one of my best buddies. David Harper's parents were sold on Chandler and mine on Barkley. When Barkley appeared and spoke from the courthouse steps, Davey and I stood in line to shake his hand. As we walked away, Davey made some remark as to how he hoped Happy would put old Barkley in his place. I retaliated by noting that "Crappy" had sneaked aboard President Roosevelt's train so he could show off at every train station when the president spoke for Barkley. Before long I was calling Chandler a "blabbermouth," trying to offset Harper's repeated cries that "Barkley is a fleahead, fleahead, fleahead!" Fists flew, and when Pat Conley and some older boys stopped us, Davey had a bloody nose and I had a black eye.

Davey and I were on bad terms until the following Saturday afternoon, when both of us showed up at church to go to confession. He was in line ahead of me. When he came out he gave me the sort of look and headshake that signaled it was time to forgive and forget. A few minutes later the priest, Father John Danz, suggested the same thing. And from that time on, I never spoke ill of "Crappy Handler" to David, and he always referred to Senator Barkley with respect—at least I *think* he did.

My black eye had scarcely healed before I won a whopping five dollars for a student poster advertising the state PTA convention. I had drawn a balloon basket with two aviators aboard and angled down from an upper corner of the poster. One aviator had a telescope pointing down to Louisville, a tiny crosshatch on the earth's great curvature below. I printed words for him saying, "Look, Captain, everybody is going to the state PTA convention!"

Whether they went or not, I had the feelings of a man of wealth when the money arrived. It was my first payment from the broad world of art, but dreams of further posters and payments encountered a blank wall. I had no idea of what to do with my talent, for the school system lacked an art teacher who might have directed me. But I still had my music.

In 1939 I started playing sax with Bob Hughes and His Constipated Crew. The listeners who stuck this nickname on our band knew what they were talking about. Hughes was a likable store clerk and trumpeter in his thirties who hoped to form a dance band. He purchased several stock arrangements of such hit tunes as "So Rare" and "Imagination." The musicians fashioned typical desklike dance bandstands out of cardboard boxes. There were seven of us and we were optimistic.

Our optimism faded after a few rehearsals, and we would have admitted with Pogo the Possum (had he been of our era) that "we have met the enemy and he is us!" Jazz markings, syncopated rhythms, ad-lib slots, and much else caused musical confusion as we quickly learned that sight-reading concert band music in no way meant we could do the same to "The Dipsey Doodle" or "Southern Fried." I correctly felt we could work these things out, but most did not have my overwhelming desire to do so. Rehearsals dwindled to three kids: pianist and guitarist Emory Griffith "Griff" Asbury, drummer Bobby Cunningham, and me. Hughes faced the fact that Carlisle did not have the population, as did Maysville and Paris, to man a big dance band. We disbanded.

Our classmates laughed, some joking that the Constipated Crew had finally had a "movement." The laugh was on them, however, for Bobby, Griff, and I formed a trio and began playing for money at club and farmhouse dances. In keeping with an old musicians' joke, we may not have played very well, but at least we sounded bad.

Our first job—we had never heard of "gig" as musician slang for job—was a three-hour dance at the Paris VFW club. We had no contract nor did we set any price on our music. Cunningham kept a steady beat, and this satisfied the dancers. When the dance ended, the ticket-taker handed us a bag of coins. The lights dimmed as we poured them out on Bobby's drumhead. I watched greedily as they tumbled and rolled in a monetary manner around the smoothly stretched hide. A neon window sign reflected off the silver coins, turning them to gold. That matched my emotions exactly. Asbury counted them out, giving each of us about five dollars. This was a huge payment for the music we made, but greed overpowered any sense of guilt. We were elated and confident, and we set out to get more jobs.

Our next job was typical of a dozen or so farmhouse dances that followed. We found that farmhouse front doors nearly always opened into a stubby hallway with a big room on each side, with second-story stairs ascending about ten feet back from the entrance. We played loudly in these hallways, allowing dancers to use both rooms yet pass easily back and forth. Griff knew country music as well as swing, and I could play fifteen or twenty ballads and fox-trots. We played by ear and began singing as our confidence soared. This got laughs at times, for we were not much over five feet tall and blushed easily. My face reddened when told the meaning of the lyrics to "Careless Love," a song I often sang to Asbury's guitar background. To say we had confidence is an understatement. We played all requests whether we knew them or not, nor did it seem to make any difference. We received compliments for playing songs we had never heard of! Our pay averaged about six dollars a dance. We felt well paid, and we were.

Griff was a talented guitarist and pianist, and we became buddies, bound tightly by our music. When a dance was near his family's farm, I often spent the night there. Coming in from such a dance around midnight, we checked in with his mom, then rambled for an hour on moonlit Hinkston Creek to gig frogs or grab fish run up barricaded riffles. His mother set the frog legs jumping about the skillet for our breakfast next morning.

Before driving me back to Carlisle, Griff usually picked up his well-worn .22 rifle and challenged me to a shoot-out. Our targets were often sycamore balls high up in the great trees down by the creek. When hit, ripe ones explode into a puff of smokelike fuzz. I could hold my own with a lot of kids but never with Griff. He was the best shot I ever saw and a few years later proved his prowess by winning a major army rifle event at Camp Howze, Texas. I was at Fort Benning at the time. News of his victory brought back recent memories of us driving down nighttime country lanes, our .22 poking from under the raised windshield of his car as we plinked at rabbits scared out of the weeds into our headlights. But the world had changed immensely for both of since then. We were being taught how to kill men instead of rabbits.

Griff, Bobby, and I could not know that we were part of what was later called "the big band era." To us they were dance bands because they played for dancers and seldom for seated audiences. I had never closely observed a big dance band until the junior-senior prom of 1939. The dance was held in the gymnasium. Colorful crepe paper streamers combined with latticeworks of flowers and Japanese lanterns to change the gym, I thought, into a fairyland. Cornmeal was sprinkled on the hardwood floor to slicken it under the gliding feet of people who thought nothing of dancing for four hours. David Harper and I landed the "pop job," that of handing out soft drinks from an iced cooler. It paid one dollar each and all we could drink. We came early to get our stock in shape.

I looked up from loading the cooler to see black men walking into the gym. This "just wasn't done" at white dances, no matter that everyone knew that jazz had black birthrights. But these men were wearing tuxedos, carrying instrument cases, drums, cymbals, and music. Now I was elated and correctly assumed that the school had hired Smoke Richardson's well-known Lexington dance band. I marveled as they set up monogrammed stands, plugged in small lights on each, riffled through stacks of arrangements, and joked with each other. Next day I told everyone what a trumpeter said to the drummer: "If you don't quit picking on me I'm gonna stick a deaf mute in your ear!" I felt like a true musical "insider."

Richardson was an exuberant soul and led an easygoing group of musicians. The outside tenor sax man grinned with a big "OK" when I asked if I might stand beside him and watch him play. Davey also said "OK" so long as I did not stay away from the pop job too long. Dancers were now filing in, but I had trouble recognizing some of the girls in their evening gowns. They looked beautiful. I was fourteen years old and noticing such things. When the jovial leader kicked the band off, girls and pop took second place as I hovered beside the amiable sax man. I was amazed at his facility in reading the music and enthralled with how the band blended as a whole. Soloists popped up and took lengthy ad-lib solos, improvising as they played. I knew that "ad-lib" translated as "at liberty," but I had never seen it in action. Smoke took the mike and belted out the song that had become his trademark throughout the Bluegrass:

> Shake it and break it and hang it on the wall,
> Jump out the window and catch it when it falls!

By this time the gym was rocking. Scores of jitterbuggers crowded the floor as the band pumped out such killer-dillers as "Bugle Call Rag," "One O'clock Jump," "Roll 'em," "Muskrat Ramble," and "Perdido." Momentary calm came with "No-breaks," dances when stags could not cut in on couples. Sweaty jitterbugs ruled the floor, however, for most of the time after midnight. At 2:00 A.M. Richardson thanked the crowd for its applause and for being such good dancers. "Be careful drivin' home," he joked, "'cause most of the band is walkin'." He turned to his band and they played the final number. I am certain I was sadder to hear "Goodnight Sweetheart" than any of the dancers. It seemed that the best thing I had ever seen or heard was being taken away from me. I was at an age when parents, school, and town bored me beyond belief. Some kids ran away with carnivals, others with circuses, and some just plain ran away, but given the opportunity I would have hit the road that night with any dance band that would have had me!

The ball was over and Dave and I were left to pick up bottles, fold chairs, and help sweep the floor. Twenty 7–Ups were left in the cooler; we looked cautiously about, then sacked and smuggled them across the street to Harper's house. It was 3:30 A.M. "slow time," and dawn was breaking, giving light enough to hide the pop in Harper's low, back porch gutter. "This will keep 'the General' out of it," Dave said, using the nickname of his rambunctious younger brother, Charles. I walked home, climbed into bed with Speck, and quickly went to sleep in spite of a head ringing with the sound of Smoke's music.

Next day, while drinking our pop at Harper's house, Dave and I were discovered. Speck and the General demanded to know where the 7–Ups came from. We lied but still had to give them swigs out of our bottles. Suddenly the General pulled a .32 caliber automatic from his pocket. He had found where his dad had "hidden" it in a bedroom closet. Speck was seated on the toilet when the General walked up, aimed the pistol at him, and said with a laugh, "Let's shoot old Speck's dingus off!" Snap! went the gun's hammer, just as expected. But when Charles slid the automatic's barrel back to cock it, we were horrified when a bullet was ejected! We were stunned and speechless. I picked it up; the cartridge showed a hammer mark— it had been a dud, a one in a million chance! Charles, of course, had earlier removed the clip from the handle, not knowing that in a cocked automatic there is still a bullet in the chamber.

A mixture of politics and music eventually erased wistful memories of the Junior-Senior Prom and chilling ones of Speck's narrow escape. Keen Johnson easily defeated King Swope in Kentucky's 1939 gubernatorial race. The CHS Musketeer Band was among many invited to participate in the inaugural parade. This event introduced us to the colorful world of marching bands—big ones from Louisville, small ones like ours, bad ones, and high-stepping ones, but all in snazzy uniforms with rolling drums and blaring brasses. We played our way up the long mall to the state capitol, listened to speeches, then enjoyed a reward of punch, sandwiches, and cake. I was happy with music and no longer disturbed about my size and recent failure as a football player.

I lost out in football the same autumn Keen Johnson scored his victory. As an entering freshman, I was pressured into football even though I weighed less than ninety pounds. CHS was a small school in a powerful conference, and every male body, large and small, was at a premium. I dutifully "suited up" one September afternoon and trotted to the practice field with lads twice my size. I wore a loose leather helmet, ill-fitting shoulder pads and shoes, and bulky canvas pants. I kept telling myself that everything would be all right, but I was scared, and with good reason.

The coach put me in the line and the fullback ran over me in the first play. I was knocked out but revived after several minutes. I got back in the line and here came the same fullback. I was knocked out again. This time I did not shake off the impact. I stumbled around seeing things and trying to solve uninvited algebra problems in an addled mind. Recovery came the next day, and with it a valuable lesson: football was not for me. Music, not sports, would hereafter be my game. Even had I played (and survived), I would have played my last organized game when I was seventeen, but music offered lifelong personal participation. I owe Dick Long, that ferocious fullback, a song of gratitude, undoubtedly in the key of B-flat!

The sound of music was ever present during my high school years, whether in practice, parades, concerts, or contests. My most attractive concert and contest solo was "Estrellita," a haunting melody by Mexican composer Manuel Ponce. Frances Henry, my grade school "sweetheart," was by this time an accomplished pianist and my accompanist. We offered the song first at the CHS spring concert, then at the state regional music contest. The competition was fierce. Andy Clark, a Maysville saxophonist, undermined my shaky confidence as he played beautifully throughout his solo.

I was up next. Frances took her seat at the piano while I nervously stepped up on a small podium. The eyes and ears of the judges and audience were riveted on me, much to my discomfort. A daze enveloped me until the piano introduction forced me from myself to the job at hand. I played well. "He is rated superior," the judges wrote, "but needs wariness of a tendency to drift into jazz sounds." They were correct, but my jazz tendency was something I viewed with pride, not wariness. Most white music teachers, however, were leery of "emotional Negro music," and contest judges graded down on even a few too many "jazz sounds."

My dream of playing in a good dance band did not come true until my senior year, but I made many nice trips with the CHS concert and marching band. We traveled to out-of-town games, performing on the fields and playing on the sidelines. I played various solos in programs at the Lexington Veterans Hospital, the Masonic Orphans Home in Louisville, and numerous concerts in neighboring towns and high schools. That shiny little alto sax had become a "horn of plenty" for me as well as one of Nannie's best investments.

17

Camp Black Hawk and Carlisle Christianity

A bad day comes to everyone now and then, but few post an advance lookout against it by pinning down exactly its date on the calendar. I did. The worst of all days for me was Labor Day, the last day of summer vacation. I was usually swimming at Black Hawk with my buddies, and the sun was going down. The day was going to end. I wanted the good times to go on endlessly, so we could be free to swim and be pals forever. "Hey, Bobby, Steamboat; hey, Popeye, Davey, don't put your clothes on yet. C'mon, let's drop off the swing one more time!" But the waning sun went down right on schedule and the day did end.

The last day of summer vacation was good at teaching the timeless impartiality of life. I was sad, but my mind had to admit that everything, even life itself, must end. My heart, however, picked up the slack, urging that somehow these summertime boyhood vacations would keep repeating themselves forever; thus my pals and I would always have Black Hawk, the river, the good times, and each other. War came and hastened maturity, dampening and gradually extinguishing such romantic dreams.

Camp Black Hawk meant more to me as a high schooler than ever before. Although Scoutmaster Sapp retired in 1939, the year I entered high school, two good men took his place—Roger Womack and Hubbard Endicott—giving the same loosely structured yet able guidance so successfully employed by Sapp.

Black Hawk was near the center of a legendary (and prehistoric) Indian and pioneer area. Blue Licks was just down the river, and through the ages animals had licked at the one hundred acres of oozing salt and mineral springs. Huge prehistoric mastodon bones by the hundreds were uncovered here by paleontologists and placed with Indian and pioneer artifacts in a nearby museum in 1931. These springs were hosts to such noted pioneers as Christopher Gist, Simon Kenton, John Finley, George Rogers Clark, and Daniel Drake, all of whom paused here to make salt, much as countless Native Americans had for ages before them. But Blue Licks was also host to deadly turmoil. Daniel Boone was captured by Shawnee warriors while making salt at the springs in 1778. He eventually escaped but four years later returned to the springs as a participant in one of the most disastrous battles of frontier history.

The American Revolution halted but did not end at Yorktown. It dribbled to its end out on the American frontier. Skirmishes between the pioneers and the British and their Indian allies flared continuously west of the Appalachians. The British were hoping in this way to retain claims to the western country at the peace table. In early August 1782, Captain William Caldwell, a British officer commanding sixty Canadians and three hundred Wyandot warriors, attacked a pioneer fort in central Kentucky. When unable to overcome the defenders, the disgruntled force headed north along a buffalo trace soon to be known as Smith's Wagon Road, later as the Maysville Road, and finally as U.S. Route 68. They made no effort to conceal their tracks, and for good reason—an ambush was planned and laid at Blue Licks in the forest's edge above the gentle, open, northern slope of Licking River.

Meanwhile, a vengeful 180-man pioneer army was racing after them. Daniel Boone and his son Israel were with the force. When the frontiersmen gathered along the bluffs above Blue Licks, Boone was wary, advising caution before fording the river, but a few hotheads foolishly ran down the steep bluff and charged into the river, shouting and whooping and daring others to follow. Most did and were soon committed on the far side of the river. The trap was sprung when rifles blazed from the forest's edge, followed by 360 screaming Canadians and Indians wielding swords and tomahawks. The Kentuckians fought heroically as they retreated back across the river, losing seventy men to the enemy's ten. Israel Boone was among those killed, and he and others are buried in a mass grave at what is now a state park. We scouts at Black Hawk were proud to think that "the last battle of the American Revolution," as it is always called by local folks, took place just a whipstitch down the river from camp.

What happened after the pioneer and Indian epic at Blue Licks held but passing interest for my pals and me but bears mentioning. Early in the next century, many people began "taking the water" at the springs. In 1845 a three-hundred-room hotel was built to answer the demand. This successful antebellum spa attracted many Deep South planters and their families; it was as far north as they could come and safely bring their slaves. They came north, of course, to escape the deadly summer yellow fever epidemics that frequently wracked the Gulf States. The spa's success led to the opening of the short-lived Western Military Academy in 1847, notable only for having James G. Blaine on its staff as mathematics professor. He was later several times a candidate for the presidency, claimed by opponents to be "James G. Blaine, the continental liar from the state of Maine!"

As if having Lower Blue Licks was not enough, we also had Upper Licks, a one-hour canoe ride up the river. Near these mineral springs, on July 9, 1776, Daniel Boone's party rescued Betsy and Fanny Callaway and Jemima Boone from several Shawnee warriors. The girls had been abducted the day before near Boonesboro, leading Boone to an all-out effort to overtake them while still south of the Ohio River. He reasoned correctly that the Indians and their captives were using the well-known Shawnee trail leading from Kentucky's interior to Old Chillicothe. Upper Licks sits astride this trail. Little wonder that Camp Black Hawk worked an almost magical charm on its guests.

Scoutmaster Endicott often said, with truth, that "it's impossible for anyone to walk far in Nicholas County without stepping in Indian or pioneer footprints." But there were footprints in the smooth rock bottom of shallow Cassidy Creek that far predated the pioneers. A prehistoric man or woman left a startling line of human footprints easily visible across the bottom of one placid pool. Scouts freely fit their feet into the prints. Neither bears nor anything other than human beings made them, yet no one paid attention to our "tall tale," no matter who we told. "Children are to be seen, not heard," was the unspoken but implied reception to our discovery. Years went by until I was a postwar student in Professor Dan Hamilton's geology class at the University of Kentucky. He suggested I relocate and photograph the footprints, but modern technology had done in minutes what thousands of years had failed to do. Bulldozers had ripped up parts of the creek bottom, piling it along the banks to "prevent flooding." A tourist and scientific attraction of great value was forever destroyed.

Watermelons were more immediately attractive to boys than footprints anyway, and they were to be had for the stealing at Flora's Farm across the river from Black Hawk. The farm occupied several hundred acres of fertile bottomland in appropriately named Pleasant Valley. Earlie Flora grew many things, but along the low river bluff he usually put in a big crop of watermelons. He probably knew the Black Hawk boys were watching his melons ripen, but like any good farmer he trusted God with the weather and his own watchful eye for the safety of his watermelons.

Watermelon harvest time was near when James Henry "Red" Wade decided it was time to launch a raiding party against the watermelon patch. Seven or eight of us swam in the river. We sneaked up the weedy bank around noon, counting on the farmer being at dinner. No one was in sight. Red opened his pocketknife and began plugging melons, cutting out small dripping wedges to spot melons that were "just right." Before long we each had a big melon, leaving a dozen or more plugged ones behind. We pushed the bobbing melons before us as we swam slowly for the other side. A big voice suddenly boomed from the top of the bank behind us: "You boys have been stealing my melons; I've found a lot of them plugged and ruined!"

Each of us was by now sitting on a melon, treading water and easily holding it out of sight. Innocence marked our faces. Red looked most innocent of all and affected a bit of anger as he replied, "Why Mr. Flora, how can you accuse us of such a thing? We are honest and good boys. We would never think of. . . ."

Red's melon had gotten loose while he was making his speech, and it bobbed up in his lying face. The game was up and we began paddling furiously for the opposite shore. This caused Flora to shout all the louder: "Boy! Boys! Don't let the melons get away. Keep the dadblasted things. If you don't the whole pack of you will be back to plug and ruin another batch!" So we did, sitting down in a ravine out of sight of the scoutmaster. Red looked up, his florid, freckled face wet with melon, and grinned widely: "You know, fellers, I just don't know what we'd do without Mr. Flora." Red was to wind up watermelonless in the U.S. Navy!

Kentucky has more than its share of caves, and a half dozen or so are near Black Hawk. One of these, Coon Cave, is a walk-in cavern in the sloping hillside surrounding the camp area. Spring water running out of it was trapped for camp use in a cistern. Another cave is a drop-in cave, and a big one, on a hilltop overlooking Cassidy Creek. We entered by sliding down a rope, but once inside, the cave boasted a big cavern with a forty-foot ceiling. It also boasted abandoned thump barrels, tubs, and copper coils used by moonshiners. But the favorite cave was Hawkins Cave. It was a quarter-mile past the trestle and opened into a hillside near the railroad tracks. An outlaw named Hawkins gave his name to the cave and was said to have died in it from wounds inflicted by lawmen. Many believed his ghost was still there, guarding his dead body somewhere deep within the cave. Sometimes I believed this and sometimes I did not depending on how close I was to the cave. Hawkins's legendary status, however, was a sure attraction for boys in their teens.

Taking guests to Hawkins Cave was to Black Hawk etiquette as tipping one's hat to ladies was to street etiquette. I showed two Maysville lads, Clarence Moore and Glenn Mattingly, the honor of a cave jaunt. We squirmed through the thirty feet of tubelike entry passage, relieved finally to stand and shine flashlights around a bathroom-sized cavern. Names and dates were scratched into the smooth cavern walls. Not to be outdone, we scratched something on the walls, joked about Hawkins's ghost, laid back down, and squirmed our way out to the welcome sunshine.

I returned a year later to find that the cave's opening and inner narrow passage had collapsed into an impassable heap. No one the year before knew that my guests and I were in Hawkins Cave. Had we budged or unbalanced some crucial rock or support, Hawkins's ghost would have had eternal company!

Uncle Joe often said, but with a touch of envy in his voice, "There's just no tellin' what you boys do down there at that camp, and if I was you, I wouldn't tell nobody neither!" He was right. We never told of spelunking in the caves, or swimming in treacherous flood currents, or stealing watermelons, or splattering telephone-wire glass insulators with .22s, or of painting out the GR on SCRUBGRASS CREEK highway signs, nor did we even hint at our dangerous capers on the dizzily high railroad bridge we all called "the trestle." We generally operated on the rather perilous principle that what the scoutmaster did not know could neither hurt him nor us.

The trestle is a six-hundred-foot-long railroad bridge spanning the shallow confluence of Licking River and Fleming Creek. Stonemasons fashioned and formed its massive sixty-foot center pier, which supports a geometrically perfect latticework of girders and beams under the thick track deck—all of this together making a bridge one hundred feet high. It is a mid-nineteenth-century engineering masterpiece but a dangerous playground.

My trestle initiation, and that of my pals, was frightening. Pat Conley, Charles Sexton, and other older scouts herded us "tenderfeet" to see it, trotting boldly across gaps between the ties. These gaps offer walkers flickering and dizzying views of river, land, and treetops far below. Several of us panicked, dropped to our knees, and crawled from tie to tie. "I'll drop between the ties," I gasped to myself, "if I ever stand up on this thing!" We were laughed at but assured that crawling was OK the first time out, that we would soon be climbing all over the trestle like everybody else.

They were correct. A few days later I earned welcome praise by scooting out steel girders to help attach a lengthy rope swing. The riffle under the trestle was too shallow to drop into, but the swing's long, swift arc made it worthwhile. The great center pier's sloping, offset stone blocks made it easy to climb or descend, thus giving access to the latticework of steel beams. In addition, a worn wooden ladder offered easy stages and platforms between the pier and the track deck. Some lads lacked even a trace of acrophobia, trotting effortlessly along narrow horizontal girders and beams or even running the high beam alongside the entire length of the track deck. O.C. Seevers, son of a Methodist preacher, won our acclaim for this feat, and he had no serious rivals. The trains that occasionally puffed across the trestle only added to the fun, when leaky fireboxes showered hot coals, cinders, and sparks through the ties and past laughing boys swatting at them as they flashed by. Such episodes were eagerly awaited whenever distant whistles warned us of an approaching train.

Tragedy awaited a call one afternoon ten feet below the track deck. I lay on the sunny deck, watching the mounting drama through sun-warmed, creosote-scented ties. Three buddies had marooned themselves on the flat top of one of the high masonry arches supporting the south end of the bridge. They had jumped down onto the arch with no though of getting back. The only escape was by means of the next arch, from which one could easily move to solid ground. But the next arch was some ten feet away, too far to jump. The only connections between the arches are two continuous, ten-foot-high, welded steel walls that run the length of the south end of the bridge, providing cover and support to the track deck above. They are, in effect, giant I-beams, with horizontal flanges protruding six inches on each side at the bottom. Impatience won out over waiting for ropes and harness. The boys decided to use the six-inch-wide flanges to get to the next arch. Ralph Shearer coached from the "good" arch as Frank Reynolds began inching his way, spread-eagled with palms against the steel wall and fifty feet above a graveled path beneath. After a few feet he was able to leap the remaining distance to Shearer. Nate Young and Bill Hopkins followed in cat-like fashion, their every move thoughtfully correct. I was dry-mouthed and bug-eyed by the time Shearer grabbed Hopkins. Hop escaped this peril only to be killed in action four years later in France with the Ninety-first Infantry Division.

Black Hawk's value to Nicholas County youth extended far beyond shenanigans with watermelons, trestles, and caves. For boys there was total freedom of expression. Twelve- to eighteen-year-old boys annually had a chance to mix, learn, compete, compare, and grow with new and old friends of all ages, instead of "old shoe" buddies. Girls and sex, for example, occupied ever-expanding space in our thoughts as each year came and went.

Deeply felt needs, wild and wooly jokes, off-color stories, and rolling on the ground gasping with laughter—things a boy could neither ask, do, nor tell parents or girlfriends—were all OK with buddies. Admittedly dirty jokes, such as "Johnny Rule," "The Old Log Inn," "Our Gal Lil," and "The Night of the King's Corona-tion," were recited year after year, always brand new to recently ini-tiated scouts. Beyond this silliness, however, were shared experiences and insights. Parents came up for comparison, most coming off bet-ter than expected by ever more critical sons. Genuine tolerance was offered any boy who did his best, no matter his failures. It was a time and place that gave lads a chance to develop confidence in themselves, not from any planned scouting structure or from Black Hawk, except as a setting for the annual drama; instead, they some-how bubbled up through the Christian atmosphere that pervaded the community.

One could almost attend church in Carlisle simply by being there. In addition to Sunday and weekday services, there were weekly prayer meetings, Bible studies, revivals, and camp meetings; church-sponsored clubs, sports, and youth groups; Masonic lodge and East-ern Star activities, Christmas and Easter pageants, and choral groups; midnight mass, various Catholic devotions throughout the liturgi-cal year, a continual stream of visiting religious lecturers and musi-cians; denominational picnics, wiener roasts, fish fries, and hayrides; interdenominational meetings and prayers in support of Prohibition and later of our troops in World War II; and much else, all of which was faithfully and accurately reported in the town's superb weekly newspaper.

Biblical names and phrases were part of everyday language: "He thinks he can walk on water," "She's a Jezebel," "He's a Jonah," "My cup runneth over," "Grandpa's as old as Methuselah," or "Woe be unto you" (if you do so and so). Biblical information was always present. A playmate caught my attention when he told me the shortest sentence in the Bible was "Jesus wept." I have never seen any reason to doubt this. Nannie never tried to keep up with her Protestant friends in quoting from the Bible, but she often won points with pertinent quotes from other sources, such as this one from G.K. Chesterton: "The Bible tells us to love our neighbors, and also to love our enemies; probably because they are generally the same people."

A foreign observer might at first glance think a superficial religious busyness ruled instead of deeper convictions. He would be wrong. The main purpose of each church was to inculcate some denominational theology and lead its members toward a righteous way of life. All churches agreed that breaking one of the Ten Commandments or a law of the land was a sin. Beyond this there often was no general agreement on what constituted a sin. One church permitted its members to play cards; others did not. Close dancing was anathema to one, while any kind of work on Sunday was to another. Eating meat on Friday was sinful for me, while drinking wine or beer was for some of my friends. These differing views sometimes led to bickering, but love of neighbor was seldom in doubt. It was a safe county and town. One could go unafraid anywhere, for abstract, impersonal violence was unknown. "Baptist measure" was a practice of many merchants, but one scrupulous soul drove several miles into town to return thirty cents to my dad, the amount he had inadvertently overcharged him for some groceries earlier in the day. "I just couldn't live with it, Lucky," he said, probably feeling free for the first time since realizing his error. The community, of course, was in no way free of sin, but it was identified for what it was and never excused as part of some "alternate lifestyle."

My pals and I were either Protestant or Catholic because we were born that way. In later life some went in different directions, but at the time I simply accepted the church for what I thought it to be. When Saint John's church bell rang, I joined the small, mostly Irish congregation for Sunday mass, a service in celebration of the Eucharist. Speck and I were told to sit upright, not pick at anything, and pay attention to the gospel reading and the sermon. I usually managed this for the first part of the hour-and-a-half ceremony, then my mind wandered.

Artwork and donors' names on the stained-glass windows were always good for a weekly inspection. After this I examined the heads and hats of people in nearby pews. I wondered then as now why old men often have hair growing out of their ears. Warts, freckles, and birthmarks on necks and ears were studied for a moment, but women's hats were a godsend for my restless eyes. Had I known of Saint Paul's admonition that females cover their heads in church, I would have been greatly in his debt. Some hats resembled aviator helmets, while others sprouted feathers like Tarzan's jungle birds, and still others flashed with beads or drooped with fur or fruitlike appendages. Women who had forgotten their hats sat stolidly through mass with handkerchiefs pinned in their hair.

My most exciting mass moment harkened back to the shenanigans of poet Robert Burns's famed louse: "How daur ye set your fit upon her—Sae fine a lady!" But this involved a large and aggressive yet nervous blue wasp. The thing flew in through an open window and settled ever so gently atop Margaret Conway's pretty blue straw hat. Margaret, a jovial young woman and family friend, was seated in front of me but separated by a vacant pew. My eyes popped wide as the malevolent looking creature sat there, its abdomen pulsing up and down like a pump handle. Suddenly it flew down to her collar, darting back and forth and making quick turns, like an excited trial lawyer during a courtroom climax. I was almost hypnotized by the shiny blue movement of the beast yet fully aware that if Margaret felt something touch her neck or hair and slapped at it, mass would come to a screeching halt! The wasp, however, tired of her collar, lit for a moment on her shoulder, then with what I was certain was divine intervention, flew back out a window, significantly the one inscribed as donated in years past by "The B.T. Conway Family."

Humor frequently entered the service; at least most of us thought of it that way. The choir could usually tell how it was doing by watching elderly Eunice Porter. She stuck an index finger in each ear and glared at them when they were not singing up to her standards. The same Irishman who threw the men down the saloon steps was not above setting off an alarm clock in church when he deemed the sermon had outworn his patience. Unlike our Protestant neighbors, we could not dismiss the minister, but there were times our priest probably wished we could. Lucky was also a source of humor. After the sermon it was his duty to take up the collection in a long-handled basket. A well-off farmer, who was noted for his miserly ways, invariably dropped no more than a dime into the basket. Lucky never wavered but stood the Lord's ground by nudging the miser with the basket until he coughed up another dime or two. Those nearby relished this weekly interplay.

Kids love events that everyone in church notices yet cannot admit noticing—like breaking wind. Jokes supposedly centered on Confucius, the great Chinese philosopher, abounded during the 1930s. Every kid in Carlisle knew them, especially liking the pun in this one: "Confucius say: 'He who fart in church sit in own pew!'" One Sunday Speck and I were sitting with the Harper and Woodall boys when one of us broke wind loudly. Confucius immediately came to life as suppressed giggling overtook every kid in church and lasted for the rest of the mass.

There was more to church than Sunday school and sermons. There were picnics, Easter egg hunts, parties, and programs. Like the other churches, ours had a women's auxiliary that gathered clothes for the needy and conducted bake sales and other projects to raise money for the parish. Christmas was a wonderful Christ-centered time of worship, carols, treats, and love. As a high schooler, I went with others out to B.T. "Batty" Conway's farm to size, cut, transport, set up, and decorate a large bank of cedar trees around the crib scene for midnight mass. Protestant friends filled the church for this colorful service.

The Catholic church appealed to me in ways not fully shared by friends and family. There was a streak in me akin to Edwin A. Robinson's "Miniver Cheevy," who ignored the present and longed for the days of old. Unlike Miniver, I recognized the difference, but the Latin, the liturgy, the incense, the wonderful Gregorian chants, the vestments, and the mass lifted my mind and soul with the beauty and continuity of it all. "Here I sit," I often thought, "in a tiny Catholic congregation in a Kentucky village, yet I can actively participate in a language, music, rituals, and dress handed down over many centuries." I suspect I was destined to be a historian all along. It ran deeper than that, however, for old Aunt Mary.

Mary Furlong, my great-aunt, was a woman of solid faith. She was born in Maysville in 1858, the daughter of Irish immigrant parents. Mary remained single and earned her living as a cook. Later in life she often said she had spent her earthly journey "working in rich people's kitchens." Nevertheless, Mary had a dream; she set herself the goal of buying a side altar for Saint Patrick's church. She saved pennies, nickels, and dimes toward her goal. Mary died in 1941, and her will bestowed two thousand dollars for the purchase of "a marble side altar." This much money would have purchased three new Chevrolets that year.

Mary's two thousand dollars lay in a Maysville bank accumulating interest for thirty-three years. When the church was remodeled in 1974, Mary's lovely side altar was installed. Her gift had more than doubled to five thousand dollars by this time. Saint Patrick's is justly noted for its magnificent stained glass windows, but there may well be a more telling symbol of faith sitting demurely as a side altar in this elegant church.

My brother and I were exposed to various Christian viewpoints as we matured. Grandma Furlong converted when marrying, but her Browning side of the family attended Mount Carmel Christian Church. In addition, two uncles and an aunt were mainline Protestants. This seemed normal to me and perhaps strengthened my Christian outlook by making me consider the ins, outs, and realities of loving one's neighbors as one's self.

We occasionally visited Mount Carmel Cemetery to decorate the graves of numerous relatives. One afternoon an elderly cemetery worker started a conversation with Dad. "Where yuh from?" he asked.

"Carlisle," Dad replied.

"Is that near Flemingsburg?" he inquired, a studious squint in his eyes.

"Well, it's twenty miles the other side of Flemingsburg, about twice as far as Flemingsburg is from here."

"That a fact! I was in Flemingsburg once; Maysville too, some years back." This puzzled the traveling salesman in Dad.

"You were only in those towns one time; is that what you're saying?"

"Yep I seen 'em. One time was enough for me. Didn't see no call to go back. Outside of them two I've stayed right here in Mount Carmel."

"Well, I'll be damned!" Lucky said slowly but loudly before Mom could hush him up.

18

Maysville on My Mind

Going alone to Maysville for a summer stay with kinfolks meant getting scrubbed and packed, with repeated warnings from Mom to "behave yourself and act like you've got some gumption." She sent me on the way with a kiss the first time when I was six years old.

Each summer I walked to the depot, carrying a small carpetbag with two weeks' worth of clothes. I averaged about fifty cents in spending money and, until up in grade school, always had a little sign pinned to my chest: "Frank Furlong Mathias to Maysville, c/o J.B. Furlong, 125 E. 5th Street." Dad, Mom, and Speck nearly always drove down to pick me up two weeks later. I also carried a big load of excitement within, for Maysville meant fun with many cousins and a much bigger town to explore. It meant lying cozily in bed listening to what I called "Maysville night music"—distant steamboat foghorns and lonesome C&O train whistles echoing up and around the tall Ohio River bluffs. There was just something good about Maysville; even the clocks were set an hour faster than those in Carlisle. I did not understand why this was but believed it must be in Maysville's favor.

Keenly sensing the freedom of the trip, I arrived early at the depot, getting down on all fours with an ear on the track, hoping to hear the strange noiseless noise a distant train makes. I had learned this from movies and knew it worked. By this time, Uncle Joe had arrived and added another "piece of money," as he called it, to my pocket. Suddenly the engine came into view through a cut a half mile away, the whistle blowing as it quickly loomed nearer, puffing by with its bell ringing as it ground to a halt in a cloud of steam and smoke. I picked up my bag and scrambled aboard.

Sometimes the two well-worn passenger cars had velvetlike seat coverings, but in the summer they usually sported woven cane creations. Either way, cinders left a gritty feel under one's hand. I was so little the conductor patted my head as he took my ticket, but seeing my name on the sign always brought the same question: "Are you kin to Joe Mathias?" When I said he was my uncle, I was rewarded with a smile and some story involving him and his friends on the L&N. I fancied the conductor took special care of me after that, but he usually had little else to do, for few passengers were ever with me on the twenty-eight-mile trip to Maysville.

The Maysville trip boosted my desire to be an engineer when I grew up. The tracks wind through clean green farmland with miles of rock fences and tree-shaded brooks, a Kentucky Bluegrass land Winston Churchill once said "looked more like England than England." A major attraction for me was the usual stop at Black Hawk to shove off a hundred-pound block of ice and several cases of pop for Scoutmaster Sapp. It seemed unquestionably normal that a three-hundred-ton passenger train should stop to unload just two dollars worth of freight. I thoughtlessly hung from a cinder-scarred window shouting at pals as they ran up to inspect the train. Others crawled inside a culvert so they could later brag that "the train ran over us!"

After the train chugged away from Black Hawk the hogger poured on the steam, picking up speed as we crossed the trestle, then made his whistle moan as we bore down on Tunnel Hill. Here two tunnels burrow deeply under the steep Nicholas/Fleming County border. Scouts hiked through them occasionally and safely, always on the heels of a passing train. The conductor ordered windows shut against smoke and cinders and turned on lights as we roared for a quarter-mile through the first tunnel. The next one is too short to make much difference, but taken together the tunnels were a highlight of the trip. Twenty minutes later the train began its sloping descent down and through Maysville's river bluffs to the big river and the depot. I had arrived!

The three-block walk to Grandma's house was a happy one. I knew I was halfway when I passed the Windmill, a Plum Street bar and restaurant. It looked like schoolbook windmills, its big "propellers" turning lazily. I held it in high regard, loving it as a symbol of my annual summer vacation. Soon I was trotting down Fifth Street, speeding up when I saw Granny on her porch awaiting me. After a hugging and kissing I unpacked for what was always my best vacation of the year.

The two-story frame Furlong house had features holding the fancy of grandchildren. J.B. and Elizabeth had quit active farming in 1916, bought the house, and moved to town. The house faces to within twenty feet of the street, but a high stone barrier shields the structure's rear from the steep hillside rising above it. The deep, shady, secretive ten-foot gap between the house and this wall became a cherished children's play area. Moreover, one could enter a second floor back door by crossing a dinky wooden bridge spanning the gap or use it to drop water or gravel on kids playing below. The door opened into Grandpa's bedroom, originating a tiptoe adventure of sneaking by him if he was taking his afternoon nap. If awakened, the big Irishman roared like a lion, sending the guilty kid flying and squealing into the hall and down the stairs.

I got a second hug and kiss when Aunt Lillian came home from her work as a public health nurse. She was the youngest and perhaps a shade the prettiest of the six Furlong girls. Lil was Maysville's beauty queen in a 1930s festival. I proudly watched her leading the parade as she sat high above a truck, the entire vehicle disguised as the billowing skirts of her gorgeous gown.

Lil had more going for her than beauty. She was witty and vivacious, with a marked ability to listen to, and empathize with, people of all ages. I could always confide in Lil, for she never "carried tales." And of importance to me, she was always "up to date." Aunt Lil was able to chat about things meaningful to me, whether the latest toys and games, my music, or later my heartfelt problems with girls and growing up. But a better judge than I wrote the following words to Lil in 1934: "May you ever keep young with the spirit of youth. Don't let it die." The note, which I have, is signed by Jesse Stuart, on his way to becoming one of Kentucky's and the nation's leading poets and novelists. A few years later Lil married Dr. Oliver Morris Goodloe, Maysville's health officer and a man matching her in good-humored vitality. Lil and Ollie later moved to Columbus, Ohio, where he served two decades as city health commissioner. But no matter where she was, or who she was with, or how many years piled up, Lil managed to "keep young with the spirit of youth," just as Jesse Stuart understood she should. She was the "Auntie Mame" of my boyhood, a kindred spirit offsetting "old-fashioned" parents, and a beloved and trusted friend.

Out of some forty cousins, my favorite was easygoing Walter Elrod Hines Jr. Anytime I arrived in Maysville, I phoned Walter. Since I had to stay a respectable number of days at Grandma's, "Doc," as he was called after his dentist father, always came over to Fifth Street. We laid plans for the days ahead, two of which nearly always involved the world-class river on our doorsteps.

A few yards out from Maysville's concrete boat landing are three large piers. They stand in a row, providing ice and anchorage protection for steamboats, barges, and other craft. Most every boy in town knew that steel ladderlike steps were embedded in the piers, and once on top a ten- or fifteen-foot dive or jump, depending on the river's dam-controlled height or "stage," was the exciting reward. Sewage, not chemicals, polluted the Ohio of the 1930s, but if I could drink Brushy Fork's nasty water at home, I was not likely to show concern for toilet paper and related items drifting by the piers, especially when such good times beckoned.

"We're going downtown," Doc and I shouted to Grandma as we headed for the front door. She walked out of the kitchen, drying her hands on her apron as she inspected us. "All right," she nodded. "Enjoy yourselves, but don't go near the river; hear me?"

"Yes, ma'm," we replied in unison, yet with nothing on our minds but the fun and excitement awaiting us in the forbidden river.

That's not quite true, however, for we usually detoured a block to Carl Bauder's toy shop before going on to the river. Carl was a delight in himself, meeting new and unsuspecting customers with a big smile and a handshake. As often as not, Bauder had his left thumb stuck in a light socket, and when he shook hands a startling trickle of electricity gave the customer a hair-standing surprise and a laugh from the expectant observers. He caught me this way and later with a buzzer hidden in the palm of his hand.

Tricks or not, Bauder knew his business. When Gene Autry cap pistols suddenly soared into every boy's consciousness—they closely resembled the Colt .44s used in the Old West and in cowboy movies—Carl had them before anybody. I knew this, but I was stuck in Carlisle. I wrote Aunt Lil in desperation to get me one, placing a quarter in the envelope to pay for it. She not only filled my order but mailed it to me, sensing as usual my state of mind. When I opened the package and saw that pearl-handled six-shooter, Lil climbed even higher on my list of favorite aunts. I quickly became the openly acknowledged envy of every cowboy and Indian east of the Carlisle courthouse.

Walter and I always left Bauder's with somewhat the feeling of scholars who have exhausted a subject through careful research. Toy weaponry, model planes, trains, games, and gimmicks had passed our inspection, but since we seldom had money for purchases, we sighed and continued on our way to the river. We sighed again as we passed Traxel's, a confectionery of wondrous sodas and sundaes that ranked just below Bauder's in our confident estimation of important places. Soon we skipped along Front Street, with the mighty river in full view across the Chesapeake and Ohio tracks. We were in "Maysville-before-the-Floodwall," a town with a magnificent river literally on its doorstep, but in less happy times, in its houses.

Doc and I emerged from a short passage under the railroad tracks and stood by the river. We never thought of bringing bathing suits, not so much that they would have revealed our intention, but that we never used them. We stripped to our BVD underwear and swam to the nearest pier. Once on top, we sat soaking in the sun, like two content turtles on a log. The huge suspension bridge loomed majestically a few hundred yards east of us. Other boys, some known and some unknown, but as irresponsible as ourselves, joined us. Conversation was never a problem.

"Look at that catwalk up under the bridge," said Boy 1. "I'll bet it's a good hunderd feet up there! Nobody'll ever get to it but painters or cops."

"Naw," said Boy 2, "my own big brother sneaked up there on it last week; said it took spit an hour to reach the ground!"

"Phooey!" said Boy 3, butting into the conversation. "It don't take spit no hour to reach the ground even from the tiptop of the bridge; besides, it would hit the water first, jist like me," he shouted, diving into the river as Boy 2 pretended to throw a punch at him.

All of us followed him into the river, glorying in the big hollow-sounding splashes and the appeal of a gang. We were soon back on the pier discussing a new subject—the *Island Queen*. By this time we had learned first names. "Boy, oh boy," gasped Andy, still breathing hard from the climb up the pier. "Did you all get down here last Tuesday and see the *Island Queen*?"

"Gollee, did I!" Wayne cried. "I wouldn't have missed that steamboat for anything. I stood outside listening to that Cincinnati dance band—didn't cost me a cent. I wish I could play as well as that drummer."

I was all ears now that music and dance bands had come up. "What band was it?" I asked. "Who do they play for?"

"I ain't sure whether it was Barney Rapp or Clyde Trask," Wayne said, "but boy were they smooth. They had a trumpet man that even blew better than 'Rats' Moore here. Don't you know that the *Island Queen* runs dance excursions up and down the river?"

"Well I reckon my Aunt Lil told me something about it, but I never paid close attention," I said, wishing now I *had* paid close attention.

"I guess I know your Aunt Lil," Glenn said, entering the conversation. "She's the prettiest health nurse in town and I really like her. Miss Furlong gave me my typhoid shots last month," he said, adding that his full name was Glenn Mattingly.

Andy, not having had his say-so regarding the *Island Queen*, interrupted, leaving Glenn and his shots behind. "I just up and walked aboard the *Queen* when it was here last month. Know what?" he asked with humor in his voice. "The dance floor is higher on both ends than it is in the middle, sort of like a sway-backed horse. The band was tuning up and I wanted to listen, but they spotted me and kicked me out."

We broke up several hours later. I envied them the big river, especially the excursion boats. Mattingly walked with us as far as his dad's Commerce Street grocery, then extended a welcome invitation: "If you two wanna go surfin' with Charlie Bramble, Sammy Whitaker, and me, meet us at my home, noon Saturday."

"Great idea!" Doc replied. "Frank's never done that. See ya Saturday."

Next day I moved into Doc's home in the midst of a crowd of pubescent boys, most of whom were ogling "dirty books" in the backyard garage. Doc's dad was a thriving local dentist blessed with a personality that won him high office in various veterans and fraternal societies and required him to keep many records, initiation regalia, and related items in his home. An ill-hidden "related item," discovered by my cousin, was a box of the small, paper-covered, pornographic booklets that occasionally turned up in men's clubs of the era. Each booklet featured drawings of imagined sexual adventures of particular newspaper cartoon characters: Betty Boop, Maggie and Jiggs, Tillie the Toiler, Jungle Jim, Smilin' Jack, and even Popeye and his stick-figured girlfriend, Olive Oil. Although not nearly as explicit as modern "soft porn" magazines, they were seen as "hot stuff" between the wars and definitely so by the cluster of lads noisily passing them back and forth in Hines's garage. We attracted unwanted attention. Pecolia, the African American maid, told my Aunt Alma what was going on. She walked in on us, calmly collected the evidence, and sent everyone home.

Uncle Doc and Aunt Alma were a jovial and gregarious couple, fully active in Maysville's social whirl. Their redheaded son, George, completed the family. He was five years younger than Walter and me and tacitly ignored as a nuisance. The maid, Pecolia, was a lovable household fixture during the 1930s. In short, it was a very pleasant place to visit.

Saturday broke hot and steamy, ideal for what we had in mind. We invited Doug Carpenter, a next door pal, and headed for Glenn's place. He lived on Cottage Street, a short street ending at the river beach. Glenn and the others met us as we came down the street, and within minutes the six of us were in the river.

The Ohio is a third of a mile wide here, and for most of that distance it flowed no more than chest deep over a fine, sand bottom (higher postwar dams have increased this depth). We waded far out before encountering the deep channel near the Ohio side. Federal dredges regularly worked the channel to maintain sufficient depth for commercial craft. This meant that steamboats, barges, and all heavy craft came pounding through this one, long, deep channel. Our gang eagerly awaited each one, for that is what "surfin'" was all about. Waves higher than our heads were sent rolling across our shallow side of the river by big steamers like the *Gordon C. Green, Avalon,* and *Island Queen.* Almost any commercial craft pushed out waves we rode for many yards, as lightly as the sun-flecked foam itself. I was forced to admit, to myself of course, that even Black Hawk and the trestle had nothing to match this!

We occasionally tempted the river by swimming across to an upriver beach on the Ohio side, one much nearer the dam. We thought of the river as our friend, but the river was impartial, of course, and sometimes offered no second chances. Andrew Clooney Jr., a boy about my age I possibly met but do not remember, drowned in the river not long after returning from World War II. He was Rosemary Clooney's half-brother and an uncle to George.

As if to spite our friendly river, Walter, Doug, and I devoted some Saturday afternoons to movies at the Hollywood. The Russell had the first-run movies, but we liked the fare at the Hollywood much better. And we got more for our fifteen cents. There was always a double and sometimes a triple feature, with a Three Stooges or Laurel and Hardy comedy, a Flash Gordon or Buck Rogers serial, a newsreel, and a preview of coming attractions. Even better there was audience participation, with loud booing of the cowboy in the black hat and riotous nyuck, nyuck, nyucking with Curly's laugh whenever he got the best of Larry or Moe.

By the time the last feature was under way, the audience's attention was in tatters. This was often the time several well-kidneyed boys paraded to the rear aisle and peed under the last seats of each of the four outer rows. Confederates followed each stream as it ran down the sloping concrete floor and out the gutter fronting the first row seats. The winner got nothing but the glory. This was probably the reason ushers closed the Saturday afternoon session by hosing down the floors and wooden seats, sending the residue flowing out the gutter and into the sewer, eventually piddling itself into the mighty Ohio, just two blocks to the north.

The first whale I ever saw did not swim to Maysville in the Ohio River but arrived first class, by train. Widespread promotion of a "genuine whale" on a flatcar baited Dad into driving the family down for a view. "He's a big rascal, ain't he, Mother!" a man exclaimed to his wife as Dad paid extra so we could move up close. I wondered why the man said that to a woman the same age as he was. Unfortunately, the whale was not nearly as big as its smell. It stunk up the entire railroad siding. Perhaps the embalming fluid had worn off or somehow shriveled away, like parts of the skin. The huge mouth, safely and widely propped open, seemed to be the source of the smell, as if the dead beast had supernaturally developed a live case of halitosis.

Nannie's brother-in-law Simon Clarkson emerged from the crowd, getting a warm welcome from us. Uncle Simon was as interested in the whale as Dad. When Mom, Speck, and I refused to get any closer to the smelly mammal, Dad and Simon made fun of us: "They think that fish is gonna bite 'em," Simon said. With this the two of them walked up closer, but suddenly stiffened and stepped back. "The whale seemed to move," Dad said later, "then that damned cat ran out!" A big tomcat, the same color as the whale, had moved under a loose flap of skin, giving the impression that life had reclaimed the rotting corpse. Mom laughed harder than any of us. "Well, smarty," she chortled, "next time you complain about not catching anything, just bait your hook with a tomcat!"

"I will if you'll cook it!" Dad laughed.

"That's tellin' 'er Lucky," Simon said.

Simon Clarkson worked bankers' hours for thirty-eight years at the State-National but finished each day working on his farm with his wife, four sons, and two daughters. A minor league pitcher in his youth, he sometimes viewed life's obstacles as if they were enemy batters facing him at the plate. His life was devoted passionately to four "teams": his family, the Cincinnati Reds, the Odd Fellows, and the Democratic Party. He and Doc Hines were Lucky's favorite brothers-in-law. Coon hunting was a happy pastime for these three during the Roaring Twenties. They treed a coon one night with Hines aiming his shotgun while Clarkson spotlighted the beast. Doc just stood there, however, aiming his gun. Finally, Lucky's skimpy patience gave out. "What th' hell are you waitin' on Doc? Shoot him! We ain't askin' you to pull his teeth." And Doc shot him.

Following my Maysville visits, I always spent a country week with the Clarksons. Everyone worked hard on that farm, and I did my best to fit in with Aunt Pauline and my cousins. I was not much at milking cows, but I set out tobacco plants and forked hay high up into the barn on suffocatingly hot summer afternoons. But we kids could knock off whenever the huckster truck was due, running down a rocky lane to Taylor's Mill Pike to meet it. This traveling store was a welcome sight to farm families. Sweet-smelling shelves of spices, candy, household gadgets, and hardware filled me with a sense of greedy discovery, as if such an appetizing thing had never before materialized on a lonesome country road. I was a town boy, and a week in the country had primed me for such a discovery. Cousin Alma, the oldest daughter, shopped for whatever her mother needed, but she always bought us some candy from the huckster: jelly beans, licorice sticks, B-B Bats, chocolate drops.

This is not to say that Uncle Simon did not shop in town, bringing needed items home after his day at the bank. He drove in one afternoon, his Hudson packed with day old penny-per-loaf bakery bread. Simon helped his wife unload the bread, which she would use to feed her chickens. The unloading stopped short when Aunt Pauline suddenly waved a half-empty whiskey bottle in her husband's face. "Simon," she said sternly, "look what I found under the seat; where did you get this?" Everyone knew that Pauline had nothing good to say for liquor.

Poor Simon was beside himself; he honestly did not know where the thing came from. His son Jimmy and I had been with him and he called on us to verify his innocence, which we did. But he was not really off the hook until his next stop at the bakery. "Simon," one of the bakers asked, "what did Pauline say when she found that booze under your front seat?"

Uncle Simon had a farmer's eye for the interrelation of all living things; he was an ecologist before the word was much in use. He caught Bobby and me one day just after we had killed three little barn owls in their hollow-tree nest. We were unable to tell him why we did it, so he forced us to sit until we came up with an answer. He was furious, and in our hearts we knew there *was* no answer, therefore our words left him cold. "You two might as well have turned five hundred rats and mice loose in the corn crib as killed those owls," he said, a helpless, hopeless tone to his voice. He shook his head and went on to work, leaving his son and me guilt-ridden but still with no idea as to why we did it. "Never again," we vowed, and I never did.

The only unpleasant thing about visiting the Clarksons' was sleeping with Bobby. Bobby wet the bed. Everybody offered thoughts on "housebreaking" him: no liquids after supper, no spicy foods, and never upset him emotionally at bedtime. We even joked about staging a wet-dry election and voting him dry. But feeling a puddle in the center of the rubber sheet told me another touted cure had failed. "Oh no, not again," I whispered in the dark, now wide-eyed and serenaded by pot-racking guineas outside. But as a grade schooler it took more than a puddle of pee in the bed to keep me awake. A year or two later, Bobby dried up for good.

One hot dry day in late summer of 1940, I was standing with Uncle Simon beside his stock pond. He was about to give me a lesson in one-party political loyalty, but neither of us knew it. "Damn it, Frank," he complained. "It's rained on every side of my farm this month, but not here—just look at it raining over there to the east. We're not likely to get any of that."

I agreed with him as I looked at the brown grass and parched, cracked earth. He seemed blue, so I thought I might get his mind off the drought by bringing up politics. "Uncle Simon," I ventured, "a lot of people over in Carlisle say Willkie will beat Roosevelt because nobody wants a president past two terms. Who do you think will win?"

Simon's face suddenly became dark as the rain clouds to the east. His voice shimmered with passion: "If we Democrats go down, we'll sure as hell go down fighting!" He suddenly picked up a clod and punctuated his statement by blasting a stick out in the pond with the easy accuracy I had come to expect from this old pitcher. I was on his side now, sensing the thrill of politics in spite of my fifteen years. Uncle Simon would have had my vote no matter what he was running for, and President Roosevelt became even more of a hero to me than before.

Uncle Simon and I strolled back to the house to find my newest uncle, Dr. Ollie Morris Goodloe, waiting to drive me back to Grandma's, then on to Carlisle. He was going to a medical meeting in Lexington and had called Mom, offering to drop me off at home, thus saving Dad a trip. Goodloe had married Aunt Lil a few years before, quickly becoming a family favorite. He was a gifted physician but, like Lil, also a tolerant yet shrewd judge of people, qualities that took him from his Paducah birthplace to several high posts as a public health official.

I kissed Grandma good-bye and settled down in the soft front seat of Uncle Doc's new Olds. I had no inkling I was starting my life's most unforgettable ride. "I'll have you home in under thirty minutes," Doc said, as the tires on the big Olds screeched around the multiple U curves winding up the high bluff from Maysville and the river. "Just listen to that hydramatic purr!" he exclaimed, pushing the speed into the eighties as we raced south. Doc loved speed. By this time I had both hands on the dashboard, peeking cautiously across the hood as the lumpy, curvy highway, built originally over an ancient buffalo trace, disappeared with alarming speed under our wheels. Doc passed everything on the road with abandon, laughing and chatting for most of the thirty miles.

By the time we reached Blue Licks I had shifted emotional gears and was happily racing along with Doc. Nothing before had equaled this overpowering adventure; how could I ever have put up with the crummy forty-five-mile-per-hour speeds Dad always drove?

When we pulled into Carlisle, under thirty minutes out of Maysville as Doc had promised, I had the feeling of a successful pony express rider. I told Uncle Doc how older lads, like Andy Metcalfe, celebrated New Year's at midnight in Maysville, which was on "fast time," then sped back to Carlisle to do it all over again. "I'll bet you and I could outrun them all," I bragged, wondering why Mom, now listening to the details of the ride, stared at Doc and me with anger in her eyes. The odds, be it said, were never to catch up with this fast-flying physician who lived a long life with never even a bent fender!

While Doc Goodloe and I whizzed along U.S. 68 in August 1940, World War II was about to enter its second year, with five more to go. France had succumbed quickly to the Nazi juggernaut, but Royal Air Force Spitfires and Hurricanes were successfully holding democracy's "thin red line" against fascism as the Battle of Britain raged. Like most, I recall easily the moment I first heard of this new war, a war then without a name but one certain to be as big as the Great War, with its now senseless title: "The War to End All Wars."

I was at Grandma's on September 3, 1939. The family had driven down the day before to take me back to start my freshman year at CHS. I came downstairs that morning and walked into the kitchen for breakfast. Dad spoke solemnly: "Did you know that another big war has started in Europe?" I did not know exactly how to feel, or what to say, but I knew history was in the making. I stood there, my mind soaking up the late summer sunlight flooding in through Granny's lacy window curtains. Also her white GE refrigerator, with its round motor on top—somehow it, the curtains, and the kitchen's peaceful décor conflicted with Dad's unusually serious manner and the stark reality of the news he announced. I knew I was expected to hate war, but I did not yet know how to go about it. I sat down and ate my breakfast, probably irked that another summer vacation was over and a fearsome unknown called high school was about to begin. Four years later, almost to the day, I arrived at Fort Thomas, Kentucky, to take up a two-and-one-half-year career as an infantry soldier. Before that was over, I knew how to go about hating war.

19

The Queen City
and the Kings

Travel was safe between the wars. In the summer of 1935, when I was ten, I went by bus from downtown Carlisle to downtown Cincinnati. Once I arrived, a bystander directed me to a streetcar routed out Warsaw Avenue to Price Hill, where I visited Mom's widowed sister Anna Martin Gilkey and family. Nannie had spent 1916 with the Gilkeys in El Paso, Texas.

A strange thing happened as we chugged up Warsaw; men and women began crying throughout the car. I was worriedly puzzled—only at funerals had I heard or seen such sobs and tears. "Will Rogers has died," the lady next to me sighed. "He and Wiley Post were killed in a plane crash." I knew Dad thought a lot of Rogers, mostly I believed for saying such dumb things as "All I know is what I read in the papers." Nevertheless, I was caught up in the mood of the crowd and cried with the others. Fortunately, I had shown the conductor a card showing my destination or I might have ridden far beyond it with the distracted passengers. He let me off at Seton Avenue, and I was soon at home with my aunt and her four sons and five daughters.

Six years earlier tragedy had overtaken the Gilkey family when Joseph, the forty-four-year-old father, died an untimely death three months before the onslaught of the Great Depression. The family had moved from El Paso to Cincinnati not long before, and now the mother was left to support and raise nine children in the very teeth of seemingly endless hard times. She succeeded, her successes gradually overbalancing many losses, but at the time she and her family knew and felt the urban terrors of the Depression close-up in a way her rural and small town relatives, such as the Mathiases, could guess at but never fully comprehend.

Cincinnati impressed me because it was so different. The people spoke with an accent, and the city ran for miles in every direction. The Gilkey lads attended a large boys-only high school called Elder, while the girls went to Seton—both schools were named for noted Catholic religious leaders. Unlike familiar Kentucky towns, large Catholic churches, such as Saint Lawrence, the Gilkeys' parish, were prominent throughout Price Hill and the city. Movies, parks, and fascinating shops were along Glenway Avenue, the main thoroughfare. I knew Price Hill as well as most before many summer vacations went by, but David Gilkey took me to an ice cream shop that first summer that allied me with Price Hill for good. I was given four dips—two of chocolate and two of vanilla—on each side of a divided cone for a nickel. This was the Depression at its best, if one had a nickel. No matter, Price Hill was "two dips up" on Carlisle, Maysville, or any other place I knew of!

I was playing cards with new Price Hill friends at a neighbor's house when I learned the hard way that Jews existed outside Bible studies. The mother, in perhaps typical pre-Holocaust innocence, asked me to run an errand for her: "Go up to the corner and get me a loaf of bread from Ben Greenstein the Jew," she said, handing me a nickel. I skipped up the sidewalk, saw the grocery, entered, and approached a silver-haired man in an apron, stating with the directness of any ten-year-old: "I wanna buy a loaf of bread from Ben Greenstein the Jew."

"No, no, sonny," came the response. "I'm not Ben Greenstein the Jew; I'm just plain Ben Greenstein. Don't tack my religion on my name if you don't tack your religion on yours." But he said this gently with a smile.

I knew I had done something wrong yet was unable to define it, so I stood staring at the poor grocer in wide-eyed, open-mouthed silence. Greenstein won me over when he handed me a chocolate drop along with the potato bread. When I got back, Johnny, the oldest boy, explained it to me, stressing that Jesus was also a Jew. Ben Greenstein was my first acquaintance outside the Carlisle pattern of people. There were no Jews in Carlisle. Price Hill people often attached "Jew" to Greenstein's name after this, but it made me uneasy to hear it.

Sunday was a red letter day for Dave, Jim, and me. After mass, if we had the money, we spent a quarter each for Sunday streetcar passes. These entitled us to ride all over the city, no matter the route, car, or anything else. Sundays were slack days, so we often rode empty cars and got to know the conductor. We were free of all authority as we stuck our heads out of windows and ran back and forth up the aisles. The cars penetrated most areas of Cincinnati, making us ever more familiar with the city. Apples and cheese sandwiches fueled us as we logged mile after mile crisscrossing the town. It was high adventure for us and seldom tiresome; moreover, a quarter was a quarter, and we knew how to get our money's worth. By 1938 I knew car routes and geography of the Queen City better than many of its natives, all this for two bits a lesson.

My cousins and I knew which streetcar to take to Crosley Field for the soon to be famous Reds-Braves game of Saturday, June 11, 1938, but we did not have enough sense to stay once we got there. It may have been a "Knot-hole" or "Milk Bottle Cap Day" when kids got in for a cylindrical cardboard cap from a milk bottle; if not, we probably winced but paid fifty cents each for bleacher seats. We had started caddying at Western Hills Country Club and had seen today's Reds pitcher, Johnny Vander Meer, playing golf out there.

Crosley Field bore the same family name as the little auto that chugged cheaply over Depression-era streets. The Gilkey boys and I loved the Reds, but we seldom paid for games unless the St. Louis "Gashouse Gang" was in town with Ducky Medwick, Paul Dean, and his rambunctious brother Jay Hanna "Dizzy" Dean. We loved to hate them, and we always had good seats to do so, for Crosley Field was so sized and shaped that good views were offered everyone. But this particular Reds-Braves game bored us. "Dumb old Boston," we grumbled, "isn't getting any hits," meaning that for us, not much was happening. We remedied this by parroting a popular radio commercial whenever the Burger Beer salesman walked by hawking his wares to the sparse crowd:

"What's yours?" Dave shouted.

"*Red* Top Beer!" I replied, stressing "Red."

"And yours?" he repeated, pointing at Jim.

"Red Top *Beer!*" Jim shouted, accenting the last world.

"And yours?" he cried, getting back to me.

"Red *Top* Beer!" I shouted, with the play on "Top."

"Well, all we ever hear is Red Top Beer!" the three of us shouted in unison, then laughed loudly at our joke. After the third or fourth time, fans sitting nearby began ignoring us, sending the message that it was time to shut up.

We watched for another inning or two as the Reds built a one- or two-run lead, but Braves batters came and went, leaving nothing behind but their hitless bats. "Nothin' going on here," Dave said. "Let's walk down to the station and have some fun." Jim and I agreed, unknowingly leaving behind us the first of the only back-to-back no-hit games in major league history. Vander Meer beat the Braves 3–0, and the next Wednesday, June 15, no-hit the Brooklyn Dodgers 6–0, in the first night game ever played at Ebbets Field. Interestingly, the Reds' pitcher Ewell Blackwell missed duplicating Vander Meer's feat when he gave up a single in the ninth inning of the second game—but this was in 1947.

After leaving the game we spent a half hour at Cincinnati's monumental Union Railroad Station. In 1933, it had replaced a dingy old riverfront station and was probably the most attractive station in the land. A wide mall with many fountains, gardens, and steps led up and into the breathtaking rotunda. The top of this great half-dome was perhaps one hundred feet above the tile floor. Inside the dome, a series of mosaic murals reviewed Ohio's role in national development. The artwork and much else was mostly lost on Dave, Jim, and me, for our eyes were glued on two fountains, one on each side of the great dome. No one can ever say who first discovers such things, but my cousins knew that the curve of the dome had created unique acoustics so that one could stand by one fountain, say something in an ordinary voice, and be heard distinctly three hundred feet away at the other.

We waited eagerly, then grinned at each other as a woman approached the distant fountain to take a drink. Dave lowered his voice, saying confidentially, "Your slip is showing." Invariably the reaction was the same: a quick turning around to see who had spoken, then a check of clothing, finally followed by a puzzled and cautious inspection of the surroundings.

The forty-nine-story Carew Tower lured us as strongly as the great terminal. Our first adventure in this downtown skyscraper amounted to no more than foot races up the stairs to a top floor, huffing and laughing as we arrived. Soon we noticed that window screens in the men's rooms opened enough for us to sail paper planes out into the shifting winds generated by the tall building. Some of these frail flyers made it to a watery grave in the river, but most flew bumpy circular routes down to the city streets. We took the obvious next step, bought and built a Piper Cub from a fifteen-cent model kit, smuggled it to a top floor, and launched it with highest hopes. Our excitement mounted as the Cub's rubber band motor pulled it clear of wind currents. Soon the little yellow plane was gliding on a straight path out over the Ohio River. We yelled and whooped like cheerleaders, urging our spunky creation to keep going, to make it all the way to the Kentucky shore. It did its best for us before gliding gracefully lower, finally plopping with our hopes and shouts into the river.

As the plane hit the water we heard a man's voice behind us ask, "What are you boys making all the noise about; what are you up to?" We turned to face a well-dressed gentleman, a salesman or owner of an insurance office next to the men's room. We told him with an excited mingling of voices and boyish passion; he smiled broadly, friendly eyes perhaps lit with memories. "Boys," he said, "I wish I could've gotten here in time to have seen that flight!"

Our hard-earned adventure was over; we left the building with happy memories, one being that our spunky little plane had set a Carew Tower distance record. As the insurance man perceived, its flight was to Dave, Jim, and me worthy of the *Spirit of St. Louis,* and as of this writing, our fifty-eight-year-old record still stands!

The Carew Tower rose next to the impressive Netherland Plaza Hotel, with lobbies and halls done in the best art deco style. We knew nothing of architectural styles, but we did know how to sneak a free view of the hotel's daytime ice shows. The Restaurant Continentale was located on the first floor under a partial second floor balcony. A small ice rink fronted the bandstand and featured various acts during scheduled meals and gatherings. My cousins and I hid behind potted palms and ferns in a corner alcove of the balcony, peering through gaps in the balustrade at what was to us the "swanky" scene below. We ogled dressy diners eating rich foods with shiny utensils on white tablecloths. Meanwhile, Burt Farber's superb dance and show band, dressed in white jackets and tuxedo trousers, played the most wonderful music I had ever heard in person. The flashing skates of the performers and the music blended perfectly. "Gee," I always whispered to my cousins, "if I could only play in a band like that," but I shook my head negatively, resigned to my Nicholas County fate. If a genie had said, "When you are eighteen years old, just three years from now, you will be playing in an army band easily the equal of Farber's," I would have developed a very healthy suspicion of genies. But the genie would have been correct.

It was hard to slip in and remain long in the Old Vienna, a Carew Tower rathskeller bar and restaurant. A solidly German motif prevailed here, with Freddie Fischer's Schnickelfritz Band pumping out "Vas You Effer in Zinzinnati" or backing the jolly customers singing such German question and answer songs as "Ist das nicht ein dicky frau?" I loved to hear the Schnickelfritz clarinetist play "slap-tongue," a style making a smacking sound typical in small comic bands of the era. Dave, Jim, and I often invaded Old Vienna even though we were quickly evicted. A few minutes was long enough to catch Fischer's well-known "Korn Kobblers" at their corny best.

We three sidled in one time as the leader poured a stream of tawny water back and forth between spotlighted chamber pots, keeping in time as his band oom-pah-pahed a schmaltzy German waltz. Just as the waltz ended, a string of frankfurters slid with plopping, splashy sounds into one of the pots. We laughed so long and loud we were spotted for what we were and hustled out into the bright downtown daylight.

Joe Gilkey was older than Dave, Jim, and me and knew how to slip us into a downtown movie. We pooled our money to buy Joe's ticket. He then entered and let us in through an unguarded rear fire door. We enjoyed whatever movie was playing. To paraphrase Wimpy and hamburgers, we never met a movie we didn't like. The miracle of seeing people move across a screen was thrill enough, even if it was a soupy love story. Sneaking in greatly blunted any criticism.

Whenever my cousins and I needed money we hitched a ride to Western Hills Country Club and checked in at the caddy barn. We were small and inexperienced and had to take golfers no one else wanted. Golfers and caddies alike walked, for golf carts were shunned as unsportsmanlike, OK for the aged and crippled but an affectation for lovers of the game. I sensed this, but had I studied it I might have wished my old duffers had used the putt-putt carts of the era. More often than not, my golfers handed me a leather bag with ten clubs, a fifth of bourbon and chasers, a book on winning golf (the pages like new), a bag of balls and tees, a large umbrella, and a raincoat and hat. To add insult to injury, some of the heavy bags had sling straps with "KADDY KOMFORT" printed on them in large lying letters! No matter, the lure of a dollar at the end of eighteen holes made it all worthwhile.

By the time I was a high schooler I felt at home at Western Hills for two weeks each summer. I knew each club and its use, whether the mashie, brassie, spoon, driver, putter, mid-iron, niblick, jigger, or the various irons. Modern golf has changed many of the names but none of the uses. Most clubs had hickory shafts, but some golfers preferred steel ones. They cost the same. I was some-times "winked at" to move the ball "just a tiny bit" in favor of my duffer, especially when caddying in a heavy-drinking foursome play-ing for low holes and money, and I did so, reaping a dime or more for my cheating ways. I learned more about life than golf at West-ern Hills.

Golf offers no way to hid one's talent, or lack of it, on a well-designed course. Western Hills's first nine holes lie rather flat, but the back nine are steep, tricky, and pitiless to any but good golfers, but I seldom got to caddy for good ones. Many breezed through the first nine, only to wreck themselves on the back side. One duffer became so furiously frustrated that he pushed his caddy into the lake and threw the clubs in after him. It was around sunset so the golfer, now embarrassed and apologetic, slipped away, not returning until the next day to retrieve his clubs. The clubs, of course, were never seen again. Older caddies often swam after dark, especially during a big dance, "feeling" balls off accessible parts of the lake bottom with bare feet. The man's clubs went the same way.

A major attraction at the club were Reds baseball stars who came as members or guests. These included Bucky Walters, Mike and Frank McCormick, Johnny Vander Meer, and others of lesser fame. A club regular was Paul Derringer, a fellow Kentuckian, and like Walters, one of Cincinnati's all-time best pitchers. Derringer hit the bottle as hard as he hit the golf ball, probably to relax after a hot day on the mound. I was not nearly high enough in caddydom to carry his clubs, but I joined the rest in ogling his every move. The first nine holes always found "Oom Paul" doing well, driving and putting with the best. But he seldom made it far into the back nine. By that time he had drained his bottle and headed happily back to his wife, who always waited patiently for him in the cab of their small pickup truck. All envied his caddy, who was paid for a full eighteen holes even though Derringer seldom played more than nine or ten.

I dragged in from the last hole one hot afternoon with a foursome, all of whom had shot over one hundred, even with cheating. One duffer paid for all, handing me a dollar, then another dollar a minute or two later. Twice more he mistook me for other caddies still arriving off the course, so I wound up holding four dollars. I was uncertain why he kept paying me, even though he was tipsy, but I knew I had better hitchhike back to Gilkeys' before anyone challenged my windfall.

My luck ran out next day when I showed up at the caddy barn. The caddymaster, a tongue-tied soul, had been shouting for me every few minutes: "Has anyboty teen Matice?" When I answered his call, he looked me over with scorn: "Matice, where is da tree bucks you 'tole yetterday? You took it and da utter catties din't get nutting." He waited impatiently as I tried to devise an answer.

"I took the money because he gave it to me a dollar at a time. I couldn't read his mind; I just sort of thought he liked me."

This brought whistles and laughs from caddies looking on. There was no getting out of it so I pulled out three dollars and handed it to the caddymaster. The three caddies received their money, and I received unfriendly stares. But they were understanding lads, and I was back caddying with them the next day. My conscience hurt for some time, however, for I had ever so easily drifted off what in Carlisle was called "the straight and narrow." For the first time I appreciated the anonymity of a big city.

I caddied for only one top-flight golfer at Western Hills between 1937 and 1942. Johnny Fisher, U.S. Amateur champion, came to the course one day with a friend and chose Dave Gilkey and me for caddies. We watched in awe as the two of them boomed drive after drive straight down the fairways. They putted beautifully at each hole. We simply handed out clubs and walked to the next hole or tee. After our years with time-consuming and patience-exhausting duffers, Fisher and his pal came as a glorious revelation. It made us want to play golf as well as they did. We practiced with fame on our minds, but only a few years later Dave was placing his shots as a gunner aboard a B-17, and I was thinking "fore!" as I dodged coconuts dropping into the "sand traps" of lovely South Pacific beaches.

Going home from Cincinnati sometimes proved as interesting as the city itself. While I was hitchhiking east along Route 52 to Maysville a driver stopped for me. When I got in I saw a sparkling white and gold drum set crammed into the backseat. My eyes bulged! "You play drums with a dance band, don't you?" I asked breathlessly. The driver, a young man in his twenties, glanced my way.

"Yeah, I'm Frankie Carle's drummer. We're playing a gig in Portsmouth tonight."

He soon realized he had a fifteen-year-old idolater in his car. I had heard Carle's band on the radio and knew he had composed "Sunrise Serenade." By the time we reached the Maysville bridge we were on such good terms he drove me over to Grandma's house. I waved good-bye, hitchhiked on to Carlisle, kissed Mom as I came in, got my sax out, and practiced hard for several days in a row.

Another interesting return trip from Cincinnati came the year before when I had been given enough money to take the George Washington back to Maysville. I had often seen this famous Chesapeake and Ohio train in Maysville, and now I was getting to ride it. After the conductor took my ticket, I wandered into the diner, sat down at a white tableclothed table, and happily watched the scenery speed by outside the broad window. An elderly African American waiter approached, handed me a menu, and waited for my order, pen in hand. I did not know what to do and feared making some mistake, yet I had to order something. "Do you have tea?" I asked, thinking a cup of tea would be cheap, and it also sounded up to snuff—Englishmen in movies were always asking for it.

"Yes we do; what kind would you like?"

"The hot kind," I replied, not knowing any other but the cold kind.

The waiter soon returned and placed a cup of hot water and a tea bag on my table. I had never seen a tea bag, knowing only the bulk tea Mom and my aunts mixed in hot water and poured through a strainer. I had trouble with the little bag but soon had it open and the tea floating across the top of my cup. Suddenly the waiter was at my side.

"My goodness!" he exclaimed. "I wish you would look at that cup. Why, your tea bag wasn't made right—look how that thing's broke wide open, spilling tealeaves in the water. Here now, let me get you another bag and a clean cup of hot water." He soon returned. "If anything happens to this bag, just call me back." I realized, young though I was, that I had not only been taught to use a tea bag but also given an effective lesson in tact.

The summer season shaped my life as much as or more than any other season of the year. Each summer I spent about seven weeks of my fifteen-week school vacation at Black Hawk or with relatives. I had plenty to think about as I contrasted recent visits to the Gilkeys in the exciting but impersonal arena of a major city with the easygoing ways of the historic old river port of Maysville, and finally, with the hardworking and somewhat isolated life on the Clarkson and King farms. The King farm?

Except for Black Hawk, the King farm was the closest of my summer destinations. We exchanged Sunday visits with these relatives often during the year, for their farm was just seventeen miles away, in Montgomery County. But I never stayed for a week with Uncle John, Aunt Katie, and my five cousins until summertime.

John Clancy King married my dad's sister Katie in 1911, then bought a hundred-acre farm at a high price generated by World War I. The farm depression of the 1920s resulted in very low crop and livestock prices, making it harder every year to pay off the farm. The Great Depression brought even harder times for the Kings as well as most other American farmers. As a child and boy, I had but slight knowledge of the family's ongoing and eventually successful battle to pay off the farm; I thought only of what fun I would have during my week's visit with my five cousins.

The farm was seven miles west of Mount Sterling, a county seat town of five thousand population that had suffered a small but very brutal Civil War battle. Saturday of course was the biggest day of the week. Uncle John always drove in to do business at the stockyards, creamery, or produce house, taking John Jr. and Ed—the two boys nearest my age—and me with him. We enjoyed the things all country kids enjoyed during a Saturday afternoon in town, and familiarity never bred contempt. We faced every Saturday as a fresh new chance, like dedicated gamblers holding a new deal of cards. But for me, a town lad, the farm was the thing.

There were four centers of action for John, Ed, and me on the farm: the typical two-story farmhouse, the privy, the springhouse, and the barns. The three-hole privy was in use every day of the year, whether shrunken by winter winds or reeking in July heat. Summertime guests were fat spiders, flies, and wasps. A jar of Vaseline was always sitting to one side, for Uncle John had piles. A mail order catalog with torn pages served sanitary purposes but also provided a corset section for older boys to ogle. This privy and others, I think, were underrated as places to while away a bit of time, at least in good weather. This line of thought came back to me years later, when President John Kennedy admitted that his only sure way to rid himself of unwanted people and collect his thoughts was to be excused to go to the john.

Aunt Katie's spring house was a typical little brick and wooden shed built over a spring. (I like the descriptive Spanish phrase for spring much better: *ojo de agua*, eye of water.) Spring water maintains the average annual temperature of its latitude, in Kentucky about fifty-four degrees year-round. Containers of milk or food set in this cool water stayed fresh longer. Moreover, spring water continually flowed outside, creating lush grasses and beds of mint as it drained down a slope. This cool old springhouse was a pleasant place to relax and become as detached as the dust motes drifting in the slender shafts of sunlight that slipped through cracks in the walls.

The Kings' big red tobacco barn loomed on a hilltop nearby like a giant surveying his domain, and why not—tobacco *was* the domain of all farms in view. Golden-green-brown chest-high tobacco plants brushed cousin John and me one hot afternoon as we walked through a field of burley toward the barn. He paused, pointing to some tobacco worms nibbling on the leaves. These colorful finger-sized caterpillars do much damage if uncontrolled. John suddenly picked up several and bit each one in half, spitting out the squirming pieces. "They won't come back after that," he said with a wide grin, knowing he had shocked me. I agreed, hoping he did not expect me to duplicate his feat. I did not think he would, for although he was a rugged, big farm boy, there was nothing tricky or mean about him.

We walked on to the barn. Once inside John scooped up a handful of dusty, half-dried burley tobacco leaves, rolled them into a twist, and bit off a chew. "Dad don't like me to chew," he said, talking as he wallowed the pungent leaves around in his mouth, "but I get a kick out of it, just like everybody else. My dad and your dad chew, so does Uncle Joe and Uncle Frank and all the rest. It just takes some gettin' used to, that's all."

"I might as well try a quid of long green," I thought to myself. "As John said, it probably just takes a little gettin' used to." I picked up and twisted some leaves and jammed them into my mouth. My right cheek bulged as I chewed along with my cousin, generating saliva that spun out tiny dust balls when I spit it on the barn floor. "Nothin' to it," I thought, just before dizziness struck. The barn interior swam in my vision, and a sick heaviness lay upon my stomach. "I'm sick," I told John, "real sick," and spit the quid out of my mouth. I had to have water and ran for the pond. "Oh Lord," I prayed, "keep the walkingsticks away from me." These harmless twig-shaped creatures were imagined by John, Ed, and me to be as dangerous as copperheads or black widow spiders. On this day the walkingsticks had to fend for themselves. I threw myself down in muddy cow tracks and stuck my head underwater, hoping to wash away the dizziness. I rinsed by mouth out, gulping down the thick-tasting pond water. Poor John felt bad about it all, blaming himself as he helped me to recovery some minutes later.

The peril of tobacco chewing was only one of the lessons provided me at the Kings'. Two small barns with weathered planking fronted pasture and cropland some two hundred feet from the farmhouse. Old Bob, Uncle John's powerful Percheron plowhorse, called one of the barns home. The two of them worked together for thirty years, loving and caring for each other. I was there when Bob died. My uncle hand-dug a grave for the big horse, crying as he shoveled dirt in on his gentle friend.

I was also there when a neighbor drove in a cow to be serviced by the Kings' bull. "You boys get away from here," Uncle John demanded. "This is none of your business." It was not considered proper to allow schoolboys to watch a bull mount a cow. John, Ed, and I knew that this was too good to miss, so we sneaked inside one of the barns, each taking a knothole to view the action. The men outside helped the bull find his mark. "Lordy, look at that; did'ja ever see such a tool!" sums up the excited whispers passed back and forth from the knothole crowd.

One of my daydreams was to grow up as strong as Frank King. Cousin Frank was thirteen years older than I and powerfully put together. He flexed his arm muscle for me one day as he stood grinning beside one of the mules. Frank forgot that this mule was a "stumpsucker" that chewed on the spongy pith of rotten stumps, or any likely thing at hand, to ease the pain in decayed teeth. With no hint of a warning, the big mule reached over and bit down on Frank's left shoulder. As if on a hair trigger, the farmer whirled and sank his right fist into the mule's muzzle. There was a sharp smacking sound and a spray of mule mucous, then the beast staggered, sinking to its front knees. It soon regained its senses and stood back up, much to Frank's relief. A gentle man, Frank asked us, "How do I apologize to a mule?" His blow, I think, would have floored any of the world's great prizefighters.

Frank's two sisters, Mary and Ann, who were also much older than I, gave me a lasting lesson in Latin during Forty Hours Devotion at Mount Sterling's small Catholic church. Simply stated, Forty Hours brought priests from nearer parts of the diocese who united with the host congregation to offer prayers, litanies, and supplications to the Lord. These were often in the form of chants. It was rather festive and presented a welcome opportunity to meet and discuss many things with visiting clergy.

I had always attended this devotion when it came to Carlisle but assumed that two Latin litany responses chanted by the priests were in English. They made no sense, but that was the way I heard them. During a break in the Mount Sterling services, however, I decided to ask my cousins about these bizarre responses. "Mary Margaret," I asked hopefully, "just what does it mean when the priests chant, 'Leave her on a stormy day,' and 'Oh wipe your nose off?'"

"Now, Frank," she replied in a voice tinged with suspicion, "I'll bet you're trying to pull one on me, just like Uncle Charlie." But she was intrigued and prompted me to tell her sister Ann what I had asked. While I was doing so, both of them caught on, laughing loudly as they explained it to me.

"Look, Frank," Ann smiled, "it may sound a lot like 'leave her on a stormy day' to you, but it's really Latin—*Libera nos Domine*—meaning, 'Oh Lord, deliver us.'"

"And your 'Oh wipe your nose off,'" Mary chuckled, "is *Ora pro nobis*, meaning 'Pray for us.'"

When I got back to Carlisle and told about it, Speck laughed long and hard at my "stupidity," not realizing at the time that for years he had been saying "Hail Mary full of grapes."

Before New Dealers and their REA brought electricity in the late 1930s, most American farm families lived lives little different physically from those lived centuries earlier in Virginia and New

England. The King family, for example, had a Model T Ford, but they used oil for light, cooked on a wood stove, pulled their water up by hand from a deep well, fought off winter's cold with fireplaces, milked cows by hand, churned milk for butter, smoked meat, used horsepower to grow crops, and learned by necessity to "make do" and to "waste not, want not." Water for Saturday night baths was drawn bucket by bucket from the well, heated on the stove, then poured into one big tub. Turns were taken, and the water changed often, but I was made thankful for the modern plumbing in my Carlisle home.

I was visiting the Kings when the family eagerly watched REA poles, carrying one precious strand of wire, slowly march from distant hilltops up to their home. Electricity had arrived at last! With it came electric pumps, stoves, refrigerators, toasters, heaters, cream separators, saws, washers, fans, but above all, switches and lights for homes and barns. Appliance dealers in many rural communities found their bank accounts expanding so rapidly that Republicans among them may have wondered why they had ever doubted "that man in the White House."

"That man in the White House" was undoubtedly as upset as most Americans with widespread news reports in early 1938 of the ghastly slaughter of over three hundred thousand Chinese civilians by the Japanese military, soon to be known as the Rape of Nanking. It was a source of conversation between Lucky and grocers for weeks: "Lucky, what in God's name do you make of people who would do a thing like that?"

"I don't know," Dad replied, shaking his head. "It's way beyond me and everybody I call on; even cannibals have more religion than that."

China was well liked, my parents and others admonishing children to "clean your plate, think of the starving little children in China." But how stunned Lucky and Nannie would have been to know that their son would eventually have a personal link to two great Japanese atrocities! My infantry division, the Thirty-seventh, annihilated the Japanese Sixth Division of Nanking infamy on Bougainville in 1944. A year later we helped do the same thing in

Manila, but not before the Japanese had brutally slaughtered over one hundred thousand Filipino men, women, and children in a repeat of the Nanking affair.

Summer 1938 ended with regrets that school had started and that I had walked out on the now famous Vander Meer. I was given an undeserved second chance, however, meeting a pitcher easily Vander Meer's equal, yet I still lacked enough judgment to be impressed. Leaving school one day, I saw Popeye Clark, Junior Smart, Bobby Harper, and Pat Conley pitching baseball with a man I had never seen before. He had on a wrinkled gray suit and a loose tie, and he looked almost as old as Lucky, who was fifty-seven in 1938. "Wanna pitch with us?" he asked as I stood staring.

"Yessir, I'd like to," I replied, wondering what an old man like him was doing pitching ball on our playground.

"This here is Mr. Grover Cleveland Alexander," Popeye said as he handed me a glove. "Mr. Alexander was a big league pitcher for the Cards in the old days."

"Glad to meet you, sir," I said, shaking his hand and telling him my name.

"Glad to meet you too, Frank. I gave a speech to the high school, and your buddies and I are fooling around until my ride shows up."

Alexander, I think, was on one of those typical, low-pay, Depression-era high school speaking tours. High schools often had "has-beens" from many backgrounds as speakers, but few of these had the credentials of Alexander. My pals and I stood there passing the ball back and forth with no inkling that this friendly old man had been one of baseball's greatest pitchers. The *World Book Encyclopedia* (1971) reveals that between 1911 and 1930, Alexander won 373 games, 90 of which were shutouts. He won the deciding game of the 1926 World Series for St. Louis when he struck out the New York Yankees' heavy-hitting Tony Lazzeri with the bases loaded and two out.

The old pitcher had chosen to relax with five unassuming kids before going on to a Maysville hotel and another speech the following day. He showed us some of the ins and outs of pitching, did some tricks with the ball, and warned us sternly against smoking (probably at Pfanstiel's behest). After twenty minutes or so of pitching and listening, the five of us wandered off to other things, each as carelessly unaware as schoolboys can be as to who it *really* was we had passed time with.

20

Life Went on as Usual

Nicholas Countians, like most Americans, had little fear that the United States would be, or even could be, sucked into another European war. I had never seen a chestnut, but I knew what adults meant when they said, "We'll not pull Britain's chestnuts out of the fire this time." We joined most of our countrymen in hunkering determinedly behind traditional Atlantic, Pacific, and Arctic Ocean barricades, following the ups and downs of the new war as pictured in *Life* magazine, a sanitized version of the horrible mess unfolding in Europe. Meanwhile, the war, like the proverbial camel, soon had more than its nose inside America's tent. We admitted this yet discounted it at the same time, and life went on as usual. Well, almost as usual.

Life in 1939 did not go on as usual insofar as basketball was concerned. Nearby Brooksville, a county seat town of seven hundred people, astonished Kentuckians by winning the state basketball tournament. The tiny town's team whipped overconfident cagers from big schools across the state. This was easily enough to shove Hitler and Mussolini out of the minds of area fans.

No one, however, needed much of a mind to follow donkey baseball, a summer pseudo-sport of the late 1930s. It was pure show business. Volunteers—teachers, businessmen, politicians—rode little burros without bridles or saddles. A small fee was collected at the ballpark gate; the game was played on the regulation softball diamond. The proceeds, I think, were split between the promoter who owned the burros and a town businessman or charity. Circles on the ground served as bases. Only the pitcher and catcher were not riders, but they had to stay in a marked lane between the pitcher's box and home plate. The names of the donkeys reflect the times: Amos, Andy, Madam Queen, Huey Long, Moon Mullins, Mae West, Wimpy, Jiggs, Betty Boop, Hoover, and so on. Uncle Ed Metcalfe played undertaker for the teams, rushing onto the field dressed in a black frockcoat and stovepipe hat with a tape measure and a coffin, fitting a fallen player—all pretense—into the coffin and wheeling him away to the cheers of the crowd. They were especially loud if it was someone like G.B. Leonard, the well-liked high school teacher. Unexpected antics of the riders and the little donkeys lent a spice to the game lacking in most entertainment. It was good Depression fare—it was cheap, it was entertaining, and it offered temporary escape from the worries of the day.

Movies offered a major escape from Depression and war worries. Most were entertaining and little more, but that was enough. I remember the plots of only seven: *Snow White*, *The Wizard of Oz*, *Trader Horn*, *King Kong*, *All Quiet on the Western Front*, *The Hurricane*, and *Gone with the Wind*. Cowboys and comics, of course, were the major fare of grade school boys, with unforgettable performers: Tom Mix, Bob Steele, Ken Meynard, Buck Jones, and several great comics in Laurel and Hardy and the Three Stooges. The Andy Hardy movies with Mickey Rooney and Judy Garland attracted viewers of all ages.

I was fully prepared to get the most out of *Gone with the Wind*. Nannie read the book to the family every evening for a month or so before we saw the movie. Moreover, we often drove by the Maysville home of John Marsh, Margaret Mitchell's husband, and in addition, my pal David Harper's mother spoke of dating Marsh before Mitchell got him. I was very pleased and thrilled as the movie mirrored the book.

King Kong scared me so badly I stood shouting outside the house's big, dark spirea bushes after the movie for Dad to come and get me. *Trader Horn* also etched fear into my childhood memory. But Erich Remarque's *All Quiet on the Western Front* showed me that war was not at all the exciting affair that Uncle Ed promoted in his tales of the AEF, a lesson of value when I needed it in the South Pacific. *Snow White* and *The Wizard of Oz* were unforgettable hallmarks to everyone in my generation. *The Hurricane* was a superb movie, but its theme song, "Moon of Manakoora," made it memorable for me.

King Kong scared my pals and me, but we knew it was movie fakery; the 1940 creature we turned up in a dump, however, came from real life and left us shuddering. Several of us were poking around in a small dump between East Main and the L&N tracks. It was a temporary refuse site that had grown by itself, then later disappeared. One of the lads picked up a large jar, gasped, then rushed to show us. At first we thought we were looking at a perfectly formed doll, but it was no doll. "What is it?" we asked in unison. "It sure looks like a real baby," one commented, "but it's awful small."

We were fifteen and had heard of abortion, but it took time for us to get our wits together and conclude that that was why the baby was in the jar. One of the boys lived nearby so we ran to his home to talk to his mother. She said the baby must be given a Christian burial. When we returned the baby was missing. We had been observed and protective action taken, either by the abortionist or the dead baby's mother or father.

When I entered high school, the East End, or Rock Quarry Gang, was at the zenith of its power. Our headquarters was an abandoned quarry a block from school but shielded along the top rim by a tangle of trees and thorny shrubs. During gang get-togethers sentries sat in upside-down auto hoods nailed high in trees, from whence slingshots harassed invaders. On the quarry's bottom were headquarters buildings. They resembled the shacky cardboard and rusty metal hovels seen strung around the hillside slums of modern Third World cities. But we had bragging rights on a weapon of real power. Near the quarry's center a twenty-foot-high mound of rocky earth had spawned a forked tree. Pertinent branches were pruned to turn the fork into a high-powered slingshot. Stretchy red rubber inner tubes were sliced into proven widths and lengths to power the weapon, while a fabric and screen pouch was fashioned to hold the ammo. We easily shot rocks the size of milk bottles or fired withering buckshotlike blasts of gravel. Best of all, the slingshot tree faced the only true attack route into our lair. The West End Gang would not stand a chance against us.

Unfortunately, no attack ever came—we just rotted away with our superweapon like Japanese on some godforsaken, bypassed Pacific island. But we enjoyed a single moment of glory on New Year's Eve 1940. Bobby Harper produced a quart jar of blasting powder and a fuse. He and Pokey Pumphrey buried it atop the mound and the gang watched eagerly, our faces reflecting the red light from a roaring wood fire. When the courthouse clock began intoning the midnight hour, Bobby lit the fuse. There was a cannonlike roar, followed by an exciting shower of dirt, snow, and gravel.

Somehow, the gang ended its existence, not all at once but in a withering away of membership. Friends, brothers, and uncles were soon being called up in the draft, and newsreels showed the fearful carnage in China and Europe. The camel had gotten much more than his nose inside our tent. Even super slingshots seemed childish and out of place.

The Rock Quarry Gang had hardly invented its memorable slingshot before another invention brought notice to Carlisle. It had to do with nuts. The Myers and Mulligan Walnut Kernel Factory had long operated from an old barn near the Catholic church. A dozen or so women worked at the slow task of cracking hard black walnut shells and extracting salable sized kernels. The shells themselves were sold to make top-grade charcoal for gas mask filters, soon to be a wartime need. Although Carlislians lusted for an imagined golden touch of "industry," this nut operation ranked as the town's only factory until the 1940s, when a tiny new factory began manufacturing such unthought-of items as spindles for yo-yos.

By then a new era in walnut kernel extraction was under way owing to a local inventor. The *Mercury* reported on January 12, 1939, that Ira Hunter had invented a walnut cracker: "The machine sells for $75 and will fill a long-felt need in the walnut kernel industry." The device was well received by the workers. Ed Metcalfe reported more than modest enthusiasm on the part of one who told him that "Ira Hunter is another Edison and that's all they are to it!"

Walnut crackers were the least of my thoughts on May 23, 1941, the day I turned sixteen. It was an eagerly anticipated milestone, with a seemingly interminable childhood standing on one side and a driver's license on the other. I drove home in glory after getting mine. A few days later David Harper dropped by to offer congratulations and propose a trip to Newport. He had a stranger with him.

Dave loved to gamble. If we were standing on Main Street and a truck came up the street, he might say, "Mat, five'll getcha ten he turns down Broadway at the stoplight." He usually knew the odds, got my five cents, and left me betting to myself that I would never be sucked in again. I was, of course, and today was no different.

Dave introduced me to his new friend, Loyall Kontz of Lexington. Loyall was visiting Carlisle kin, met David, and the two had struck friendly sparks. He also introduced me to their exciting plan, one deftly geared to my new driver's license. Dave had long had an illicit key to his dad's Ford garage basement, often slipping out the business's perky pickup truck for practice driving. Their plan was starkly simple and seemed foolproof. "Mat," Dave said, "Loyall and I plan to take the pickup and make a quick trip to Newport, win some bucks, and hurry back before anyone catches on. We don't have drivers' licenses, but you do in case we're stopped. Loyall, show Frank why we've got a sure thing!"

"Know what these are, Frank?" Loyall asked, smiling smugly as he held out a handful of copperish looking metal disks.

"Nope," I replied, wondering what they were and what they meant to Loyall.

"These are five-cent Lexington bus tokens, old buddy, and they fit quarter slot machines to a T. When we get down to those Newport casinos we'll clean up!" His expression and tone of voice left not the slightest doubt that he meant exactly what he said, forcing me to agree.

"We'll clean up," I echoed hopefully.

Newport, Kentucky, was a major gambling center across the

Ohio River from Cincinnati. Staid old Cincinnati played the role of a pure but put-upon mother whose daughter has sunk into whoredom. Thousands of conventioneers came to the great hotels of the Queen City only to find that the Kentucky side of the river was where the action was. There were nationally famous nightclubs such as Beverly Hills and the Lookout House, gambling casinos galore, and enough whorehouses to make any true Cincinnatian blush. During the Depression and World War II eras, organized syndicate crime was a dominant force in Newport and northern Kentucky. Scores of confiscated slot machines, for example, were held in a city jail, then "stolen" back out of the jail! Newport later underwent a lengthy, painful, but thorough postwar cleaning, making it almost as staid and wholesome as its big mother across the river. But the old, sinful Newport was the city in which three naïve high school country bumpkins confidently intended to "clean up."

Dave sneaked the pickup out and by noon we were eating lunch at Jack's Shack, a small and cheap roadhouse featuring jack salmon near the Beverly Hills Supper Club. "We've got to strike fast," Loyall insisted, pushing us to finish our fish sandwiches and drive on into Newport. Once downtown, we looked things over, then strolled into one of the casinos. I had never seen anything like it. Rows of slot machines lined the aisles of the gymnasium-sized room. No great number of customers were in the place, but those there were playing cards or the slots or betting on a variety of sports with horse racing foremost. An old Kentucky ham hung from a ceiling pillar; a small sign advertised chances on it. This surprised me, reminding me of our nonsinful attic hams at home.

Kontz put his plan to the test. He was built like a high school halfback, but a pallid complexion belied his athletic abilities. These abilities were soon pushed to the limit. While Dave and I gawked at the customers and their games, Kontz busily played a quarter slot machine. He fed tokens in as fast as he could pull the lever, setting the drums spinning with oranges, cherries, lemons, plums, or, he hoped, to line them up as a jackpot of three "Bell-Fruits." Kontz ignored the little window next to the coin feed slot. This oblong window revealed the last six coins fed into the machine, each new entry pushing the sixth one out of view. If the casino had been crowded, Loyall might have gotten away with his scheme. But it was not, and retribution was heading his way.

One of the tough floormen at the club, possibly suspicious of the speed with which Kontz belabored the machine, walked by and spotted the tokens lined up in the small safety window. He made the mistake of signaling another floorman for help before grabbing the cheater. This gave Loyall just enough warning to make a break for it, and the chase was on.

David and I heard the furor and turned in time to see Kontz and two floormen barreling through an open back door. This open door, Kontz later said, saved his hide. By the time the outside air hit him, Loyall was showing Olympic speed as he raced for the river and its cluster of moored boats, floating docks, and restaurants. If he was caught, a severe beating would be his lot. He made it, plunged into the river, and disappeared amid the clutter of docks, walkways, and boats. His pursuers were satisfied; he was just a two-bit gambler. Dave and I awaited him at the parked pickup. Eventually he walked up grinning—a damp, disheveled, but not much wiser Kontz. "I guess I showed 'em!" he bragged. In fact, Loyall was still trying to "show 'em" four years later when, as Seaman Kontz, he sneaked into the cockpit of an idling navy fighter plane, taxied it "for fun" around the airstrip, but damaged it and spent considerable time in the brig.

Turning sixteen meant even more than getting a driver's license. This magical milestone also gave the owner the legal right to drop out of school or to enter the adult workaday world. I wanted to enter this world, but the pickings were slim. The Depression had not gone away. It had ransacked the nation almost as badly in 1938 as it had in 1933, and even in the early 1940s jobs and salaries had yet to recover. Nicholas County judge Walter Shepherd had a monthly salary of $141.66, while county attorney William Conley earned $85. The *Mercury* of September 30, 1943, also reported that fiscal court clerk John Sugg garnered but $50, and courthouse janitor Bob Curtis made do with $75. My dad was, as he said, "ticking along" with some $85 monthly in commissions. In addition, government spending produced great concern. The national debt of

$40 billion was, by 1939, the highest in all history. The deficit for that year was $3,580,000,000. Compared to past spending, this looked terrible. The 364-mile-long Erie Canal had been built in the 1820s for $7,000,000. The Civil War had cost $4,000,000,000, yet here was a government that had spent ten times that amount, and still the Depression ground on as usual. My pals and I showed little concern for these "hard facts"; girls and jobs were on our minds.

By 1941 a noticeable job advantage had come my way. The 1940 draft had taken many young men into the service, leaving vacancies in some Carlisle businesses, one of which was at the small Kroger store. Stanley Galbraith, the likable manager, let word out that he was hiring clerks. The local A&P was also hiring, but the fact that Galbraith had a lovely daughter probably led to the excess of hopeful high school boys he interviewed. He hired five or six of us, sent to Cincinnati for our social security papers, and set our salaries at twenty-eight cents an hour. I like the sound of that. In one hour I made enough to get a haircut, or buy a meal at the Little House with the Big Eats, or ride the bus to Maysville. This was weekend work, from the time school let out on Friday until midnight on Saturday, amounting to enough hours to amass $4.20. Best of all, it did not interfere with the occasional farmhouse dances I played, for they came during the week so as not to interfere with the farmers' Saturdays in town.

When I showed up for work I was assigned as meat clerk to Russell Glenn, the jovial butcher. I like him right off. My job was to chip ice for the fish and meat display cases, slice endless amounts of bloody and quivering pork and beef livers, grind Kroger brand sausage as well as private sausage meat for customers (some of it amazingly bristly, hairy, and dirty), grind hamburger, slice bologna and ham, make standing rib roasts, and pretend to show no fear of the mystical looking blue light permeating our big walk-in refrigerator.

"This blue light," Butch explained, "that makes the insides of our refrigerator look like a haunted house, is caused by Kroger's 'Tenderay.' Have you heard of that?"

"Yes, sir," I replied. "I've seen in Kroger ads that it's supposed to tenderize meat."

"Well, that's what they say, and I guess they're right. Actually, what it is is a doo-dad called a Westinghouse 'Sterilamp,' but that darned name is about the reason you won't be here a week before some nut will come up and tell you that blue light will make you sterile."

"Will it!" I exclaimed, suddenly paying full attention to a now suspicious looking blue glow fogging the interior of our refrigerator.

"I doubt it," Butch chuckled. "From what I've seen of all the Kroger boys I know, it seems to work in the opposite direction!"

"Butch, the A&P probably started the rumor," I said with a grin, and this went over well with Glenn. Nevertheless, from that moment on, thoughts of being "tenderized" kept me clear of the subtly glowing blue light whenever possible.

I had mixed feelings when I took the job at Kroger; Dad had always growled that he hated chain stores "like the devil hates holy water." Working for the "enemy," I thought, might make him mad. Instead, he was delighted I had the job. He and Galbraith were good friends; the Kroger manager bought Lucky's early tomatoes and each summer gave him many pounds of overripe grapes for wine making. Moreover, Dad intended to leave Bryan-Hunt whenever income from his rental property made it possible. That day would come soon, for he and Mom had almost paid off all of their buildings. With five or six classmates working with me, and with two good bosses, I looked forward to fun as well as money from the job.

I had seen one of America's first supermarkets in Cincinnati, a huge Alber's store along Glenway Avenue, and my cousin Neil O'Connor managed a nearby Kroger, but the tiny Carlisle store was light-years behind these and those to come in the postwar world. The store was about thirty-five by sixty feet, with additional enclosed space in the back for bulky sacks of sugar, flour, meal, and various animal feeds. The manager's small office was here and had a peephole to view the sales floor. There was no self-service; all items were on shelves, and the shelves ran from the floor to ceiling height around the store, except for the big front windows. Clerks stood behind counters, took customers' orders, brought items from shelves, added prices up on paper sacks, sacked the groceries, took the customers' cash to the big NCR cash register, and returned with change, if necessary. Joking and conversation between clerks and customers were part of the scene, for friends, acquaintances, or relatives were nearly always involved. A massive three-doored electric refrigerator for soft drinks and milk products centered one side of the store.

The butcher shop occupied a ten- by twenty-foot space along the wall opposite the refrigerator. On one end was the entrance to our refrigerator with its blue light, while on the other stood an imposing big butcher's block. "It's sycamore," Glenn explained, "because the wood doesn't have any stinky stuff in it and it won't split and splinter like everything else—nobody likes splinters in their steak!" Butch used the block to carve out his artistic offerings of lamb chops "with two pairs of pants," steaks, fowls, roasts, and much else. Whenever Butch or I finished using the block, Tommy, an oversized and fluffy calico cat, effortlessly hopped back up to his usual place on the block and lay there, licking his fur and arrogantly watching us, the store, and the customers. He was valuable and, like any cat, seemed to know it, for he killed his weight in mice and rats every week.

Tommy and I put an act together one slow Saturday morning. It was unplanned but grew out of my fooling around with a string and some liver trimmings. I wondered if Tommy would swallow liver tied to my string, so I tried him. He gulped it down, then I pulled it up and out. Since Butch Glenn was not around, I did it again, Tommy taking the string and all like a big catfish hitting one of Lucky's lines. At this moment Miss Nancy Talbert, the high school principal, walked up to my counter. Miss Nancy was a very prim and proper maiden lady.

"How are you, Frank?" she asked.

"Just fine, Miss Nancy."

"I'm glad to see so many of my boys have gotten jobs," she added, looking around the store and nodding at Bob Cunningham, Tom Carter, John Haizlip, Van Crabbe, and several others. But a puzzled expression accompanied her next question: "What in the world is wrong with that cat?" she asked, emphasizing *world*.

Tommy lay in front of her on the block with the string reaching from inside his mouth over to my hand behind the counter. He was licking at it and shaking his head. I sensed that my big moment had arrived. "Miss Nancy, I think Tommy has something on his

246

stomach," I said as I pulled out the string and liver—this with the big cat's rather impolite "urp!"

Miss Nancy was not flustered; she had seen a thing or two during her many years as a teacher. "Well, I never!" she said, trapping my eyes behind her gold-rimmed glasses in her famous "sideways stare." She calmly ordered two pounds of ground round and left with a pleasant "good-bye." Neither Tommy, nor I, nor anyone else ever got the best of Miss Nancy!

Slicing liver and serving sow belly was tough work. The quivering movement of liver caused slips of my knife and many nicks and slices on hands and fingers. I paid little attention to this until the first time I sold sow belly, or, to give it a more polite name, salt pork. A bedraggled and impoverished looking farmhand came up to my counter: "Ah 'onta buy some mate," he said, "ifini tis 'at they is ary?"

"I'm sorry," I said. "I didn't understand what you wanted."

"Ah 'onta buy some mate, ifini tis 'at they is ary?" He was now suspicious and a little worried. Fortunately, Butch Glenn overheard us and whispered: "He wants to buy some sow belly—some meat—if we have any."

Sow belly has no secrets; it comes from the hog's belly and flanks and is packed in barrels of salt brine. It provided much of the wintertime energy for pioneer America. When I stuck my hand into our barrel to pull out his ten-pound order, I winced as the brine stung the many nicks and cuts in my hand. Butch grinned so I put up a good front, wrapped it up, and collected $1.50 for the meat. "Thank 'e," my customer said as he left the store, probably glad to be shut of city boys and their dumb questions.

Marion Prather Evans did not like friends to use his "girlish sounding" first name: "Just call me Steamboat," he demanded. His father had worked as a deckhand on steamboats out of Higginsport, Ohio, and passed his nickname on to his son. Some, noting the size of his towering father, insisted on calling him Tugboat: "You're too small to be a steamboat!" they chortled, proud of their wit. The same thinking applied to James "Shotgun" Cannon. But by whatever name or nickname, Evans, our classmate and buddy, worked long and hard on the Kroger crew with the rest of us.

Bad habits occasionally come to all of us; in Steamboat's case a severe one developed in relation to Wescola. Steamy was simply unable to pass Kroger's huge wall refrigerator without swinging open one of the heavy doors and taking a swig of Wescola. Stanley Galbraith did not mind us drinking this Kroger brand pop, but he complained that Evans was overdoing a good thing: "His constant recourse to the bottle is airing out my refrigerator." Steamboat, as was his way, paid scant attention to Galbraith's complaints, his breath reeking of Wescola even as the manager threatened to "piss in your bottle."

Later that day, when Evans was elsewhere, all of watched as Galbraith poured a mixture of salt, vinegar, and lemon juice in with the Wescola in Evans's quart bottle. We were delighted and eagerly awaited Steamboat's return. For me, it promised to be a sanitary reenactment of the sterner solution employed six years earlier by Grandpa Smith.

When Steamboat returned he reverted quickly to his Wescola-holic ways. As he passed the refrigerator he swung the door open, held his bottle on high, and drank deeply for a second. "P-f-f-f-f-f-t-t-t-t-t, Stanley pissed in my bottle!" he screamed, spitting and jumping up and down. "He has pissed in my . . . in my . . . bottle," he mumbled, for he saw the entire crew doubled up in laughter. The joke was on him, he admitted, and began laughing with everyone else. By this time customers had joined the happy uproar, friends Kenneth Jolly and Ollie Guthrie hoisting Evans's hand and bottle as if in victory. That may have been the last time I saw Jolly and Guthrie together, for both were soon in the service and both were killed in action, the former with the Third Infantry Division in Italy, the latter with the Third Marine Division on Iwo Jima.

At midnight after a hard Saturday at Kroger's, most of the crew piled into Howard Rice's car for a relaxing hour or two down at Licking River bridge. We took neither beer nor booze, just pop, with tobacco for some. Few autos passed, and if the moon was full a lovely greenish cast lay over the peaceful river and silent countryside. Our pockets held our wages in crinkly bills and jingling coins made of real silver.

Jokes were shared and explosive blasts of laughter blew pop

over heedless buddies. O.C. Seevers, caught up in the exuberance, often shed his shoes and pranced back and forth along the bridge's top girders, some eighty feet above the river. We cheered him on—just as we always did at the trestle—but we also worried about him as we watched his white shirttail flutter in the moonlight. We worried about little else, however, even though we knew there must be plenty to worry about somewhere in our war-torn world. Life went on as usual for us and our Nicholas County moonlight. But it was 1941, and the camel was poised fully to enter our tent, changing our lives forever.

21

Poetry and War

For years I had no idea that my education had been "Oh so tragically flawed!" as some sighed, by the Depression. There was, I suppose, good reason to think so. From the first grade through high school, there were no math teams, no debate teams, no chemistry courses, no math beyond geometry, no school newspaper or yearbook, no advanced placement classes, no guidance counselors, and no drivers' training. The town had no library, and the school library held no more than two hundred books and a set of the *World Book Encyclopedia*. I of course accepted things as they were, giving the situation no thought until I was in high school.

During high school I often entered or noticed schools in neighboring communities and in Cincinnati. Most were much larger and better equipped than CHS. Friends and cousins talked of "trig," yearbooks, chemistry lab, school dance bands, and the like. I envied them and for the first time felt uneasy about my schooling. Gradually I sensed that I would be out of place in most of the larger schools. Some pushed their students toward achievements beyond my reckoning or capacity at that time. A large Catholic high school in Cincinnati reveled in producing more than its share of priests, monks, nuns, and bishops, while down the street an even larger public school boasted loudly of an annual crop of prize-winning athletes, which in later years included Pete Rose. Average students in such schools were too often engaged in a painful effort to find their bearings in a

250

pressurized environment. I could not have explained it at the time, but I gradually understood that I was happier back in Carlisle High School than some of my friends and cousins in much larger schools. We had only two things well worthy of boasts at CHS: disciplined students and dedicated teachers. That is always more than enough.

I was not a dedicated student. Except for music and English, I studied only to make a passing grade, thereby driving Nannie to distraction. I flunked the last semester of Latin for lack of study. Lucky's fishing friend Pfanstiel taught Latin, but I quickly shattered his reasonable expectations for me. Asked to translate orally a passage for the class, from a textbook assignment I had ignored, I stood up and took my chances. I would say later that I was like a jazz musician trying to fake a tune he had never heard. A blush tinted my brow as I stood there, hoping for inspiration. The superintendent stood nearby, smelling of cigars and cinnamon balls, watching me for some small sign of scholarship. My classmates listened hopefully as I offered my first word: "Caesar," I said, knowing this had to be correct for I recognized the name; "Caesar," I repeated, "climbed a tree." The entire class erupted in a spontaneous uproar of very un-Latin-like laughter.

I earned one-half credit for the one-credit Latin course, and I did not deserve that. But I was peeved and told several classmates I was going to hold a book burning in front of Carlisle Drugs after school. I tore half the pages out of the Latin text and burned them in a revengeful little fire as J.E. Soper, Betsey Simons, James Lowe, and other good Latin students watched in amazement.

When I got home I told Nannie what I had accomplished. She was instantly enraged: "You, sir, are a nut—that's exactly what you are! What do you think education is? What do you think books are? You're nice and secure now, but let me tell you, young man, hard times are coming your way. Unless you've got a lot more in your skull than you have now, you'll be a goner. What you did to that book shows a lack of respect—shows you haven't grown up yet. You're staying home until you've thought this thing through. You're going to tell me how you and education are connected before you ever leave this house again. And you are most certainly going to pay for that book out of your own pocket. I've taught for years and I've never heard of such a thing! You're like that Hitler gang in Germany." Dad backed her to the hilt. It took several months for this stressful affair to work itself out. And I paid for the book. But all was not lost, I still loved English.

Lucky and Nannie laid the foundations for my love of the English language and its writers. They read to their boys from the start, not only from *Mother Goose* but from any and everything they might be reading at the time. Dad, for example, was a fan of James Fenimore Cooper and often read or quoted from *The Last of the Mohicans, The Pathfinder, The Deerslayer,* and other of his novels. He obtained these and other books from two Scottish immigrant brothers, the Mialls, one of whom ran a small grocery in the Fleming County village of Nepton. Mr. Miall was elderly and gentle of manner, but he kept knitting needles going furiously as he fashioned beautiful sweaters, "just like back in Scotland," he smiled. He could tell he amused Speck and me, for we had never seen a man doing what we assumed to be woman's work. But the Mialls had some nice books, and Dad read through Cooper every few years, and whenever he did, he read to us. We three could exchange comparisons of our adventures with those of Leatherstocking, Uncas, Hardheart, and other Cooper characters.

Since Carlisle had no library, Dad bought and borrowed books as he went along. He read *Hiawatha* to us so often that we memorized the Indian lad's names for fireflies and other forest creatures, but Mom finally forced us to quit calling her "Old Nakomis." Our cowboy neighbor, Ed Metcalfe, loaned Dad books on the West and Zane Grey novels from his large collection. The three of us were thrilled as "riders of the purple sage" chased bad hombres up in the "rimrock" of an "enchanted mesa." It was soothing to call up such images later as I viewed western scenery through the windows of a troop train on my way to the South Pacific.

Speck and I read a wide variety of material for entertainment in addition to school, church, and Boy Scout magazines and books. Although I read the comics in the *Cincinnati Times Star,* the weekly *Grit,* which I delivered, offered most of the coming Sunday's comics as well as excellent serials and advice columns for boys. Christ-mases or birthdays always brought a number of the latest *Big Little Books* and hardcover boys' serials such as *Tom Swift* and *Don Sturdy*. *Superman, Captain Marvel, Flash Gordon,* and other comic books were skimmed quickly on drugstore racks to save money. *G-8 and His Battle Aces* was far and away my favorite pulp magazine, but druggist Doc Bradshaw frequently interrupted G-8 and me just as the going got good, showing me the door and huffing G-8 back to his ignominious place on the rack.

While chasing Fokker D-7s above the Western Front with G-8 and his Spad, or fishing in the "shining big sea water" with Hiawatha, I was also mundanely memorizing a heaping pile of poetry. Jane Ross, and especially Nancy Talbert, were superb English teachers, and I was a willing pupil. We broke sentences apart in grammar, stud-ied the etymology of words, reviewed the lives of English and Ameri-can authors, read offerings as varied as *The Rubáiyát of Omar Khayyám* and *Macbeth*, and nearly always had a poem recital hanging fire. These poems became old and trusted friends, not only to me but to most American students of my generation. James Michener thought so much of them that he quoted more than a dozen in *Journey*.

I have never been in a "mossy cavern" since my high school days without becoming conscious of John Keats's "Mermaid Tav-ern." Nor do I ever read his poem "The Eve of St. Agnes" without a happy memory of nervous Lucy Jane Smoot reciting the opening line to the class: "Saint Agnes Eve, Ah, chitter bill it was. . . ." Know-ing Sidney Lanier's poem "Song of the Chattahoochee" boosted flagging spirits when the army sent me to Georgia, for I found my-self literally listening to the "song" of this river as it flowed by my Fort Benning campground. "I Have a Rendezvous with Death," claimed Alan Seeger, soldier-poet of the Great War. I did too, one war later, during combat on Luzon, but unlike Seeger, I failed "to keep my rendezvous." Country churchyards have never seemed the same since I memorized Thomas Gray's famous "Elegy," and daffo-dils have danced to an ever more sprightly tempo since I encoun-tered William Wordsworth's poem of the same name. I memorized Leigh Hunt's "Jenny" as a sophomore and quickly fell in love with her. Would that some gal like her would turn up and have mercy on me, the shortest guy in the class. (One eventually did, but her name was Florence):

Jenny kissed me when we met,
    Jumping from the chair she sat in;
Time, you thief, who love to get
    Sweets into your list, put that in!
Say I'm weary, say I'm sad,
    Say that health and wealth have missed me,
Say I'm growing old, but add,
    Jenny kissed me.

These poems and more came to me unexpectedly two years after high school. My buddy and I had just sighted our machine gun down a Manila street from a Far Eastern university balcony fronting offices vacated minutes before by the Kempetai, the Japanese equivalent of the Nazi Gestapo. Lying on the floor amid the clutter was a paperback book, *The Pocket Book of Verse*, rubber-stamped: "Censored by Hodobu, Jun 6, 1944." It was intended for Yank POWs. Favorite poems, so recently memorized in high school, were there like old friends when I needed them the most. I read the book lovingly for the remainder of the war and retain it today as a precious souvenir of tough times.

The only live stage production ever seen by most Nicholas Countians was the annual junior-senior class play. I had a nice role in a typical one titled *Mad March Heirs*. The play is set in the living room of the millionaire March family's Park Avenue penthouse in New York City. My pal John Soper played Obadiah March. All were after his millions. June Stewart played his daughter, Henrietta, and my role was that of Baron Kurt DuBois, Henrietta's European "catch." Late in the play I was to embrace Jane Kenning, Obadiah's stenographer, giving her a hearty kiss. This appealed to me greatly because Jane Kenning was played by Idell Smith, a lovely blonde classmate. I argued repeatedly with Idell for private rehearsals of this scene but was turned down every time. All good things come to him who waits, however, and on the night of the play I hung in there until the audience began whistling and shouting.

It was a sunny and dry December day, cold but nice for the month. Speck and I, the Harper boys, Charlie Sexton, Pokey Pumphrey, Popeye Clark, and others met for a touch football game in a cow pasture within a rock throw of the school. Within minutes I was dragged through a cow pie. After cleaning up in a nearby pond, I played with damp pants until the game broke up. The Harper boys and I went to their house and encountered sister Jane running down the second story stairs. She was excited and shouting: "Pearl Harbor's been attacked! Pearl Harbor's been attacked!" Then she ran back up the stairs. I knew Jane was very serious and very upset, but the only Pearl I knew was Pearl Gill, and I could hardly imagine him being attacked, so I thought this other one must be some friend of Jane's. Quickly of course I learned the facts and ran home to break the news. Dad and Uncle Joe were hunched up close to the radio, grumbling and cursing the Japanese, when I arrived.

As the Pacific war unfurled, it became obvious that the Japanese were far more capable than we thought. Tension built as they enjoyed success after success in a seemingly unstoppable progress toward Australia. Little Carlisle was as unprepared as other places. Pearl Harbor was such an overwhelming surprise it briefly undid the knowledge that America had made measurable progress toward preparations for war. We in Carlisle soon regained our bearings, recalling that our draft board had been operating since late 1940. The first number of the first draft call was 158, and Clifton Waugh, a young farmer, had this number; forty-four others joined him in this first time around. These men were part of the peacetime draft, supposed to last just twelve months, but extended and then caught up by Pearl Harbor. Carlisle's National Guard unit was already training with the Thirty-eighth "Cyclone" Division, their parent outfit and one destined to destroy Japanese forces on Bataan in 1945. Young Americans unlucky enough to have been born in the "soldiers' slot"—roughly the years between 1910 and 1927—were to bear the brunt of the bloodiest war in the bloodiest century in the history of this planet.

Although Carlisle was ten thousand miles from Japan and four thousand from Germany, there was a short-lived fear that the enemy might have us in mind. It was said that our unusual twin water tanks identified us for enemy bombers. "They ought to tear them down," Uncle Joe grumbled, before thinking better of it. Ed Metcalfe held that camouflaging the tanks with green and brown paint and tree branches "just might work." Most concluded that our town might or might not be a target, but all were certain the big Lexington Signal Depot at Avon would be one if enemy planes could reach it.

The federal government built the Signal Depot in 1941 as part of Roosevelt's effort to prepare for a war he was sure was coming, despite the powerful isolationist sentiment. Many depot workers commuted from Carlisle; it was an economic godsend for the community. We were correct in thinking it was a valuable target, for it soon became the center of the army's radar training program. As late as July 6, 1997, the *Lexington Herald-Leader*, in a major article on this now closed installation, noted that during 1942 and 1943 more than twelve thousand civilians were taught how to use and maintain what was then secret radar equipment.

Powerful searchlights were among the items stored and tested at the depot. Although they were twenty miles away, we watched breathlessly as they swept the night skies, their beams chasing one another and reflecting brightly off passing clouds. The scene reminded me of the unusually bright aurora borealis of 1937. The flickering, pulsating light brought Prim Roundtree, a favorite neighbor, running into our living room with startling news: "Mrs. Mathias! Mrs. Mathias! Hurry outside quick and look at the sky; Cincinnati is on fire!" We all had a good laugh at this, Prim included, but the skies to our south were no laughing matter. These slowly shifting searchlights proved that although we were a village deeply set in North America, we shared a sight already long familiar to embattled citizens in London and Coventry.

If Carlisle's citizenry needed something to take their minds off the war, the Home Guard filled the bill. The *Mercury* of March 12, 1942, reported that uniforms for the "home militia" would be issued. Officers and staff had been appointed, with the capable AEF veteran Everett Earl Pfanstiel in charge of most units. There were 172 male and female volunteers, a nice turnout for a town of just over 1,400 souls. The Guard was divided into fourteen units, probably patterned on similar groups in England: air raid wardens, fire watchers, first aid squad, bomb (removal) squad, auxiliary firemen, rescue squad, emergency food and housing, and the remainder in various housekeeping, maintenance, and service units. Speck and I were messengers, along with classmates Emily Asbury, Marie Shrout, Frank Reynolds, Custer Blair, Anne Colliver, and others. Mom and her best friend, Mae Conley, were in the Victory Home Committee, a large unit embracing homemakers and probably aimed at giving everybody a role. Finally, there was a decontamination squad, but it boasted only one member, Allan Hopkins, a local druggist. Carlisle, Kentucky, was ready for the enemy, whether he arrived in Messerschmidts or Zeros.

The time came to test our team. Carlisle's first official blackout was declared for Friday, November 20, 1942. All citizens were to turn out their lights from 8:00 to 9:00. The "Regulations" were published in the *Mercury*:

1. Air Raid Warning Siren, 3 blasts. Turn out lights.
2. Blanket grate fires
3. Confine dogs
4. Traffic to curb
5. No pedestrians on streets
6. All roads into and out of town blocked
7. All clear on long blast of siren

My messenger classmates and I were poised and ready when three siren blasts sounded. We thrilled as Carlisle's lights went out. The darkness appealed to our romantic natures since the nearest enemy bombers were certainly no closer than the British Isles. Shadowy outlines were the only visible remnants of our old hometown. I was assigned to a unit patrolling the hilly working-class Dorseyville section of town. We walked the streets, our flashlights showing red through tinted cellophane covers. This reminded me more of Halloween or Christmas than of wartime. Messengers Bobby Cunningham, Spud Marshall, and Nate Young joined me. Suddenly a sight to terrible to contemplate assaulted our senses—a porch light blazing bright enough to vector in a squadron of Nazi bombers! We rushed over to the shabby little house. An auxiliary policeman banged loudly on the tattered screen door. We waited, our sense of authority blazing as brightly as the light.

Abruptly the door opened and a gnarled, gray-haired old man stepped out, his rumpled bib overalls covering his long johns. He shook his fist at us: "Play your damned games somewhere else!" he shouted. "I ain't turnin' out nary a light, and that's fur damned certain. To hell with all of it!" He stepped back into his house, slamming the door behind him.

There was no doubting him; he meant exactly what he said. For a moment, however, real danger flared, the kind that comes from placing undue authority in ignorant, vicious, or inexperienced hands. "We ought'a shoot the old sonza-bitch!" someone shouted angrily from the shadows. "Yeah," growled another, "we ought at least shoot that damned light out!" Just as I began fearing that some nut might start shooting, another voice broke the tension: "The old codger thinks the Civil War is still on and we're nothing but a bunch of damned Yankees!" We all laughed, then walked on, leaving the codger's porch light brightly shining to lead in nothing more dangerous than moths.

Unlike this codger, who saw only the rather foolish side of Carlisle's blackout, my dad had good historical insights into World War II itself. Lucky was willing to argue that "if Germany had won the first war by Christmas 1914 as planned and expected, we wouldn't be in the fix we're in today." Few modern historians would disagree, knowing as he did that it was the dreadful four-year extension of this conflict that made possible the rise of communism, the entrance of the United States, the sapping of empires, and the emergence of Hitler and World War II. In addition, Lucky argued that "carriers will doom battlewagons," a belief most of us ridiculed until the Japanese sank the *Repulse* and *Prince of Wales* early in the war. His education had stopped with the eighth grade, but his sharp, analytical mind had educated itself through a lifetime of reading.

The blackout was hailed as a great success. "It must have been," Nate Young laughed, "for we didn't see one enemy bomber all night!" Although we took some pride in our successful blackout, we took much more in the big Honor Roll sign erected at this time in the courthouse yard. The CHS band played for the unveiling and County Attorney William Conley presided and spoke at the affair. The names of all local servicemen were on the sign. When I left for the army in 1943, it held 468 names.

I felt much better about myself during Christmas 1942 than I had the year before. My growth spurt had finally come, leaving me with a height of five feet, nine inches. My weight was keeping pace and would finally level off at 155 pounds. Since most of this had taken place in a year's time, I hardly believed that Santa Claus could possibly do anything more for me. I was wrong. A late December phone call not only changed my life but may well have saved it during the army years ahead. I answered the phone, assuring the voice on the other end that he had the right number and that I was Frank Mathias. Then came a stunning offer.

"Frank, Mrs. Martha Comer, a friend of your mother's, tells me that you're a pretty good sax man. Is that right?"

"Well," I replied, somewhat puzzled at his question, "I've played for seven years now and play in a combo here. I don't know whether I'm good or not."

"I'm glad to hear that. My name is Clarence Moore and I lead a fourteen-piece Maysville dance band called the Kentucky Kavaliers. The army is gobbling up our musicians and we need a sax man. Could you come and audition with us?"

I barely managed to utter a hoarse but happy "Yes sir!"

22

The Music Goes Round and Round

My audition came during a rehearsal of the Kentucky Kavaliers in the century-old Maysville Armory. My pulse pounded as I walked into the big drill and dance hall. The musicians were seated on a bandstand behind swank silver and blue "Portadesks" with KAVALIERS stylishly lettered across the fronts. I was frightened and prayed silently for help. Moore, a small but attractive man in his mid-twenties, introduced himself and then turned to his band: "Hey everybody, quiet, let me introduce Frank Mathias; he's trying out for the second tenor seat tonight."

Band members, some as old as forty but most much younger, nodded with interest at me as I took my seat in the sax section. Two in the section were young women, as was the pianist, evidence that "Rosie the Riveter" was not the only wartime female to break into a male domain. A trumpet bell tapped my shoulder. I turned and, to my surprise, saw Glenn Mattingly, a swimming buddy from summer surfing on the river. Another, Donnie Wood, was in the sax section; both gave me a "thumbs up" sign. I needed all the encouragement I could get for I was dizzy with anxiety and wanted the music to get under way.

The thick Kavalier "book" held over two hundred stock arrangements as well as my fate. The leader held his trumpet in one hand as he riffled through the book with the other, finally calling up "The Music Goes Round and Round," Tommy Dorsey's swingy

1936 novelty hit sung by vocalist Edythe Wright. I had long since memorized the words and music from hearing Dorsey's recording on radio and jukebox and was relieved to find the Kavaliers' stock arrangement practically the same. This eased my initial anxiety as I joined the band in backing the singing of Charlotte Newell, one of the two attractive "girl vocalists." Moore called up "Hindustan" next, then "Southern Fried," after which I lost track of titles, for I was reading fairly well, gaining confidence, and experiencing joy in the music. Whenever a difficult arrangement came up, I followed Gayle Clark's facile alto sax lead as she blithely fingered her way through several troublesome passages. I knew I was earning a passing grade from the grins and winks of my fellow musicians. After some thirty minutes Moore told me I had the job.

I was wildly elated as I rode the bus back to Carlisle, and my joy did not subside the next day at school. "Are you *really* going to play with the Kavaliers?" old girlfriends asked, but with a delicious new meaning in their voices. "Sure," I replied, relishing the questions and the perfume as the sweatered bobby-soxers clustered about me. They were amazed to hear that I would make six dollars for three easy hours of work, half again what I made at Kroger's on a weekend. We were all frugal children of the Depression, so such information was important and gladly shared. What I could not know at the time was that infinitely more than money was involved. Clarence Moore and the Kavaliers gave me experience that undoubtedly paved my way into two army bands the next year, possibly saving my life. At Fort Benning I won an audition into a post band instead of continuing with an infantry division that was later shot to pieces during the Battle of the Bulge. When the Benning band broke up after six months, I wound up in an infantry company, this time on embattled Bougainville in the South Pacific. In short order I won a transfer into the division band. We suffered casualties but nothing like those in the company I left behind.

I never knew life could be so wonderful as it was from January through August, 1943. I was playing in a big band in what later would be remembered as the legendary big band era. The songs we played were on every jukebox, and jukeboxes were everywhere, from drugstores to bus stations to restaurants. No American music has ever been as popular as swing, with some 90 percent of the people, young and old, listening or dancing to it. It follows that the musicians who created it were also popular, and nowhere more so than at the high school and college levels. Suddenly, I had shed my Carlisle cocoon as "little Frank" and in my eyes emerged stylishly as "that new tenor man with the Kavaliers." Music, I learned, had charms much more widespread and lasting than football, basketball, or any other sport.

There was an interesting mix of people and professions among the musicians. Their ages ran from fifteen to forty, with trumpeter Gene White, son of the Owl Drug owner, as the youngest, to Hans Hirschfeld, a talented German immigrant who often arrived at rehearsals with Glenn Mattingly on his motorcycle, the latter clutching and balancing Hans's big bass fiddle as they slid to a stop at the armory door. Another older musician and motorcycle owner was trombonist Leo Caproni, who served as fatherly adviser to the younger musicians and "in between times," as he put it, ran Maysville's best restaurant. Sitting next to Caproni in the trombone section was Shelby Cox, a genial lettercarrier from Manchester, Ohio, who delivered good brass sounds as well as the mail. Baritone sax man Don Wood and I argued about Verna Ellis's age. It was a tossup, for although she was in the sax section she carried a special ageless aura as Maysville High School's principal secretary, in our eyes a position of power transcending her twenty-five-plus years. But the ongoing war matured our ideas of power and preference, especially in Wood's case, for a year or so later he found himself completely powerless in a Nazi prisoner of war camp.

My playing improved as quickly as my understanding of the unique relationships between a dance band and the dancers or audience. Moore, although only in his mid-twenties, was an experienced leader. He used various tricks to get a dance crowd up from their tables and out on the floor. Everybody's favorite ballad was "Stardust," and Moore invariably called it up to get a slow dance moving. This was especially effective at high school dances, for it was always one of the six tunes on their "No Break" cards, and as

Charlotte Newell sang it, we in the band watched couples pairing off for a dance banning any breaking in from the stag line. Sometimes, however, a dance got off to a good start, then sagged, a problem I watched Moore solve one night by calling up the latest swingy pop hit, "Shoo Fly Pie," and signaling our other vocalist, Wenonah Jones, to sing it. Nonie grabbed the mike and belted it out: "Shoo fly pie, and apple pan dowdy, makes your eyes light up and your tummy say howdy." In no time a chattering, cheering crowd gathered around the bandstand and Moore smiled a foxy smile at us.

At all dances, whether slow, sagging, or swinging, Moore was quick to answer demands to "turn the drummer loose." This meant giving Wayne Cablish or, later, Wyman Wyatt, a thirty-six-bar Gene Krupa–style drum solo on "Drumboogie" or any of the big band killer-diller jump tunes. This brought almost any audience to its feet and thoroughly satisfied even the tone deaf. The usual dance, however, required little prompting or pushing, for a good leader called up sets tailored to that night's crowd: two ballads, a waltz (or perhaps Latin number), and a jump tune for jitterbugs: "Body and Soul," "I Had the Craziest Dream," "Three O'Clock in the Morning," and "One O'Clock Jump." But Moore was ready for anything. He broke up a fistfight on a Portsmouth, Ohio, dance floor one night by calling up "The Star Spangled Banner." Wartime patriotism stopped the fight in its tracks when the entire crowd stood at attention. I was amazed at how suddenly the uproar ended. The fight was over and we in the band laughingly backed Virgie Whitaker when she stood up from her piano and pronounced Clarence Moore "our fearless leader and flyweight champion!"

Few old-timers are left to remember and fewer still to have heard in person the great African American dance band of Jimmy Lunceford. Most musicians find it hard to choose between Lunceford, Tommy Dorsey, and Duke Ellington as to who had the best *all-around* band of the swing era. I doubt that any of the Kavaliers ever heard Lunceford in person, but it was our honor to fill in for this great band in one of the most memorable dances any of us ever played. Lunceford was scheduled and widely advertised to play a one-night stand for an African American dance at the Maysville Armory but for some reason was unable to free himself from a Columbus engagement and bring his band to Maysville for the date. A huge crowd had assembled, awaiting his arrival, but no Lunceford. By ten o'clock the desperate promoters called Moore: "Can the Kavaliers play in Lunceford's place? He can't make it."

"Glad to," Moore replied. "Just give me thirty minutes or so to get them together and set up in the armory." Caproni and Hirschfeld ran their motorcycles out to several musicians who didn't have cars, but phone calls brought in the rest. By eleven o'clock all was ready. Moore did not open with our theme but kicked the dance off with "White Heat," an honestly named killer-diller. Immediately the dancers in the jam-packed armory gave living proof to the lyrics of the Fats Waller song "The Joint Is Jumpin'!" The crowd was there to have fun, Lunceford or no Lunceford, seething, moving, dancing, and applauding us no matter what we played. Every soloist had a huge cheering section, inspiring all of us to even greater efforts. When there was no longer an inch of extra room inside, dancers overflowed outside to a flat adjoining roof or into the street to jitterbug.

A month earlier an overpumped beer barrel had exploded and drenched the crowd at a riotous factory dance at the armory. The same thing happened at this dance, spewing a geyser of beer over many of the ersatz wartime crepe paper dresses. Jitterbugging soon tore the wet paper away and bandsmen had trouble keeping their eyes on the music.

The trumpets and trombones gave up by dawn's early light, packed their instruments, and nursed sore lips to bed. Several hundred dancers were still going strong, so the rhythm and saxes hung in there until 7:30 A.M. I passed Saint Patrick parishioners going to early mass as I lugged my tenor and clarinet up to the Furlongs' Fifth Street home. I peeled off my sweat-soaked clothes and flopped into bed, vaguely aware that dances like that one come only once in a lifetime. Unfortunately, I was right.

The Kavaliers played club, school, and industrial dances in some twenty counties stretching from New Richmond to Portsmouth on the Ohio side of the river and from Alexandria to Ashland on the

Kentucky side. It was a joyous and exciting new world for me. I had more money than I needed, new friends in every town within range of the band, and complete acceptance in front of every jukebox in Maysville. And there were the girls—new ones, lovely ones, interesting ones—clustered like butterflies around these drugstore jukeboxes. I abandoned all dry analysis of music in such pleasant situations, content to sense the soft, sweatered presence beside me in the booth, sip cokes together, or get up and jitterbug in a flash of bobby sox and saddle shoes. Although I had my favorites, I think I was exuberantly in love with all of them, as only a seventeen-year-old can be.

Always in the back of my mind during these happy months were whispered hints that a war was going on. The *Maysville Independent* headlined some place called Guadalcanal—"must be somewhere in Holland where all the canals are," I thought, turning to more interesting news, such as a report of the last dance we played. A year later I would see Guadalcanal from the rail of a troopship taking me to New Guinea. Had I read war news I would have read of places and troops I had never heard of but which I soon would never forget. I might have noted that the Thirty-seventh Infantry Division was in a life-and-death struggle at Munda, New Georgia. A year later I would join this division. Instead of comic strips and the sports pages, I could have read that the "Fifth Air Force is pounding Jap installations on the New Guinea coast." I would soon land as an infantry replacement at Oro Bay, one of those installations. Ongoing high-level debate as to whether to invade or bypass the Philippines would have been news to me, but two years after I joined the Kavaliers I was making news as one of the thousands of Yanks landing on Luzon, a long way in body and mind from those joyous, carefree days with the Kavaliers now seemingly "so long ago!"

In spite of scores of bus rides back and forth to Maysville, I managed to qualify for graduation. I had to turn down a chance for a part in *Foot Loose,* the senior class play, but I played a sax solo during the annual commencement program, its theme in its title: "Behind the Guns: A Pageant of School Activities in Wartime." We graduated thirteen boys and twenty-six girls, each with a part in the program. John Soper, the class prophet, failed to foresee that a year or so later he would be ten thousand miles away on Luzon with his classmate Frank Mathias. Miss Mary Frances Fisher, Carlisle's life-long second grade teacher, pounded out "Pomp and Circumstance" on the grand piano as we filed offstage, out of high school and into times as uncertain as any in American history.

By midsummer I entertained long thoughts as the war finally caught up with me; my draft call could not be far off. I felt good, however, about passing entry exams into the Army Specialized Training Program once I was drafted. The ASTP was to provide college training for young men throughout a war of as yet unknown length, thus preventing a shortage of engineers and physicians. I was sure this would free me from war's worst dangers, proving I had yet to learn that scarcely anything works out as planned in any army. Many months later I finally realized that the best thing I took into the army was my music and experience with the Kavaliers.

Nicholas County's August draft call was followed by physical exams in Cincinnati. On the morning of August 25, 1943, with Mom crying as I kissed her and my little brother good-bye, Dad walked me uptown where I joined twenty-nine other draftees milling around in front of the courthouse. Louis Reibold, a playmate from our Indian cigar days was there, as well as four buddies from the class of 1943. Most, I think, believed with me that our luck would hold, that we would be alive at war's end. Nevertheless, I was concerned enough to wish that some sort of "red mark" would appear above those destined to die. If such marks had hovered over the heads of those boarding the bus, one would have shown itself above my classmate Marion Letcher and another over my older friend Nick Feeback. Both were killed in action a year later, Pfc. Letcher in France with the Third Infantry Division and Pvt. Feeback in Italy with the Thirty-fourth Infantry Division.

I was no longer "Little Hoover," or "Little Lucky," or "tenor man with the Kavaliers." Instead, I was now an American soldier and very proud of it. Doc Bradshaw emerged from his Carlisle Drugs to hand each of us a "flat fifty" tin of Lucky Strike cigarettes. I saw this as an open acknowledgment of manhood. In my innocence I felt grown up at last, fully able to leave old Carlisle behind and take on bigger things. Dad knew better. Tears were in old Lucky's eyes as he hugged a loving father's farewell into his son. I joined the rest aboard the Fort Thomas bus, all of us burdened with a confusing mixture of thoughts and emotion. As the bus roared away, I waved back to Dad, loving him as much as ever but joining with the others of my star-crossed generation in beginning brand new and never to be forgotten chapters in our lives.

Postscript

As the scream of the eagle is heard after she passes so the memory of men remains after they die.

Inscription on the veterans' memorial, Carlisle Cemetery

I wish to honor the following classmates and friends who were killed in action defending the United States during World War II:

Donnell Baugus
Nick Feeback
Ollie Guthrie
William Hopkins
Kenneth Jolly
Fred Kendall
Marion Letcher
Robert Mathias
Andrew Metcalfe
Franklin Sousely